THE

Improbable

VICTORY

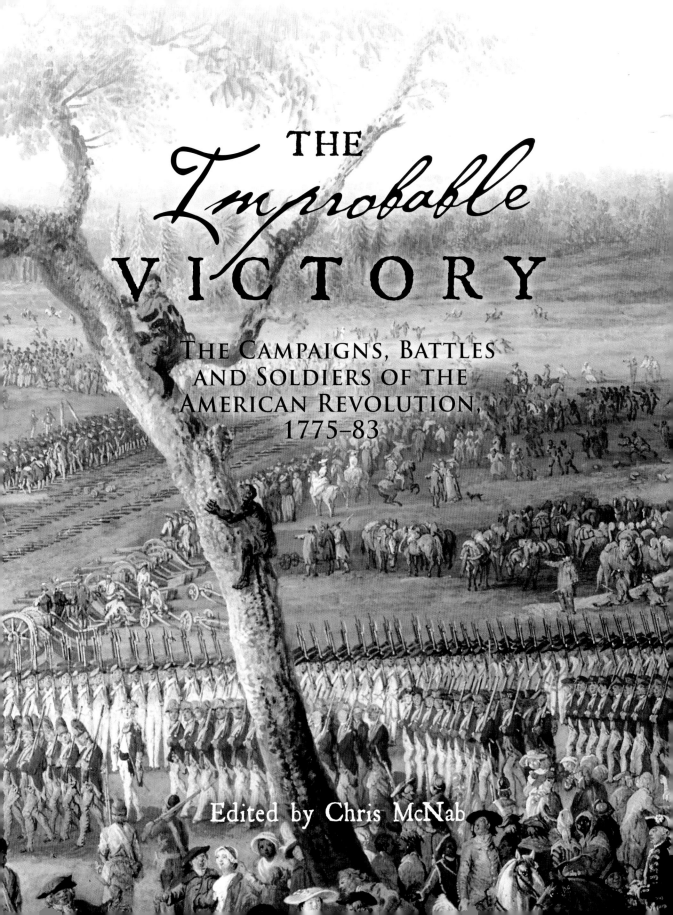

THE *Improbable* VICTORY

THE CAMPAIGNS, BATTLES AND SOLDIERS OF THE AMERICAN REVOLUTION, 1775–83

Edited by Chris McNab

First published in Great Britain in 2017 by Osprey Publishing,
PO Box 883, Oxford, OX1 9PL, UK
1385 Broadway, 5th Floor, New York, NY 10018, USA

E-mail: info@ospreypublishing.com

Osprey Publishing, part of Bloomsbury Publishing Plc

OSPREY is a trademark of Osprey Publishing, a division of Bloomsbury Publishing Plc.

Material previously published in Battle Orders 31: *The Royal Navy 1793–1815* by Gregory Fremont-Barnes, Campaign 37: *Boston 1775: The Shot Heard around the World*, by Brendan Morrissey, Campaign 47: *Yorktown 1781: The World Turned Upside Down* by Brendan Morrissey, CAM 67: Sarratoga 1777: *Turning Point of a Revolution* by Brendan Morrissey, Campaign 109: *Guildford Courthouse 1781: Lord Cornwallis's Ruinous Victory* by Angus Konstam, Campaign 176: *Philadelphia 1777: Taking the Capital* by Justin Clement, Campaign 203: *Trenton and Princeton 1776–77: Washington Crosses the Delaware*, Campaign 273: *Point Pleasant 1774: Prelude to the American Revolution* by John F. Winkler, Combat 9: *Continental versus Redcoat: American Revolutionary War* by David Bonk, Combat 17: *British Redcoat versus French Fusilier: North America 1755–63* by Stuart Reid, Command 21: *George Washington*, by Mark Lardas, Duel 44: *Bonhomme Richard vs Serapis: Flamborough Head 1779* by Mark Lardas, Essential Histories 45: The *American Revolution 1774–1783* by Daniel Marston, Men-At-Arms 1: *The American Provincial Corps 1775–84* by Philip Katcher, Men-At-Arms 39: *The British Army in North America 1775–83* by Robin May, Men-At-Arms 214: *US Infantry Equipments 1775–1910* by Philip Katcher, Men-At-Arms 244: *The French Army in the American War of Independence*, by René Chartrand, Men-At-Arms 450: *American Loyalist Troops 1775–84* by René Chartrand, Men-At-Arms 475: *The Spanish Army in North America 1700–1793* by René Chartrand, New Vanguard 161: *Ships of the American Revolutionary Navy*, by Mark Lardas, Osprey Wargames 9: *Fighting Sail: Fleet Actions 1775–1815*, Warrior 19: *British Redcoat 1740–93* by Stuart Reid, Warrior 68: *Continental Infantryman of the American Revolution* by John Milsop, Warrior 176: *Patriot Militiaman in the American Revolution: 1775–82* by Ed Gilbert and Catherine Gilbert.

ISBN: 978 1 47282 314 4
PDF e-book ISBN: 978 1 47282 315 1
ePub e-book ISBN: 978 1 47282 316 8

Page layout by: Myriam Bell Design, UK
Index by Sandra Shotter
Typeset in Goudy Old Style, Roman Antique, Cezanne
Originated by PDQ Media, Bungay, UK
Printed in China through World Print Ltd

17 18 19 20 21 10 9 8 7 6 5 4 3 2 1

Title page: Anne S.K. Brown Collection, Brown University

Osprey Publishing supports the Woodland Trust, the UK's leading woodland conservation charity. Between 2014 and 2018 our donations are being spent on their Centenary Woods project in the UK.

www.ospreypublishing.com

CONTENTS

FOREWORD

E LIVE TODAY IN A NEW revolution, where with the touch of a button, a finger on a keyboard or a voice command to a device in our pocket we can discover the history of the world in a few seconds. We can ask Siri, or Google, or Yahoo or any number of search engines, when was the Battle of Trenton? Who was the British Commander at Saratoga? What were the number of causalities at Brandywine? And within an instant we will have five of Kipling's Honest men: who, what, when, where and how. However the search becomes more difficult, and therefore more rewarding, when we find the much more elusive **why**.

Why would a group of colonists who had little in common other than their links to the mother country go to war against arguably the greatest army in the world and undoubtedly the greatest navy? **Why** would a Pennsylvanian farmer or a Virginian freeman risk their lives for something as intangible as freedom and liberty?

It is that search for why that has motivated both the writing of this book and, for my own part, has driven the ambitious construction of the American Revolution Museum at Yorktown in the past three years.

The content of a museum, much like the content of a book, is based on a collective decision of stories that need to be told. From the grumblings of discontent and the Boston massacre to the "shot heard around the world". From the despair at Valley Forge, to the last great victory at Yorktown and the founding of a new nation. The story of the American Revolution is ultimately the story of the people who lived through it. The story of ordinary people in extraordinary times.

While most Americans know that the United States of America owes its independence to the Revolutionary War, and all have heard of George Washington, the details after that become blurry to say the least. Polls and testing indicate that most Americans don't know the causes of the Revolution, cannot identify the events leading to its outcome, or what the Revolution even means to Americans today. This isn't just unfortunate, it's dangerous. For the American Revolution is the American evolution. The end of the war is the start of the ongoing idea of democracy and until we understand the creation of the republic that changed the course of world history, we cannot fully understand our own liberties, our own duties as citizens, and our place in the world.

And that is what makes the search for **why** so important both in this book and within the walls of the American Revolution Museum at Yorktown - for it was that last great victory that forever made Yorktown, Virginia, the place where a king's subjects became citizens of a new nation.

Peter Armstrong
Senior Director, The Museum of the Revolution at Yorktown

INTRODUCTION

THE HISTORY OF THE AMERICAN REVOLUTIONARY War (1775–83), aka the American War of Independence, has been steeped in nationalistic myth, and much we know about the conflict tends to focus on the larger-than-life personalities such as General George Washington, Lieutenant-General Sir Henry Clinton, or General Sir William Howe. Beyond that handful of recognizable names we know little about the lives and struggles of senior officers such as Nathanael Greene, Anthony Wayne, or Sir Charles Grey. We know even less about the men who fought in the ranks to secure their independence, or who fought for their king. Much of the written record of the war has been left by officers in the form of diaries and post-war memoirs. There were rare enlisted soldiers on both sides who kept diaries or corresponded regularly with family. It is interesting to note that for both officers and lower ranks their writing tended to focus on mundane daily activities—food, accommodation, how far and where they marched—rather than descriptions of combat. When they did write about combat was surprisingly cursory. Such reflects the timeless reality of life in a war zone: continual drudgery and hardship, rarely punctuated by moments of terror and adrenaline.

The American Revolutionary War was fought across a broad landscape, ranging from the frozen forests of northern New York to the humid backcountry of the Carolinas. The geography and climate of the American colonies largely dictated the strategy and tactics of the Revolutionary War. While British tactical doctrine, as embodied in the 1764 Regulations, did reflect an emphasis on linear tactics based on a three-rank formation, the army that engaged the American patriots around Boston in 1775 was in transition.

The evolution of British tactics in North America can be traced back to their experience in the French and Indian War fought against France between 1754 and 1763. That experience led key members of the British military leadership, many of whom had fought in the war, to develop innovative approaches to the deployment and operations of their armies. This included following the practice used in Europe of organizing light infantry and grenadier companies into composite battalions and the adoption of different formations that involved reducing the number of ranks from three to two and requiring greater separation between the men in the lines. As the war progressed British commanders revised and adapted their tactics, including the formations they used, to better address local conditions and their enemy.

Continental counterattack at Cowpens. The Delaware Continentals, dressed in hunting shirts, are rushing forward; they will capture or kill the British artillery crew defending their gun and shatter the 7th Royal Fusiliers. (Johnny Shumate © Osprey Publishing)

The initial approach of the American military leadership to both tactics and doctrine reflected the unique attributes of the men who volunteered to serve. It was also influenced by the experience many senior commanders had while serving with their British counterparts during the French and Indian War. As the war progressed the American commanders trained their men to fight in the more rigid formations, while British practice stressed more open formations, so that by the end of the war both sides had adopted a wide range of options.

The innovation in battlefield tactics was just one aspect of this landmark conflict. For the American Revolution was not simply a war in which, as popularly represented, plucky but tough American amateurs took on the might of a British imperial army. The war evolved to become a truly international conflict, drawing in French, Spanish, Dutch, German, and Indian forces, among others, the French in particular being a critical partner in the eventual American victory. The involvement of such nations meant that the fighting spread well beyond the ill-defined borders of the formative United States. If we include the naval clashes, the War of Independence was conducted in places such as the West Indies and Caribbean, the Mediterranean islands of Gibraltar and Minorca, and the Indian subcontinent, theaters that were in some cases half a world away from the primary warzone. Arguably, here we have an early example of what was virtually a world war. We must also factor into the equation that in large part the War of Independence was a civil war, with tens of thousands of American individuals remaining loyal to the British, and many taking up arms against the rebels, shoulder to shoulder with the British Redcoat. At its heart, the American War of Independence was a conflict as complex as it was historically significant.

*General George Washington at the battle of Yorktown, October 19 1781
(Granger, NYC/Topfoto.co.uk)*

PART 1

Birth of a Nation

A painting of the battle of Long Island, fought in the late summer of 1776. It was a stinging early defeat in the military career of George Washington (North Wind Picture Archive/ Alamy Stock Photo)

Chapter 1

SPARKS OF REVOLUTION

*T*HE END OF THE SEVEN YEARS' War (more commonly know as the French and Indian War) in North America sparked a dispute that would eventually lead to a rebellion among the Thirteen Colonies of New Hampshire, Massachusetts, Rhode Island, Connecticut, New York, Pennsylvania, New Jersey, Delaware, Maryland, Virginia, North Carolina, South Carolina, and Georgia. Britain had emerged victorious from the Seven Years' War, but in so doing had amassed a considerable debt. Before the war, the British government had intended minimal contact with or interference in the internal affairs of the North American colonies, aside from passing Navigation Acts that required the transportation of exports from the colonies in British ships. Tensions with the French Britain's great international rival increased as the 18th century progressed, however, prompting the British to consider the North American colonies from a more "imperial" perspective. The government began to examine ways that the colonies could be tied into a more efficient trading system with British colonies in the Caribbean and India.

The North American theater of the Seven Years' War had provided the British government with some very negative impressions. Officials had encountered considerable difficulty in gathering supplies for the war effort, and problems

with locally-raised colonial militia had resulted in the deployment of British regulars to the region. There has been debate over the importance of provincial militia in the French and Indian War, but there is no doubt that colonial troops could not have won the war without the support of British regulars. Some provincial forces fought well as irregular units, but others lacked the training and discipline necessary to wage a linear-style conflict. The discipline of the

British regular was required in this theater as in all the others, and following the war's end the British government decided that a large contingent of British regulars should be stationed permanently in North America to offset French, Spanish, and Native American ambitions in the area.

The British government settled upon a series of new taxes on the colonies as the best way to fund establishing troops in North America. The first of these was the Sugar Act of 1764. The second, the Stamp Act of 1765, charged a duty on newspapers and other official documents. This initiative provoked an understandably negative reaction from the American colonists. Their principal grievance was that the taxes had been levied by the British Parliament, rather than by the local colonial assemblies. Popular opinion held that it was appropriate for taxation to be levied only by locally-elected officials. Groups of men formed organizations known as the "Sons of Liberty" to protest the Acts. Serious rioting erupted in the colonies, to which the local British government officials felt powerless to respond, and which resulted in the repeal of the Stamp Act in 1766 following a change of government in Great Britain.

A leather-covered box commemorating the repeal of the Stamp Act, London 1766. (The Museum of the Revolution at Yorkown)

A new method of Macarony making as practiced at Boston. *Tarring and feathering a British official, a brutal act of rebellion against the British government. (Ann Bettman/Getty Images)*

The British government's next move in 1765 was the Quartering Act. This was principally devised to address the supply problems that had been common during the French and Indian War, and its requirements included the provision of wagons and drivers to supply the army in the field. It was, however, the clause concerning the housing of soldiers that created problems. This provision stipulated that British regulars were to be lodged in public houses, inns, even empty homes, if barracks were overcrowded or unavailable. Furthermore, this lodging was to be at the expense of the local colonial authorities. The reaction of the Reverend John Tucker of Boston in 1768 was fairly typical: "I think we are very afflicted and in a distressed state having the Ensigns of war at our doors ... a tax laid on us to pay the exorbitant charge of providing barracks and for those undesired troops." Initially this did not seem a very odious imposition, as most of the troops were to be stationed on the frontier or in territory recently gained from France and Spain, such as Niagara, Crown Point, St. Augustine, Mobile, and Detroit. In practice, however, the movement of troops en route to their final postings was extremely disruptive. Further protest ensued, and in 1769 the colonial assemblies and the British government met to work out agreements

This is a romanticized and inaccurate depiction of the Boston Massacre, although a minor clash, provided the rebellion with a powerful propaganda tool. (H. Armstrong Roberts/ ClassicStock/Getty Images)

concerning particulars of the Quartering Act, in an attempt to appease both sides. The transfer of British regulars to the Atlantic seaboard in 1770, however, strained the arrangement still further.

The Townshend Revenue Act, proposed by the Chancellor of the Exchequer, Charles Townshend, was to create yet more problems. This act, passed in 1767, imposed customs duties on tea, paper, paint, glass, and lead. It sparked the ire of the colonists afresh, and assemblies from New England to the Middle Atlantic expressed anger at its provisions. A Virginia militia colonel, George Washington, spoke in the Virginia House of Burgesses (legislature) in 1769, contending that only Virginians could tax Virginians, and local merchants in most ports swore not to sell British goods or to order items from Great Britain.

Tensions rose in Boston when customs commissioners were attacked by a mob. The British government responded by dispatching 4,000 British regulars to Boston to impose control. This was a role for which regulars were not trained, and their incapability only served to incite the local population to complain of a "standing army" imposing order on a "just" civilian society. Stories of robberies and assaults by soldiers were circulated, further alienating the civilian population. Events reached a crisis on March 5, 1770, when a small contingent of British regulars, attacked by an angry mob, opened fire, killing three men and wounding five. The incident, dubbed the "Boston Massacre," was exaggerated and used as propaganda against the British. The regulars were pulled out of Boston after this episode, but tension remained.

The British government changed again in 1770, and the new Parliament, led by Frederick North, First Lord of the Treasury, repealed all duties of the Townshend Act, except for the duty on tea. The new government, in agreement with its predecessor, believed in its right to levy taxes upon the colonies, although Lord North did feel that this stance only hurt British merchants in the end, when their goods were boycotted in the colonies.

The next crisis arose in 1773, when Lord North imposed the Tea Act, a second tax on tea. This initiative was an attempt to boost revenue for the British East India Company. The plan was to undercut the Dutch tea supply and shift the surplus of tea to the Thirteen Colonies. Americans, however, interpreted this as a further attempt to subvert their liberty. In December 1773 a small flotilla of Company ships arrived in Boston. While docked in Boston Harbor, they were

The Boston Tea Party was just one of several similar incidents throughout the colonies, and it was inspired as much (if not more) by the financial ruin facing wealthy smugglers, like John Hancock, as by any fine political principles. (Anne S.K. Brown Collection, Brown University Library)

Lord Frederick North, Britain's Prime Minister from 1770 to 1782. (Hulton Archive/Getty Images)

boarded in the middle of the night by a group of men dressed as Indians. The interlopers dumped the tea into the harbor, in an act of defiance that came to be known as the Boston Tea Party.

The British government, alarmed by the situation, passed the Coercive Acts in 1774 in an attempt to restore order, especially in Boston. Lord North felt that this would be sufficient to contain the small fringe element of rebellious individuals, failing to recognize the broad base of support for some of the actions being taken. John Hancock, a prominent Boston merchant, and Samuel Adams, one of the leaders of the opposition to the British government, were identified as the main troublemakers in Massachusetts. The port of Boston was closed and notice given that provincial government officials implicated in any wrongdoing could be tried in Great Britain. Lieutenant-General Thomas Gage returned to Boston with 3,500 regulars and with powers to assume the role of governor of Massachusetts. The Acts achieved the opposite effect to that intended, provoking a rebellious reaction throughout the colonies.

The Québec Act of 1774 also played a role in fomenting discontent among turbulent colonists. In an attempt to resolve the future of the French settlements of Québec, the British government passed an act that has had repercussions to the present day. The colony of Québec was allowed to keep its French language, laws, customs, and Roman Catholic religion intact, with no interference from London. Furthermore, the boundaries of the colony were extended as far west as the Mississippi, encompassing land treaties made between the British government and Indian tribes following the end of the Seven Years' War. The understanding was that the laws described in the Act would apply to this area, in recognition of the fact that many of the Indian tribes west of the Appalachian Mountains had been allied with France, and had thus been influenced by French customs and converted to the Catholic Church.

The Thirteen Colonies reacted strongly against the Québec Act. Long-standing prejudice made them deeply distrustful of French Catholics, and many of the colonies resented this incursion into land west of the Appalachians, which they believed was theirs by right. They protested at being hemmed in by a Catholic colony and denied access to the rich lands to the west. Many leading figures throughout the colonies felt that their liberties were gradually being worn away. Their dissatisfaction led to the First Continental Congress, formed in Philadelphia to discuss the Coercive Acts, the Québec Act, and issues in Massachusetts. The First Continental Congress was convened by colonial leaders, including John Adams, George Washington, Samuel Adams, Benjamin Franklin, and Patrick Henry, with the aim of organizing formal, legally recognized opposition to Parliament's actions. The Congress issued a declaration condemning the Coercive Acts as unjust and unconstitutional, and rejected the appointment of Gage as governor. The Congress additionally addressed issues of parliamentary control over the colonies, especially with regard to taxation. At this point the Congress was not interested in independence, merely the redress of perceived injustices. It was not until July 4, 1776–after the bloodletting of 1775 and early 1776–that the Second Continental Congress, led by John Hancock, decided to declare independence from Great Britain. From this point, the Thirteen Colonies referred to themselves as "the United States of America," but as this title was not officially recognized until after the Treaty of Paris in 1783, we will continue to refer to the Thirteen Colonies throughout this work.

It is significant that the British government failed to recognize that the formation of the Congress indicated not just a local Massachusetts or New England rebellion, but the beginnings of a large-scale insurrection. The military situation in North America began to worsen as 1774 drew to a close: British regulars were stationed in Boston; the Quartering Act came into effect once again, increasing tension between civilians and soldiers; the delegates of the First Congress, although they considered military action a last resort, did not help the situation by calling on colonial militia to strengthen and drill more frequently; weapons of various sizes were seized by colonists and stored away. Royal government representatives were slowly being replaced by committees who supported the conclusions of the First Continental Congress. The colonies and the British government were moving towards all-out conflict.

John Hancock, President of the Second Continental Congress. (De Agostini Picture Library/ Getty Images)

OUTBREAK

The year 1775 marked the formal outbreak of hostilities between the British and Americans. A small skirmish in Lexington led to a larger confrontation in Concord, and the British withdrawal from Concord sparked a savage fight for survival and the beginning of outright conflict. The battle of Breed's

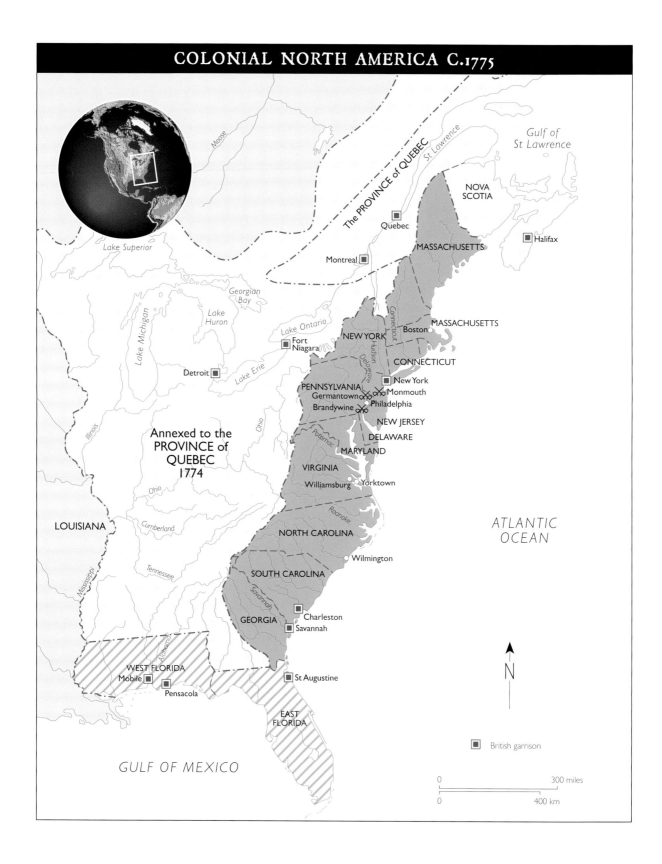

COLONIAL NORTH AMERICA C.1775

Moose

*Gulf of
St Lawrence*

The PROVINCE of QUEBEC

St Lawrence

NOVA
SCOTIA

■ Quebec

■ Halifax

Lake Superior

MASSACHUSETTS

Montreal ■

*Georgian
Bay*

Lake Huron

Lake Michigan

Lake Ontario

Fort ■
Niagara

NEW YORK

Connecticut

Boston ■ MASSACHUSETTS

Detroit ■ *Lake Erie*

Hudson

CONNECTICUT

Delaware

New York ■

✕ Monmouth

PENNSYLVANIA

Germantown ✕

Brandywine ✕ Philadelphia

Ohio

Annexed to the
PROVINCE of
QUEBEC
1774

NEW JERSEY

DELAWARE

Potomac

MARYLAND

Illinois

VIRGINIA

Williamsburg ○ Yorktown

Ohio

Cumberland

LOUISIANA

Tennessee

Roanoke

NORTH CAROLINA

○ Wilmington

SOUTH CAROLINA

Savannah

Mississippi

GEORGIA

■ Charleston

■ Savannah

Alabama

WEST FLORIDA

Mobile ■

■ St Augustine

Pensacola ■

EAST
FLORIDA

*ATLANTIC
OCEAN*

N

■ British garrison

GULF OF MEXICO

| 0 | | 300 miles |
| 0 | | 400 km |

Hill (Bunker Hill) in June was the first pitched battle of the war. This was followed by a bold American attempt, in December 1775, to seize and conquer Canada. After these events there could be no turning back. It was war.

The armed struggle for America began on April 19, 1775, in the towns of Lexington and Concord, Massachusetts. It could easily have been sooner. By late 1774, the British government was growing tired of its contentious North American colonists. General Gage, commander-in-chief in North America, received orders in December to arrest the instigators, but he considered the number of British troops available locally too small to be effective. Most of the British forces in North America were gathered and sent to Boston, nearly 13 battalions of infantry by the spring of 1775. Gage still considered this inadequate to deal with a possible insurrection.

In early April, Gage received reports that a large cache of weapons and gunpowder was being stored at Concord, 16 miles (26km) northwest of Boston. The local militia was aware that the British knew about the stores, but not when the British might move against it. Senior members of the Continental Congress, such as John Adams and John Hancock, were in Lexington, and there was fear that the British would move to arrest them.

American troops fire a ragged volley at the battle of Lexington. A 20th-century recreation, the clothing and kit featured is not entirely accurate. (Hulton Archive/ Getty Images)

General Thomas Gage had long experience of serving in North America, and was the supreme commander of the British forces in the theater from 1763 to 1776. (Bettmann/Getty Images)

On April 18 at 8:00pm the commanding officers of the British regiments in Boston were ordered to send their light and grenadier companies to the beach by 10:00pm. These troops numbered between 600 and 700 men and were commanded by Lieutenant-Colonel Francis Smith of the 10th Foot and Major John Pitcairn of the marines. The troops were ferried across the Charles River towards Cambridge. All of the troops landed on Cambridge Marsh by midnight, but had to wait till 2:00am before moving, in order to allow the shipping and unloading of provisions to be completed. One Lieutenant Barker noted, "few but the commanding officers knew what expedition we were going upon" (Barker, p.31.) The legendary Paul Revere and William Dawes secretly left Boston and rode towards Lexington and Concord to raise the alarm that the British were marching on the stores.

As the British troops marched towards Lexington, they began to receive intelligence that a large group of armed men was forming near the common at Lexington. Lieutenant-Colonel Smith sent a messenger back to Boston for reinforcements. A reinforcement brigade was ordered ready to move from Boston overland to Lexington. Due to orders not being conveyed correctly and time wasted to correct the mistake, the brigade was delayed and did not march until 8:45am. The Lexington militia formed a company of 70 men on Lexington Green, under the command of Captain John Parker, a veteran of the Seven Years' War.

Major Pitcairn and his companies arrived at Lexington Green just as the militia was forming up at around 6:00am. Pitcairn called upon the militia to lay down their arms and return to their homes. The American commander, Parker, told his men not to fire; the British moved forward and a shot was fired. There has been extensive debate about who actually fired the first shot. Barker contends that "on our coming near them they [the American militia] fired one or two shots." The situation was confusing for both sides, and Barker mentions that, after the initial shots, "our men without any orders rushed in upon them, fired and put them to flight." The firing lasted for 15–20 minutes, when Pitcairn managed to restore order. Eight militiamen lay dead and ten more were wounded. The British had suffered one wounded man.

Following this engagement, Pitcairn and the light infantry moved on to Concord to destroy the cache of weapons. The militia surrounding Concord was mobilized and moved to intercept the British column. The British seized Concord, and the light infantry was sent to secure bridges north and south of the town, while the grenadiers dealt with destroying the weapons and gunpowder in the area. A fight broke out at the North Bridge after the British had occupied both sides. As the militia moved forward, the British withdrew from one side and fired a volley into the militia. An American stated that "we were all ordered to load [muskets] and had strict orders not to fire till they fired first then to fire as fast as we could ... the British ... fired three guns one after another ... we then was all ordered to fire ... and not to kill our own men." The Concord militia opened fire and according to a British officer, "the weight of their fire was such that we were obliged to give way."

The British suffered one killed and 11 wounded, including four officers. They withdrew towards Concord, and orders were received at around midday for all units to fall back towards Boston, the military stores having been destroyed. As the troops left Concord, sniping began from houses along the road to Boston. About 1 mile (1.6km) outside of Concord, the British column crossed at Meriam's Corner, where it became bunched up. Militiamen opened up on the large column, inflicting heavy casualties on the flanks and rear.

The relieving brigade from Boston met up with the remainder of the British column at Lexington, bringing the numbers of British troops close to 1,500 men. The combined force marched out towards Boston. As a British officer noted: "we were attacked on all sides from woods, and orchards and from stone walls and from every house on the road side." The British reaction to this sort of attack was described as follows: "the soldiers were so enraged at suffering from an unseen enemy, that they forced open many a house from which the fire proceeded, and put to death all those found in them."

"The British are coming!" In this print by Felix Darnley, local militiamen are depicted responding to the call to arms. All the southern colonies boasted efficient well-organized militia organizations. (PhotoQuest/Getty Images)

The weapon of the great majority of infantrymen on both sides was the musket. This photo shows a British Long Land pattern musket, a bayonet belt and sword, all marked to the 15th Regiment (East Yorkshire). (Private collection/Photo © Don Troiania/Bridgeman Images)

Militiamen poured in from all the surrounding towns to fight against the withdrawing British column, but the British were able to keep them at a distance with the use of flanking parties and a very good rearguard formation. When they arrived in Cambridge, the British column decided to head towards Charlestown, as the bridge from Cambridge to Boston had either been destroyed or was heavily defended. The column arrived at Charlestown at 7:00pm and occupied the area until boats were sent to ferry the troops back over to Boston. The militia did not pursue the British into Charlestown because the area was open terrain. As Barker noted: "the rebels did not chuse [sic] to follow us to the Hill as they must have fought us on open ground and that they did not like."

The British lost about 70 killed and 170 wounded during the day's fighting, while the Americans are estimated to have lost 100 men killed and wounded. The British had been successful in extricating themselves from the area and had applied good light infantry tactics in clearing the militia from the stone walls and houses that lined the road to Boston.

TACTICS—LINEAR AND IRREGULAR WARFARE

Before progressing with our narrative of the early events of the American Revolution, an overview of the war's tactical context (expanded in Part 2) is useful. Popular images of the American Revolution feature American "minutemen" (militia) hidden behind stone walls and trees, firing into Continental-style linear formations of British Redcoats. While this type of warfare occurred occasionally, a more accurate image would show Americans assembling for battle in linear formations opposite British forces similarly arrayed and supported by their German allies. The American Revolution had more in common with the linear warfare used in the European theaters of the Seven Years' War than with the irregular skirmishes fought on the frontiers of North America in the same conflict.

The flintlock musket of the Seven Years' War was still the chief weapon for all sides. The ability of an army to deploy in linear formation and maintain fire discipline with the musket was of considerable importance in training. Formations were required to march in step over open terrain, maintaining cohesion, and then deploy effectively from columns to linear formations. The British ability to accomplish this at the Battle of Monmouth in 1778 saved the army from destruction, as will be described later. Following deployment in linear formation, the men were required to deliver devastating repeat volleys against the enemy. Consistent fire discipline was crucial to the success of this maneuver.

Lieutenant-General Sir William Howe replaced Gage as supreme commander of British forces in North America in 1776. (The Museum of the Revolution at Yorktown)

Tactics used in the Seven Years' War also continued to be employed, particularly seen with generals attempting to outflank their enemy ("oblique order") when the ground permitted. The British attack at the Battle of Long Island is a clear example of this tactic. Prussia's success during the Seven Years' War had inspired many armies, including the newly created American forces, the Continental Army, to emulate its firing techniques and discipline, with some success by 1777, many Continental regiments were capable of holding their line against British and German regulars. For the American Revolution was chiefly an infantry war. The British and Continental formations deployed in ranks of men two or three deep, with artillery deployed on the flanks of battalions or regiments to mark unit boundaries. The use of only a small amount of cavalry was mainly due to practical considerations. The British encountered difficulty in transporting mounts or purchasing them in North America, and the Americans felt that the upkeep of dragoon regiments was too costly. As a result, only a few dragoon regiments were formed in the Continental Army or deployed by the British Army.

Although use of traditional tactics remained constant, there were innovations in irregular warfare, following on from developments of the Seven Years' War. The British Army

re-employed light infantry companies in 1770–71, and by 1775–76 had begun to form these into independent battalions. The Continental Army also formed light infantry companies, and they too tended to use these in independent formations. Rifles were reintroduced for use by a small number of dedicated units, who appreciated the improved accuracy and range afforded by the rifled barrel. The British employed German *Jäger* (riflemen) and the American forces used riflemen occasionally. The numbers were small on both sides, however, and their ability to defend themselves was compromised by the amount of time it took to reload the rifle and its lack of a bayonet.

Keeping in mind the previous comments about the limited use of cavalry on the open battlefield, the use of combined mounted infantry/cavalry units for raiding and reconnaissance was another innovation of this period. The British began to develop this tactic in 1777 with the raising of the Loyalist British Legion and Queen's Rangers corps in the New York area. These troops made a name for themselves in the later Southern campaigns, with vast expanses of territory to cover. Other regiments of *Jäger* were occasionally formed into ad hoc mounted infantry units or attached to the Legion or Rangers, and the Americans followed suit with the mounting and use of irregular units made up of militiamen who preferred to fight in a less traditional role. The French also used mixed mounted units, the Lauzon Legion being the most famous.

Siege warfare, a significant component of the Seven Years' War, remained so in the American Revolution. Numerous battles and skirmishes were fought around fixed positions, which were dug in and defended from besieging opponents in the traditional European manner. The sieges of Savannah, Charleston, and Yorktown are classic examples.

BUNKER HILL

Following the first clashes, the surrounding colonies sent militia reinforcements to Boston during the remainder of April and May. By the end of May, militia numbers had swelled to about 17,000 men. The British received reinforcements in the shape of Major-Generals (later Lieutenant-Generals) Sir William Howe, Sir Henry Clinton, and Sir John Burgoyne as well as the 35th, 49th, and 63rd Regiments of Foot over the course of May and June. Gage finally felt equipped to occupy the two dominant heights commanding Boston: Dorchester Heights and Charlestown (Breed's Hill). The rebels received word of this and began to dig a redoubt on Breed's Hill on the evening of June 16, 1775.

The British decided to attack the American positions on Breed's Hill, in an episode that has come down the years of history as the Battle of Bunker Hill.

View of The ATTACK on BUNKER's HILL, with the
Burning of CHARLES TOWN, June 17, 1775.

Colonel William Prescott was in charge of the American forces on the hill; these were estimated at a few thousand men. Defensive positions had been dug from the redoubt down to the Mystic River in an attempt to rebuff any flanking attack from the British. The British sent a force of 2,500 men over to Charlestown in the early afternoon of June 17, under the command of General Howe. Howe, a veteran of the French and Indian War, understood the needs of light infantry and the difficulties of assailing a fixed position straight on, so it is surprising that his main attack was a frontal assault. This choice can perhaps be attributed to the arrogant belief that the rebels would flee once they saw the British regulars advancing.

The British left, under the command of Brigadier Robert Pigott, had marched to within yards of the American lines when a heavy volley was fired into their midst. A second volley followed, forcing the left wing to fall back. The British troops were supported by artillery, but this had no impact on the first attack. One American observer described "the balls flying almost as thick as hailstones from the ships and floating batteries … our people stood the fire some time." Howe's troops on the right flank were similarly unable to breach the American defenses. Pigott launched a second frontal attack with no more success. A British officer said, "the oldest soldiers here [Boston] say that it was the hottest fire they ever saw not even the Battle of Minden [1759] … was equal to it." Howe's second attempt on the right wing failed as well. Reinforcements arrived as the decision was made to attempt a third and final attack.

The American defenders, meanwhile, were running low on ammunition, and Prescott ordered his men to hold their fire until the last possible moment. The British line advanced, and when they were within 30–60ft (9–18m) the Americans fired their last rounds. The British pushed forward with bayonets fixed, driving the Americans from their positions. The Americans managed to retreat over the Charlestown Neck without much opposition, however, as Gage failed to translate the victory into a decisive rout.

The British had seized the hill, but it was a Pyrrhic victory. Of the 2,500 British troops involved, 228 had been killed and 800 wounded. The Americans, on the other hand, had lost only 100 killed and 270 wounded. The casualties were the worst the British suffered during the war. As Gage noted in a letter that was published in the *London Gazette*, "the tryals [sic] we have had shew that the Rebels are not the despicable Rabble too many have supposed them to be" (July 22–25, 1775). This battle also made clear to the Americans that, though they might be successful in defense, they would require a professional Continental-style army to challenge the British in the open fields of America.

After the casualties suffered at Breed's Hill, the British decided not to attack Dorchester Heights. While Charlestown was occupied, the British remained

A depiction of the British amphibious attack on Newport, Rhode Island in August 1778. (National Maritime Museum)

holed up in Boston for the rest of the year. Gage was replaced by Howe as commander-in-chief of British forces in America in October 1775.

BATTLE OF QUÉBEC

The final military campaign of 1775 took place in upstate New York and Canada. American forces had seized the British posts at Fort Ticonderoga and Crown Point in May 1775. In June, the Continental Congress created the Separate Army, giving the command to Major-General Philip Schuyler, along with orders to attack Canada. Schuyler's deputy, Brigadier Richard Montgomery, a former British regular, was given field command of the army. He was ordered to attack towards Montréal and rendezvous with a New England force under the command of Brigadier Benedict Arnold. Arnold's force followed the Penobscot River (in present-day Maine), intending to arrive outside Québec City, the principal British garrison in Canada.

Montgomery's advance went according to plan, but the British and Canadian militiamen at St. John's, Québec, unexpectedly held out for five weeks. Montréal fell on November 13, 1775, with cold weather setting in. Arnold's force had underestimated crossing the Maine frontier, and arrived fatigued and hungry outside Québec in mid-November. Montgomery arrived in early December. The British commander and governor at Québec, Lieutenant-General Sir Guy Carleton, had only 1,800 troops, nearly all of whom were newly raised militia or recruits. Most of the regulars had been sent to Boston.

RICHARD MONTGOMERY

Richard Montgomery (1736–75) was commissioned in the 17th Foot in 1756 and served at Ticonderoga and Crown Point in 1759. In 1772, he resigned his captain's commission, came back to America, married into the wealthy Livingston family in 1773, and espoused the American cause. Following the outbreak of hostilities he was made a brigadier-general in June 1775: he set out to "liberate" Canada, and took forts Saint-Jean and Chambly and the cities of Montréal and Trois-Rivières. Joined by Arnold's troops who had come up from Maine, the American laid siege to Québec. The mighty fortress city was well defended by Governor Carleton, but Montgomery opted for a two-pronged assault. On the snowy night of December 31, 1775, Montgomery was killed leading an assault column on a position defended by Canadian militiamen just below Cape Diamond.

The Americans fielded about 1,000 men. They attacked the city on December 31, one day before many of Arnold's New England troops' terms of enlistment ended. A snowstorm began as the attack was launched; an American soldier, Caleb Haskell, described the scene in his diary:

> This morning about 4 AM the time appointed to storm the city our army divided into different parts to attack the city ... we got near the walls when a heavy fire of cannon and small arms began from the enemy, they being prepared and expecting us that night ... came to the wall cannon roaring like thunder and musket balls flying like hail.

Montgomery was killed and Arnold wounded. The Americans suffered heavy losses, and, though they remained outside the city, the threat to Québec had passed.

The British strategy of 1775 had been to apply overt military action to try to resolve a problem that was essentially political in origin. Their aim in doing so was to quell the growing dissatisfaction of the colonists, and in this they failed. The concentration of British regulars in Boston had not frightened the local population into submission. On the contrary, the population had become more openly hostile in the presence of troops. The attempt to seize and destroy the weapon caches in Concord, while technically successful, had sparked an all-out rebellion. Lack of strategic planning found the bulk of the British North American forces hemmed into Boston, surrounded by a hostile citizenry. The victory at Breed's Hill, won at such great cost, had left the senior commanders in Boston hesitant to destroy the local American forces surrounding them.

Finally, the Americans had almost succeeded in capturing Canada. While an American victory would almost certainly have provoked a more definitive response from the British, the reality remained that the Americans had successfully invaded as far as Québec, conclusively demonstrating just how vulnerable the British were in dealing with the insurrection. Senior members of the British government called for a naval blockade of the colonies, but the ultimate decision was to concentrate resources in a land war.

The Americans had been able to achieve great things in 1775. They had forced the British into Boston and kept them trapped there. Some members of the Continental Congress recognized, however, that the British were not going to give in easily and stressed the need for proper military training and force to counter the British regulars.

Chapter 2

WASHINGTON TAKES OVER, 1775-77

THE LAND WAR IN NORTH AMERICA encompassed a large area, involving the interests of numerous colonial powers, and the incursions of France, Spain, and the Dutch Republic in 1778, 1779, and 1780 respectively, gave the war a more global character. Underpinning these great events is the presence of one man in particular, George Washington, who took command of the Continental Army on its formation on June 14, 1775. George Washington may be history's most underrated commander. Frederick the Great and Napoleon Bonaparte, two other great commanders, were contemporaries. Frederick's career reached its apogee when Washington was a young officer, while Bonaparte entered the world stage in the decade in which Washington last commanded an army in the field. Both are frequently believed to be better commanders than Washington. Yet measured by results, Washington trumped both.

Frederick and Napoleon inherited formidable militaries, and both had extensive military training and experience prior to assuming command of armies. Washington built his army from scratch. The manpower came from a pool of men accustomed to acting independently and who resented authority. Washington had been educated by private tutors and in private schools. He was better educated than 99 percent of the people who lived in British North America at that time but had little formal military training. Prior to assuming

OPPOSITE

This image of Washington Before Yorktown fully evokes the reverence commanded by this historical leader, a reverence warranted by his military accomplishments. (Universal Images Group/ Getty Images)

command of the Continental Army in 1775, he had never commanded anything larger than a regiment.

Frederick's victories added to Prussia's territory and prestige, yet cost Prussia much gold and blood. Ultimately, they failed to elevate Prussia into more than a regional power. Napoleon's meteoric accomplishments led only to his island exile and set France on a path where it devolved from the world's leading nation to a third-rate power. Washington's battlefield accomplishments, despite his deficiencies in background and material, took a scattering of frontier colonies and led them to independence. Because of the way he led this army, he forged the Thirteen Colonies into a unitary nation that within a century would dominate the world.

It was not that Washington did not make mistakes. He made many, perhaps more than Frederick and Napoleon combined over their much longer careers. Washington's initial plans, characteristic of amateur soldiers, were overly

George Washington, the general, a role in which he was heavily self-taught. A contemporary painting by Wilson Peale in 1776. (Culture Club/Getty Images)

complicated. They asked for more than his men could deliver and required split-second timing in an age where commands carried only as far as a human voice, at speeds no faster than that of a galloping horse. Yet Washington was a fast learner. Boston taught him the importance of artillery. The battles for New York City in 1776 taught him both the strengths and weaknesses of his army. More importantly, experience also showed him the strengths and weaknesses of the opposing British forces and provided insights on how to pit American strengths against British weaknesses. These lessons culminated in victories over British garrisons at Trenton and Princeton, victories that revived the flagging rebellion. Washington would make more mistakes notably at the Battle of Brandywine (1777) but he learned from these as well. The most important lesson he learned was that his army was more critical to ultimate victory than territory. After New York, Washington realized that so long as the Continental Congress could field an army, the British had not won and that he could lose any major city in the Thirteen Colonies as long as it remained in existence. An army capable of destroying an isolated British brigade allowed Washington to prevent the British from occupying more than three or four cities at a time.

Washington's battles took place during a transitional period of warfare. At the war's onset, wars were fought by maneuver and siege, by small professional armies. Commanders husbanded troops; they were difficult to replace. Moreover, individual soldiers were rarely trusted to act on their own initiative.

The American Revolution pointed to a new type of warfare, where individual soldiers were motivated by patriotism. Destroying the opponent's armies, not capturing cities, yielded victory. Washington's campaigns heralded this change, serving as the opening curtain for modern warfare; they foreshadowed the *levée en masse* of the French Revolutionary wars. Washington was more than a contemporary of Frederick the Great and Napoleon: he was the bridge between their two styles of fighting. Washington learned that for ultimate American victory, he needed troops capable of meeting and defeating British regulars on an open field. He also needed soldiers who thought of themselves as American first, not Pennsylvanians, Virginians, or New Yorkers. Washington knew that to win he had to chase the enemy out of all the Thirteen Colonies, requiring regiments unconstrained by regional limitations. He recruited soldiers for long terms of service, and organized them into national regiments.

By 1778 he had an army that could successfully contend with British regulars in the open as he demonstrated at Monmouth. He built this army despite several crushing handicaps. Even after the French entered the war as America's allies, Washington's troops faced critical shortages of supplies and money. The Continental Congress proved unequal to raising the funds necessary to equip, feed, and pay the Continental Army. Troops had to build their own quarters, were frequently unshod, and had a commissary system unequal to the task of securing rations.

Washington's enduring legacy lay in his ability to subordinate personal ambition and military capability to civil political objectives. Virtually uniquely among revolutionary military leaders from Oliver Cromwell to Saddam Hussein, Washington confined himself to military goals, eschewing politics when in uniform. He even quashed an attempt by his own army to make him a military dictator.

The path of military glory lured and ultimately destroyed Napoleon. Washington's ability to walk away from the battlefield, to permanently sheath his sword, and willingly relinquish the reins of power made him truly great. Understanding Washington the general the indispensable commander of the Continental cause goes far in helping us to understand how he could do so.

THE LAND WAR: 1776

The spring of 1776 marked further moves towards America's political independence from Great Britain. The fighting of the previous year and the raiding and burning of towns by the Royal Navy had pushed the American colonies beyond the reach of conciliation and closer to cutting their ties conclusively. The colonial governments authorized the use of privateers, war against Loyalists, opening of trade with European nations, and an embargo on

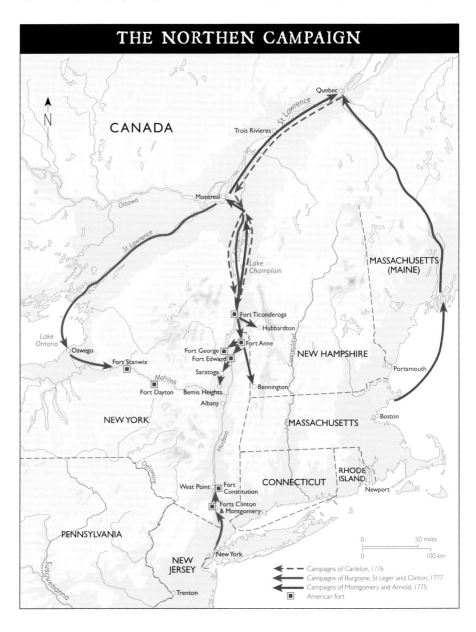

THE NORTHEN CAMPAIGN

CANADA

Quebec

St Lawrence

Trois Rivieres

Montreal

Ottawa

St Lawrence

Lake Champlain

MASSACHUSETTS (MAINE)

Lake Ontario

Oswego

Fort Stanwix

Mohawk

Fort Dayton

Fort Ticonderoga

Hubbardton

Fort Anne

Fort George

Fort Edward

Saratoga

Bemis Heights

Albany

NEW HAMPSHIRE

Connecticut

Portsmouth

Bennington

Boston

NEW YORK

MASSACHUSETTS

Hudson

RHODE ISLAND

West Point

Fort Constitution

CONNECTICUT

Newport

Forts Clinton & Montgomery

Delaware

PENNSYLVANIA

New York

NEW JERSEY

Susquehanna

Trenton

| 0 | | 50 miles |
| 0 | | 100 km |

- - - - Campaigns of Carleton, 1776
——— Campaigns of Burgoyne, St Leger and Clinton, 1777
——— Campaigns of Montgomery and Arnold, 1775
■ American fort

British goods. After much wrangling over terms and conditions, the Thirteen Colonies declared political independence from Great Britain on July 4, 1776, and recreated themselves as the "Thirteen United States of America." The political and social implications of the Declaration of Independence have been debated for decades and fall outside the scope of this work, except to say that this act galvanized some elements of society and alienated others, particularly those who considered themselves neutral on the question. Citizens who wanted outright independence felt that the Declaration of Independence was the last step towards that independence. The Second Continental Congress had finally and formally decided. Some people who sympathized with the original grievances, however, felt that the Declaration of Independence had gone too far. They did not want to sever ties with Britain.

The effect on the Continental Army appeared to be positive. Colonel Benjamin Tallmadge commented that: "the Declaration of Independence ... was announced

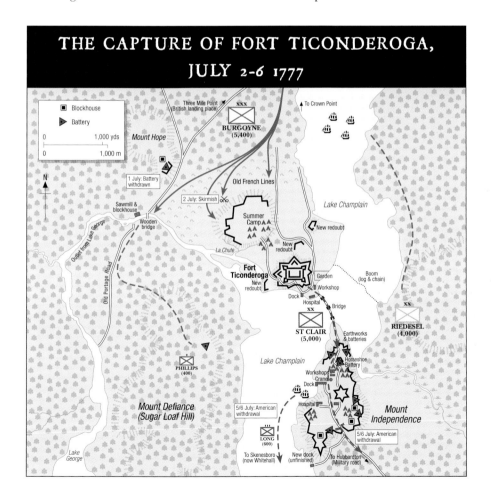

IN CONGRESS, JULY 4, 1776

The unanimous Declaration of the thirteen united States of America.

When in the course of human events it becomes necessary for one people to dissolve the political bands which have connected them with another, and to assume among the powers of the earth, the separate and equal station to which the Laws of Nature and of Nature's God entitle them, a decent respect to the opinions of mankind requires that they should declare the causes which impel them to the separation. ——— We hold these truths to be self-evident, that all men are created equal, that they are endowed by their Creator with certain unalienable Rights, that among these are Life, Liberty and the pursuit of Happiness — That to secure these rights, Governments are instituted among Men, deriving their just powers from the consent of the governed, — That whenever any Form of Government becomes destructive of these ends, it is the Right of the People to alter or to abolish it, and to institute new Government, laying its foundation on such principles, and organizing its powers in such form, as to them shall seem most likely to effect their Safety and Happiness. Prudence, indeed, will dictate that Governments long established should not be changed for light and transient causes; and accordingly all experience hath shewn, that mankind are more disposed to suffer, while evils are sufferable, than to right themselves by abolishing the forms to which they are accustomed. But when a long train of abuses and usurpations, pursuing invariably the same Object, evinces a design to reduce them under absolute Despotism, it is their right, it is their duty, to throw off such Government, and to provide new Guards for their future security. — Such has been the patient sufferance of these Colonies; and such is now the necessity which constrains them to alter their former Systems of Government. The history of the present King of Great Britain is a history of repeated injuries and usurpations, all having in direct object the establishment of an absolute Tyranny over these States. To prove this, let Facts be submitted to a candid world. ——— He has refused his Assent to Laws, the most wholesome and necessary for the public good. ——— He has forbidden his Governors to pass Laws of immediate and pressing importance, unless suspended in their operation till his Assent should be obtained; and when so suspended, he has utterly neglected to attend to them. ——— He has refused to pass other Laws for the accommodation of large districts of people, unless those people would relinquish the right of Representation in the Legislature, a right inestimable to them and formidable to tyrants only. ——— He has called together legislative bodies at places unusual, uncomfortable, and distant from the depository of their public Records, for the sole purpose of fatiguing them into compliance with his measures. ——— He has dissolved Representative Houses repeatedly, for opposing with manly firmness his invasions on the rights of the people. ——— He has refused for a long time, after such dissolutions, to cause others to be elected; whereby the Legislative powers, incapable of Annihilation, have returned to the People at large for their exercise; the State remaining in the mean time exposed to all the dangers of invasion from without, and convulsions within. ——— He has endeavoured to prevent the population of these States; for that purpose obstructing the Laws for Naturalization of Foreigners; refusing to pass others to encourage their migrations hither, and raising the conditions of new Appropriations of Lands. ——— He has obstructed the Administration of Justice, by refusing his Assent to Laws for establishing Judiciary powers. ——— He has made Judges dependent on his Will alone, for the tenure of their offices, and the amount and payment of their salaries. ——— He has erected a multitude of New Offices, and sent hither swarms of Officers to harrass our people, and eat out their substance. ——— He has kept among us, in times of peace, Standing Armies without the Consent of our legislatures. ——— He has affected to render the Military independent of and superior to the Civil power. ——— He has combined with others to subject us to a jurisdiction foreign to our constitution, and unacknowledged by our laws; giving his Assent to their Acts of pretended Legislation: ——— For Quartering large bodies of armed troops among us: ——— For protecting them, by a mock Trial, from punishment for any Murders which they should commit on the Inhabitants of these States: ——— For cutting off our Trade with all parts of the world: ——— For imposing Taxes on us without our Consent: ——— For depriving us in many cases, of the benefits of Trial by Jury: ——— For transporting us beyond Seas to be tried for pretended offences: ——— For abolishing the free System of English Laws in a neighbouring Province, establishing therein an Arbitrary government, and enlarging its Boundaries so as to render it at once an example and fit instrument for introducing the same absolute rule into these Colonies: ——— For taking away our Charters, abolishing our most valuable Laws, and altering fundamentally the Forms of our Governments: ——— For suspending our own Legislatures, and declaring themselves invested with power to legislate for us in all cases whatsoever. ——— He has abdicated Government here, by declaring us out of his Protection and waging War against us. ——— He has plundered our seas, ravaged our Coasts, burnt our towns, and destroyed the lives of our people. ——— He is at this time transporting large Armies of foreign Mercenaries to compleat the works of death, desolation and tyranny, already begun with circumstances of Cruelty & perfidy scarcely paralleled in the most barbarous ages, and totally unworthy the Head of a civilized nation. ——— He has constrained our fellow Citizens taken Captive on the high Seas to bear Arms against their Country, to become the executioners of their friends and Brethren, or to fall themselves by their Hands. ——— He has excited domestic insurrections amongst us, and has endeavoured to bring on the inhabitants of our frontiers, the merciless Indian Savages, whose known rule of warfare, is an undistinguished destruction of all ages, sexes and conditions. In every stage of these Oppressions We have Petitioned for Redress in the most humble terms: Our repeated Petitions have been answered only by repeated injury. A Prince, whose character is thus marked by every act which may define a Tyrant, is unfit to be the ruler of a free people. Nor have We been wanting in attentions to our Brittish brethren. We have warned them from time to time of attempts by their legislature to extend an unwarrantable jurisdiction over us. We have reminded them of the circumstances of our emigration and settlement here. We have appealed to their native justice and magnanimity, and we have conjured them by the ties of our common kindred to disavow these usurpations, which, would inevitably interrupt our connections and correspondence. They too have been deaf to the voice of justice and of consanguinity. We must, therefore, acquiesce in the necessity, which denounces our Separation, and hold them, as we hold the rest of mankind, Enemies in War, in Peace Friends. ———

We, therefore, the Representatives of the united States of America, in General Congress, Assembled, appealing to the Supreme Judge of the world for the rectitude of our intentions, do, in the Name, and by Authority of the good People of these Colonies, solemnly publish and declare, That these United Colonies are, and of Right ought to be Free and Independent States; that they are Absolved from all Allegiance to the British Crown, and that all political connection between them and the State of Great Britain, is and ought to be totally dissolved; and that as Free and Independent States, they have full Power to levy War, conclude Peace, contract Alliances, establish Commerce, and to do all other Acts and Things which Independent States may of right do. ——— And for the support of this Declaration, with a firm reliance on the protection of divine Providence, we mutually pledge to each other our Lives, our Fortunes and our sacred Honor.

Button Gwinnett
Lyman Hall
Geo Walton.

Wm Hooper
Joseph Hewes.
John Penn

Edward Rutledge.
Thos Heyward Junr.
Thomas Lynch Junr.
Arthur Middleton

John Hancock

Samuel Chase
Wm Paca
Thos Stone
Charles Carroll of Carrollton
George Wythe
Richard Henry Lee
Th Jefferson
Benja Harrison
Thos Nelson jr.
Francis Lightfoot Lee
Carter Braxton

Robt Morris
Benjamin Rush
Benja Franklin
John Morton
Geo Clymer
Jas Smith
Geo. Taylor
James Wilson
Geo. Ross
Caesar Rodney
Geo Read
Tho M:Kean

Wm Floyd
Phil. Livingston
Frans Lewis
Lewis Morris
Richd Stockton
Jno Witherspoon
Fras Hopkinson
John Hart
Abra Clark

Josiah Bartlett
Wm Whipple
Saml Adams
John Adams
Robt Treat Paine
Elbridge Gerry
Step Hopkins
William Ellery
Roger Sherman
Samel Huntington
Wm Williams
Oliver Wolcott
Matthew Thornton

to the army in general orders, and filled everyone with enthusiastic zeal, as the point was now forever settled, and there was no further hope of reconciliation and dependence on the mother country" (Tallmadge, p.9.) Such a state of affairs also made a clear distinction between Loyalists and American patriots, a situation that provoked a violent civil war among the civilians of North America.

The British had a strategy in place for the 1776 campaign season. Lord George Germain was the Secretary of State for the American Colonies from November 1775 to February 1782. He was a former military officer and his role was to coordinate military and political strategy with the British commanders in America. Its first component was the British Northern Army. This group, under the command of Major- (later Lieutenant-) General Sir John Burgoyne, was to sail for Québec to lift the siege, then transfer command to General Carleton to clear Canada of American forces, and strike south towards the Hudson River. A second contingent, leaving from Halifax under the command of General Howe, would attack the New York and Long Island region and link up with Carleton coming from the north. The intention was to cut off New England from the rest of the colonies, leaving it to "rot" under a Royal Navy blockade. A third and smaller expedition was to attack Charleston in the south.

NORTHERN CAMPAIGN

During the winter months of 1775–76, the British troops in Boston were hemmed in on three sides. General Howe refused to fight Washington and the New England Army, preferring to wait for reinforcements. Howe was unaware that the New England Army that surrounded him was at times barely capable of offering resistance as it tried to cope with ongoing problems of desertion and re-enlistment. In December 1775 General Washington sent Colonel Henry Knox to Fort Ticonderoga to retrieve the artillery captured by the British and bring it to Dorchester Heights. Fort Ticonderoga placed on Dorchester Heights, and by early March 1776 the guns were in place and firing upon the British in Boston. Howe ordered an attack to take place, but had to cancel the order on account of inclement weather. Howe then decided to evacuate Boston, and did so on March 17, 1776. A British officer called Kemble recorded: "troops ordered to embark

Fort Ticonderoga from the "horseshoe battery" on Mount Independence. The fort is about a half-mile away and the narrows are some 400yds (365m) wide. (Brendan Morrissey)

at 5 in the morning and completed by 8 and under sail by 9" (Kemble, p.73.) The British force sailed from Boston for Halifax, Howe considering that his troops needed rest and refitting before heading towards their next battle in New York.

In Canada, the British relieving force arrived outside Québec on May 6. The Americans lifted the siege and fell back towards Montréal, while the British pushed towards Trois-Rivières. The Continental Army suffered from smallpox and low morale over the course of winter 1775–76, but upon receiving reinforcements attacked the British camp near Trois-Rivières on June 8. The attack failed, and the American Army began to retreat towards Lake Champlain. By the end of June, the Americans had withdrawn from Montréal, Fort Chambly, and St. John's. The British halted their pursuit when they reached Lake Champlain, as Carleton wished to build a flotilla to launch an attack towards Crown Point in the south. This delay allowed the American forces to regroup and fortify the southern areas of Lake Champlain.

On October 11, Carleton sailed with his flotilla and captured Crown Point. His force then moved towards Fort Ticonderoga, where the American garrison refused to surrender. With winter coming on, Carleton decided that a blockade of Ticonderoga was not feasible; wintering in that region without adequate shelter would cause casualties, so he withdrew to winter quarters on the frontier of Canada. The Americans had been driven from Canada, but the objectives of the campaign had not been achieved. Fort Ticonderoga and the southern area of Lake Champlain were still in American hands. As a result, Carleton was branded as being too hesitant, and when the campaign resumed in 1777, the invasion force was under the command of General Burgoyne, who had to finish the job of clearing the southern areas of Lake Champlain.

SOUTHERN CAMPAIGN

A combined force was organized for British operations in the American South. One contingent, under the command of Major- (later Lieutenant-) General

Sir Henry Clinton, originated in Boston, while a second was organized to sail from Ireland. Their objectives were to coordinate the raising and support of Loyalist corps in the southern colonies. Both contingents encountered problems in reaching their destinations; Clinton arrived at Cape Fear on March 12, after the Loyalists of North Carolina had been organized and then soundly defeated at Moore's Creek Bridge on February 27, 1776. Following the arrival of the second contingent, Clinton decided to set sail for South Carolina and capture Sullivan's Island, which protected the estuary leading to Charleston.

The attack on the island highlighted the problems of coordinating an amphibious operation. The naval commander, Admiral Sir Peter Parker, and Clinton communicated poorly, failing to coordinate plans and intelligence. The fort protecting the island, commanded by Colonel William Moultrie, was well fortified, with capable gunners manning the defenses. The British attack began on June 28. The fort not only withstood the attack, but also inflicted heavy damage on the Royal Navy ships. Commanders on land could not launch their attack because the Royal Navy could not get close enough to provide support. The British withdrew and the force sailed for New York to link up with Howe's troops, arriving on August 2.

Map of Charleston, South Carolina, from an atlas of battles of the American Revolution printed in 1845. (Cascoly/Alamy Stock Photo)

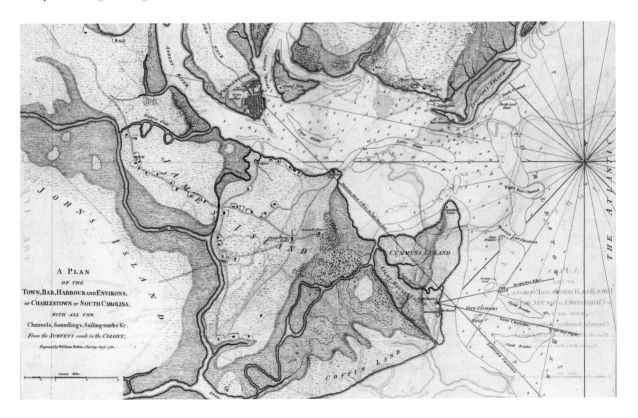

MIDDLE ATLANTIC CAMPAIGN

General Washington sent Major-General Charles Lee, a former British regular, to assess the defenses of the New York City region. Lee understood that defending the region would be too problematic, as the British would certainly have a numerical as well as a naval advantage, permitting them to land troops at will. General Lee decided to fortify areas where the Americans might at least hold up the British regulars and inflict heavy casualties. He was then directed to head south to shore up defenses in South Carolina.

In April, Washington moved to New York to make preparations for the defense of the region with the remainder of the New England Army. Forts were constructed along the Hudson and designated Forts Lee and Washington. Washington also needed men to defend the area, and summoned some 20,000 soldiers, many of them militia, from the colonies around New York. As Colonel Tallmadge noted: "the American Army [was] composed principally of levies, or troops raised for short periods, and militia." Washington sent most of his troops to Long Island and constructed fortifications along the heights of Brooklyn and the hills south of the heights. The troops on Long Island were placed under the command of Major-General Israel Putnam, whose defensive lines were poorly organized: too long and too lightly held. Washington, however, approved the plans, and they proceeded accordingly.

Unlike South Carolina, the British amphibious operations carried out in New York Harbor were an excellent example of coordinated army/navy planning. Howe and his troops reached New York from Halifax in late June. On July 2, light infantry units seized control of Staten Island. The rest of the British Army was disembarked to camp there for the remainder of July, while Howe awaited reinforcements from Europe and Clinton's forces arriving from the south. The bulk of the reinforcements arrived from Europe in early August, mainly Guards regiments and German auxiliaries.

On August 22, the first British units landed on Long Island. Lieutenant Colonel Stephen Kemble wrote: "landed about 9 in the morning ... without the smallest opposition ...

Major-General Charles Lee. His career was not generally helped by an often slovenly appearance and constant reliance upon bad language. (Anne S.K. Brown Collection, Brown University Library)

the whole on the shore by 12 o'clock making fourteen thousand seven hundred men" (Kemble, p.85.) A force of light infantry, grenadiers, and other regiments proceeded east to reconnoiter the American fortified positions in the hills south of Brooklyn Heights. The British commanders realized that a direct assault would be difficult, while forward units under the command of General Clinton noted that the American left flank was weakly defended. The British decided on a flanking attack to roll the Americans up from behind.

By August 25, all of the British troops, nearly 20,000 men, had been assembled on Long Island. The battle of Long Island was to be the largest battle of the war in terms of total numbers of men involved. General Howe sent a large force, commanded by General Clinton, to attack the American left flank. Two brigades, under the command of Major-General James Grant, were under orders to attack the American right flank while Clinton's units dealt with the left, creating a diversion. The Hessian Division, under the command of Lieutenant-General Leopold von Heister, was to attack the American center, commanded by Major-General John Sullivan.

Clinton's force moved into position overnight on August 26–27, and General Grant's brigades began to move towards the American lines. Captain Francis Rawdon described how "we got through the pass at daybreak without any opposition … we fired two pieces of cannon to let him [Grant] know we were at hand" (Scheer and Rankin, p.166.)

The battle began at 9:00am with General Grant's troops and the Hessian division attacking. The American Colonel Tallmadge commented, "before such an overwhelming force of disciplined troops, our small band could not maintain

British troops enter New York City in July 1776. (MPI/ Getty Images)

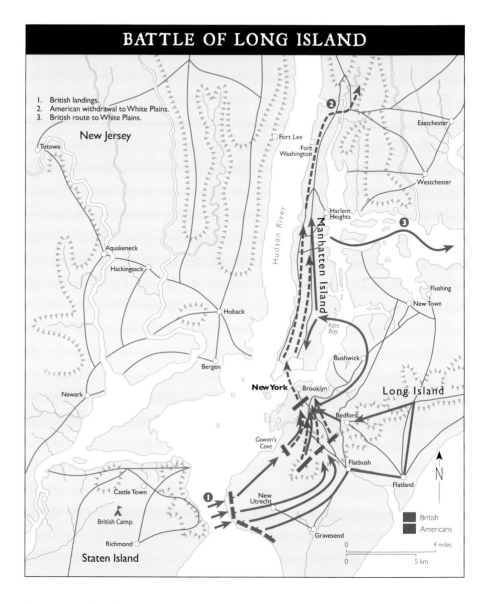

BATTLE OF LONG ISLAND

1. British landings.
2. American withdrawal to White Plains.
3. British route to White Plains.

New Jersey

Totowa

Aquakeneck

Hackingsack

Hoback

Bergen

Newark

New York

Brooklyn

Gowan's
Cove

Castle Town

British Camp

Richmond

Staten Island

New
Utrecht

Gravesend

Fort Lee

Fort
Washington

Hudson River

Manhatten Island

Harlem
Heights

Kips
Bay

Bushwick

Bedford

Flatbush

Flatland

Long Island

Eastchester

Westchester

Flushing

New Town

N

British

Americans

0   4 miles
0   5 km

their ground, and the main body retired within their lines" (Tallmadge, p.9.) The British and Hessians smashed into the American center, which began to collapse. The fighting in the trenches and redoubts was bloody. A British officer described how "the Hessians and our brave Highlanders gave no quarter and it was a fine sight to see with what alacrity they dispatched the Rebels with their bayonets after we surrounded them" (Scheer and Rankin, p.167.)

The American right flank held up better than the center line until Clinton's force began to attack from the rear. Some of the fiercest fighting took place as the American right flank attempted to pull back. The troops of the Maryland regiments acquitted themselves well in attempting to force a hole in the British lines. After a series of heavy fights in the marshes behind their positions, the American right wing broke up into small parties and attempted to reach the fortified lines at Brooklyn Heights.

Colonel Tallmadge recorded the bitterness of the fighting on Long Island: "this was the first time in my life that I had witnessed the awful scene of a battle. ... I well remember my sensations on the occasion, for they were solemn beyond description." American private Joseph Plumb Martin recalled how, when his unit was shipped over to Long Island to support the defenses at Brooklyn Heights, "[they] now began to meet the wounded men, another sight I was unacquainted with, some with broken arms, some with broken legs, and some with broken heads."

The British were outside the defenses of Brooklyn Heights by midday, but Howe decided not to attack right away. He feared that the defenses were too strong, although he was mistaken in this assumption and they might have been easily breached. By 10:00pm on August 29 the Americans had begun to withdraw 9,000 men from Long Island and retreat to Manhattan, over the East River. The British were not aware of the withdrawal and Lieutenant Colonel

The attempt to defend New York by garrisoning Long Island was Washington's greatest strategic error during the American Revolution. The British army easily routed the green American soldiers. (Universal History Archive/ Getty Images)

Stephen Kemble noted: "in the morning to our great astonishment found they had evacuated all their works on Brookland [Brooklyn]" (Kemble, p.86.) Part of the reason for this was, as pointed out by Colonel Tallmadge, that "the troops began to retire from the lines in such a manner that no chasm was made in the lines" (Tallmadge, p.10.) It is estimated that the Americans lost nearly 1,000 men killed and wounded, plus another 940–1400 captured. The British lost 300 men killed and 500 wounded.

General Howe did not move against Washington's army on Manhattan Island because peace negotiations were still a possibility. The Declaration of Independence proved a stumbling block, however, and on September 15, some 4,000 British troops landed on Manhattan Island at Kip's Bay, after clearing most of the western end of Long Island. The British decided to secure the beachhead area instead of attempting to cut off the retreating American forces from lower Manhattan. This strategy allowed the Americans to retreat up the west side of Manhattan Island.

A combined force of Hessians and British light infantry was repulsed at Harlem Heights in northern Manhattan on September 16. The Americans held fortified positions at the northern end of the island, and the British decided not to attack frontally. Instead, they embarked and landed to the north of Manhattan on October 12. Washington recognized the danger of being cut off and decided to pull most of his troops off the island and into Westchester County New York, leaving a large contingent at Fort Washington, while the majority withdrew to White Plains and entrenched themselves there.

The British forces attacked the American positions at White Plains on October 28. Colonel Tallmadge reported that "at dawn of the day, the Hessian column advanced within musket shot of our troops ... at first they fell back, but rallied again immediately" (Tallmadge, p.14.) The focus of the battle was Chadderton's Hill, which dominated the area and was held by the Americans. After two attempts, British forces took the hill, and the rest of the day was spent with the two sides exchanging cannon and small-arms fire. After a few days, Washington withdrew further afield with his troops. Here again, Howe failed to press his advantage to try to capture and destroy Washington's army. Instead he returned to Manhattan Island to besiege Fort Washington.

The British Lieutenant-General Earl Hugh Percy had previously made an attempt on Fort Washington from the south but had recognized that it was well defended. By November 15, the fort was surrounded on all sides by British troops, including Royal Navy ships on the Hudson River. Washington withdrew across the Hudson into New Jersey on November 16, but a large group of troops remained stationed on the eastern side of the river, under the command of General Lee, to forestall any British incursion into southern New England.

On November 16, Fort Washington was attacked from three sides. The fort fell with more than 3,000 American soldiers killed, wounded, or captured, and American control of the Hudson was compromised. Following this victory, Howe decided to divide his forces. He sent Major- (later Lieutenant-) General Earl Charles Cornwallis and 4,000 soldiers to Closter, New Jersey, on November 20. Cornwallis was able to threaten Fort Lee, which was evacuated. He pushed hard to entrap Washington and his army. Howe followed and landed with another contingent, meeting up with Cornwallis at New Brunswick, New Jersey, in early December. Howe also dispatched a contingent of 7,000 men under the command of General Clinton to seize Newport, Rhode Island. Both the town and the island on which it was located were in British hands by December 8, giving the British control of Narragansett Bay.

Cornwallis and Howe together chased Washington and his army across New Jersey. On December 8, Washington and his army crossed the Delaware River as the British entered Trenton. On December 14 the British were ordered into winter quarters in New Jersey. British and Hessian troops were quartered throughout the region, and Washington devised a bold scheme. He decided to attack the Hessian positions in Trenton on December 25, and his plan was completely successful. The Hessians were soundly defeated, for two reasons: the Hessian Colonel Rall had failed to fortify their positions; and the date of the attack meant that many soldiers had been celebrating the holiday. The Americans lost four men wounded, compared with more than 1,000 Hessians captured.

Small islands like these are found along the Delaware River. Washington used these islands, found near McKonkey's Ferry, to hide the boats that were used to carry the American Army across the river on the evening of December 25, 1776. (David Bonk)

Washington re-crossed the Delaware on the night of December 25, only to go back again on December 27, when he headed towards Trenton. Howe had ordered Cornwallis and 8,000 troops to find and destroy Washington's force. Cornwallis's force came into contact with Washington in Trenton on January 2, 1777. A Hessian officer, Captain Johann Ewald noted: "the *Jägers* and light infantry, supported by the Hessian Grenadiers, attacked the enemy at once, whereupon he withdrew through Trenton across the bridge." Washington was caught at Assunpink Creek. During the evening, however, Washington, realizing his position, marched first due east then due north towards Princeton. Ewald described "this clever man [Washington] who did not doubt that Lord Cornwallis would realize his mistake during the night and would dispatch a corps ... whereby he would be forced by circumstances to surrender" (Ewald, p.49.)

The British forces at Princeton were surprised and compelled to give ground. Washington, however, was forced to head to the mountains in Morristown when news arrived that Cornwallis was heading towards Princeton. Morristown offered Washington the option of counteracting a British move from either New York to the north along the Hudson or across New Jersey towards Philadelphia.

The British had lost more than 1,000 men in the course of one week. Howe pulled his forces back to New Brunswick, thus abandoning most of New Jersey. As with operations in Canada, the British were put on the defensive and would have to regain lost ground in the campaigns of 1777, when they aimed to seize Philadelphia.

The successes of late 1776 had given the American cause a significant boost in morale. An American soldier commented that "our taking the Hessians has given our affairs quite a different turn as the militia are embodying in all parts of the Jerseys." Ewald appraised public opinion of Washington and Cornwallis: [actions at Trenton and Princeton] "raised so much hubbub and sensation in the world and gave Washington the reputation of an excellent general, derived simply and solely from Lord Cornwallis' mistake of not marching in two columns to Trenton" (Ewald, p.50.)

The British had lost the initiative and were clearly no longer within striking distance of Philadelphia, the perceived governmental headquarters of the Thirteen Colonies. George Washington and the remnants of his army had survived the 1776 campaigns. The foundations of the Continental Army had been laid. A French officer writing a report described the American forces thus: "men need only the experience of defeats in order to learn how to defend themselves properly and acquire the military effectiveness necessary in order to inspire respect on the enemy" (Reicicourt, p.211.)

Lieutenant-General Earl Charles Cornwallis. Like many other commanders of the American Revolution, he was a veteran of the Seven Years' War. (Anne S.K. Brown Collection, Brown University Library)

THE LAND WAR: 1777

The British strategy for 1777, dictated by the government in London, provides the clearest example of failed strategies planned by generals in North America. General Burgoyne and his army were ordered to push south from Canada and take Albany and the Hudson River. Burgoyne was expected to wait in Albany to link up with General Howe. General Howe did not see that Burgoyne required his support, and, holed up in New York with his troops, decided that they would not link up with Burgoyne as planned. Leaving only a secondary group in New York to push north, Howe took the major part of the British army in New York and set out to seize Philadelphia by amphibious assault. Howe felt that, since Philadelphia represented the independence movement, the seizure of the Continental Congress might force an end to the conflict. Historians have debated the "what ifs" of this decision-making process thoroughly, but it is indisputably clear that both Howe and Burgoyne underestimated the American forces and paid a high price for their miscalculation. The war became global partly due to the incompetent performance of 1777. After the campaigns of 1777, Great Britain would be forced to strip her army in North America to fight a global war against France and later Spain and the Dutch Republic.

The Continental Army, under the command of General Washington, was deployed to counter the British attacks in Pennsylvania. It suffered defeats in this undertaking but survived, never being completely destroyed. The "Separate Army," now referred to as the "Northern Army," under the command of General Philip Schuyler with Major-General Horatio Gates as his subordinate, formed to fight Burgoyne's army. The majority of troops used to defend New York from the British were made up of militia from New England and New York, with Continentals representing a small corps of the total numbers.

NORTHERN CAMPAIGN

The principal northern campaign began in Canada. Lieutenant-General Burgoyne advanced from St. John's, Québec, towards Lake Champlain with 10,000 men in June 1777. A secondary drive of 1,600 troops, regulars, provincials, and Indians was sent from Fort Oswego in the west under the command of Lieutenant-Colonel Barry St. Leger. St. Leger was to march due east along the Mohawk River and link up with Burgoyne at Albany.

Burgoyne's force reached Fort Ticonderoga on July 1. The American commander at Ticonderoga, Brigadier Arthur St. Clair, expected the attack to come from the front, but Burgoyne placed cannon on a hill opposite. St. Clair, recognizing the danger, withdrew his force of 3,000 militia

Washington's Life Guard was formed from 180 men chosen from each state. During the battle of Brandywine, Count Casimer Pulaski was given command of about 30 mounted men of the Life Guard to charge the British. Later, at Valley Forge, Washington's Life Guard was re-organized and trained as a model for the rest of the Continental Army. (Troiani, Don (b.1949)/ Private Collection/ Bridgeman Images)

and Continentals to the south on July 5. Leaving a small detachment at Ticonderoga to maintain communications with Canada, Burgoyne pushed south to harry St. Clair's rearguard, reaching Skenesboro by July 10. At Skenesboro, Burgoyne decided to march overland to Forts Ann and Edward instead of returning north to travel down Lake George. The Americans anticipated Burgoyne's plan and set out

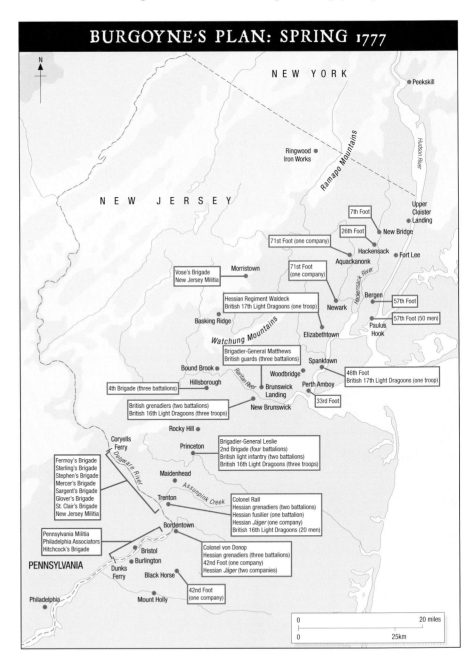

BURGOYNE'S PLAN: SPRING 1777

THE BRUNSWICK DRAGOONS AT BENNINGTON, AUGUST 16, 1777

The climax of the engagement at Bennington was the storming of the main redoubt, commanded by Lieutenant-Colonel Baum himself and held by 200 dragoons, 25 rangers, and a 3-pdr gun of the Hesse-Hanau artillery. Convinced that the Native Americans were patrolling the woods and that the Americans massing in them were Loyalist recruits, Baum did not realize his error until Nichol and Herrick attacked around 3.00pm. They were soon joined by other American units that had overcome the defenses at the bridge. Outnumbered, surrounded, and almost out of ammunition, the dragoons were forced to draw their sabers and cut their way out through the woods and meadows to the southwest. About 30 dragoons, including Baum, reached the river, but they were intercepted and Baum was mortally wounded; only seven dragoons arrived back to Burgoyne, leaving the regiment with a single troop barely quarter strength. (Adam Hook © Osprey Publishing)

to block his path. A British officer, Lieutenant William Digby, noted on July 24: "the enemy have felled large trees over the roads which were turned so narrow as not to allow more than one man ... we were obliged to cut around the wood which was attended by much fatigue and labour" (Journal of Lt. William Digby.) Supplies became a problem early in the campaign; Burgoyne commented on July 9 and 10, "the army much fatigued, many parts of it having wanted their provisions for two days" (Letters of Lord Howe, General Burgoyne and Lord George Germain.) He also described the effect of the terrain: "the toil of the march was great ... forty bridges to construct and others to repair" (Letters of Lord Howe, General Burgoyne and Lord George Germain.)

The British reached Fort Edward on the Hudson River on July 30 and occupied Fort George on the same day. The Americans were still falling back to the south and across the river in the Saratoga region, but the ever-present need for supplies forced the British to stop and rest at Fort Edward. On August 11, a detachment of 600 men, comprising German auxiliaries, provincial troops, and Indians, under the command of Lieutenant-Colonel Frederick Baum, was instructed to march southeast towards Bennington, "to obtain large supplies of cattle, horses and carriages."

Brigadier John Stark and 2,000 New England militiamen met Baum's column outside Bennington on August 16, where they surrounded and destroyed them. A second German column, which had been sent in aid of Baum's efforts on August 14, closed in on Bennington as the militia pillaged Baum's camp. The militia re-formed to destroy the second column as well. Burgoyne shortly received word of the defeat and loss of almost 1,000 men.

The "uniform" of the militia (and other units) is well depicted by this 1860 depiction of a Virginia Rifleman. (NARA)

Lieutenant Digby wrote on August 20 that "the German detachment at Bennington was destroyed and ... St. Leger was forced to retire to Oswego" (Journal of Lt. William Digby.) On August 19, Major-General Gates took over command of the Northern Army from General Schuyler. Recruits were on the rise as word of the successes at Bennington spread and raised spirits in the area. On September 13–14, Burgoyne's army crossed the Hudson River near Saratoga. Supplies were still at a premium for the British, and Lieutenant James Haddon, an officer in the Royal Artillery, described a general order that warned troops to "be cautious of expending their ammunition in case of action ... the impossibility of a fresh supply ... avoid firing on a retreating army" (Hadden, p.150.) Upon taking command, General Gates marched north towards Bemis Heights, which controlled the main Saratoga–Albany road. General Schuyler had fortified Bemis Heights in August.

The first firefight between the two armies occurred on September 18, when British soldiers foraging for food were ambushed by American forces. On September 19, Burgoyne set out to deal with Bemis Heights, only to be intercepted by Major-General Benedict Arnold, who smashed into the British column with 3,000 troops at Freeman's Farm. The fighting was heavy; Lieutenant Digby related that "the clash of cannon and musketry never ceased till darkness ... when they [Americans] retired to their camp leaving us the master of the field but it was a dear bought victory." The British suffered more than 600 men killed and wounded in this incident, while the Americans lost just over 300 men killed and wounded. Burgoyne decided to stay in the area and build a defensive position for the army after he received word from Lieutenant-General Clinton in New York, promising a push up the Hudson River. Clinton marched north with 3,000 troops on October 3, and his force moved quickly, seizing Verplanck's Point, as well as Forts Montgomery, Constitution, and Clinton by October 7. Clinton sent a detachment of 2,000 men and supplies towards Albany to meet Burgoyne, whose situation was rapidly deteriorating. The Americans had all but cut off communications between Burgoyne and Canada, seized Fort George, and threatened Fort Ticonderoga.

Lieutenant-General Sir Henry Clinton served as commander-in-chief of British forces from 1778 to 1782. (Anne S.K. Brown Collection, Brown University Library)

Burgoyne decided to attack the American positions at Bemis Heights once again on October 7, instead of falling back towards the Hudson. He sent a strong force to engage the American left flank; this was repulsed and fell back to the British lines. Major Henry Dearborn noted, "a body of the enemy [was] advancing towards our lines ... at about 4 o'clock the battle began ... the rifles and light infantry fell upon the enemy's right flank and rear ... they then retreated with great precipitation and confusion" (Dearborn p.108.) British morale was very low, and sank further when Clinton's detachment was forced to return after the pilots refused to proceed any further up the Hudson, leaving Burgoyne's troops stranded and outnumbered two to one.

On October 8, Burgoyne decided to pull back, only to discover that Gates had already cut off his retreat. Burgoyne created a defended camp north of Saratoga and the Americans began to close in. Lieutenant Digby observed: "their cannon and ours began to play on each other. They took many of our batteaus on the river as our artillery could not protect them" (Journal of Lt. William Digby.) Another British officer, Thomas Anburey, noted: "we are now become so habituated to fire that the soldiers seem to be indifferent to it" (Anburey, p. 181.)

On October 14, Burgoyne began to negotiate the surrender of his forces, and on October 17 the remains of his force marched out of camp. The British surrendered almost 6,000 men, shattering British prestige the world over. The surrender effectively removed any threat to the Hudson River region and New England from the north.

The American forces had distinguished themselves, but the British commanders had forgotten the rules they had learned in the French and Indian War about waging war in the hilly, wooded countryside of the American frontier. The American generals, especially Arnold, had demonstrated themselves equal to the task required of them. The militia had fought well when they had the advantage of terrain, as at Bennington, while the Continentals had fought well at Freeman's Farm.

MIDDLE ATLANTIC CAMPAIGN

Howe's campaign in the Middle Atlantic centered around the engagements at Brandywine and Germantown. He moved troops into New Jersey in an attempt to draw Washington and the "Main Army" out for battle. This maneuver produced a series of skirmishes but was a failure overall, prompting Howe to return to Staten Island. Over the course of July, troops embarked onto Royal Navy ships and transports, and on July 23 the fleet sailed. On August 25, the fleet landed its cargo on the northern reaches of Chesapeake Bay at the Head of Elk. Washington received word of the landing and marched south with the Main Army, 18,000 strong, to confront the British. Washington placed his army at Brandywine Creek and built up the area into a defensive position. Though strong generally, the American position had left its flanks unprotected. Howe, approaching with his troops, saw the potential for another successful flank attack. An American soldier described how, "at 8 o'clock in the morning on the 11th [September] a considerable body of the enemy appeared opposite to us" (Samuel Shaw.)

Fighting at the Breymann Redoubt during the battle of Saratoga. (Adam Hook © Osprey Publishing)

The defeat at Saratoga prompted the British "Southern Strategy." The American commander Daniel Morgan is at right center in the light-colored hunting uniform. Horatio Gates is at center, arms outspread. After a painting by John Trumbull. (NARA)

The battle commenced at 10:00am. A sizable column of Hessian and British units were sent in opposite the center and left flank of the American lines, under the command of Lieutenant-General Wilhelm von Knyphausen. A large formation of light infantry, plus Guards and Grenadiers units, under the command of General Cornwallis, moved without being detected against the American right flank, in a march 18 miles (30km) long, intending to create havoc in the American lines. The other British lines were successful in pushing the American lines back, and the British left flank finally joined the battle at about 4:00pm. As Major John Andre noted: "the rebels were driven back by the superior fire of the troops, but these troops were too much exhausted to be able to charge or pursue" (Andre, p. 46.)

The Americans reacted, but did not panic. When the British left flank finally smashed through the American lines, the Americans began to retreat, but in fairly good order, not as a rabble. A French officer serving with the American forces declared: "if the English had followed up their advantages that day, Washington's Army would have been spoken of no more" (Accounts of Brandywine, Germantown, and the Siege of Gibraltar.)

The battle at Brandywine Creek cost the Americans more than 1,000 men killed, wounded, and captured. The British lost half that number. The British had won but were not in a position to follow up their victory aggressively; they were simply too tired after their long march. The two armies fell back towards Philadelphia over the next few weeks and a series of small skirmishes took place. On September 26, the British marched into Philadelphia. This was an important achievement psychologically, but not as important strategically as Howe's continued failure to completely destroy Washington's Main Army as it withdrew to the west of the city. The Continental Congress had already been evacuated to Lancaster and later moved to Yorktown. Howe moved to the north of the city and encamped his army at Germantown.

Following the defeat and occupation of Philadelphia, Washington set out to destroy the British camp at Germantown. He deployed four columns—two militia and two Continental—intended to converge on the British lines simultaneously. Private Joseph Plumb Martin recorded that at "about daybreak [October 4] our advanced guard and the British outposts came in contact ... they soon fell back and we advanced, when the action became general. The enemy [was] driven quite through their camp. They left their kettles ... affairs went on well for some time" (Martin, pp. 72–73.)

The American advance became bogged down in trying to take a position held by the 40th Regiment at Chew House. As Major Andre noted, "these [soldiers of the 40th Regiment] not only maintained themselves a great while but drove the rebels off repeatedly" (Andre, p.55.) By the time the Americans moved on, the rest of the British forces had rallied. Colonel Tallmadge stated, "during this transaction [Chew House] time elapsed, the situation of our troops was uncomfortable, their ardor abated and the enemy obtained time to rally. In less than thirty minutes, our troops began to retire, and from the ardor of the pursuit, were in full retreat" (Tallmadge pp. 22–23.)

Not all of Washington's troops took part in the battle due to the weather, but again the British were unable to follow up their victory to encircle and destroy the Main Army. The losses for the Americans were some 1,000 killed, wounded, and captured, while the British lost 500 men. Howe pulled back his defensive lines around the city of Philadelphia, and once again the British found themselves on the defensive with

Battle of Germantown, October 4, 1777. Germantown was another early defeat, and a critical learning experience, for Washington. (Annesk Brown Collection, Brown University Library)

the Americans, although weakened, still able to inflict damage upon their troops. The British cleared defenses on the Delaware River to allow seaborne supplies to reach the city. Washington was having difficulty keeping his army together, as enlistment contracts expired for many men. This depletion convinced Washington not to attack, but Howe was left once again at the end of 1777 without a decisive victory to his credit. Washington withdrew his army into winter quarters at Valley Forge, Pennsylvania in mid-December, where the troops were retrained under the drill instructor eyes of Major-General von Steuben.

The campaign of 1777 finally ended in November. The British had been soundly defeated at Saratoga, and the war seemed likely to become a global conflict with the entrance of France. Howe had defeated the Main Army, but had been unable to destroy it conclusively. The American "capitol" had been taken, but even this decisive action did not signify the end of the war.

The year 1778 marked the true beginning of the end of the British presence in the Thirteen Colonies. Both the British Army and the Royal Navy were redirected to other parts of the world to deal with French and, later, Spanish antagonism. The years 1775–77, in retrospect, were the closest the British came to ending the uprising with military force. It is debatable whether the political rebellion would have continued if the American forces had been decisively defeated in a land war.

Frederik William Augustus, Baron von Steuben, who played a critical role in reforming the Continental Army. (ZU_09/Getty Images)

The burning of New York. British soldiers apprehended and dealt roughly with suspected rebels who were blamed for starting the fires. (Library of Congress)

Chapter 3

INTERNATIONAL WAR, 1778-81

*T*HE BRITISH FORCES IN NORTH AMERICA were by 1778 centered around New York, Philadelphia, Newport, Florida, Halifax, Québec, and Montréal. A formal alliance, signed on February 6, 1778, between the American and French governments forced a change of strategy. Over the first few months of the year, Benjamin Franklin was instrumental in lobbying the French court to support the American cause. British commanders were reassigned. General Clinton was ordered to take command of the forces in the Thirteen Colonies, replacing General Howe. In Canada General Carleton was replaced by Lieutenant-General Frederick Haldimand. Senior commanders in North America and Great Britain realized that the focus of war had shifted fundamentally and that France had become the primary threat. In March, Clinton received his orders for the whole of 1778. He was to withdraw British forces from Philadelphia and send troops to New York and then to the West Indies to fight the French. The British were to hold New York, Newport, and Canada. Naval raids were scheduled along the New England coast, and a southern campaign was planned. The overarching strategy was that the British Army would control major towns along the coast, and the navy would allow it to raid at will. Peace negotiations were to be opened between the Continental Congress and the British government.

OPPOSITE

General Washington at the Battle of Monmouth, 1778. (North Wind Picture Archives/Alamy Stock Photo)

MIDDLE ATLANTIC CAMPAIGN

General Washington and his Main Army had a difficult winter at Valley Forge, 18 miles (40km) north of Philadelphia. Many men were released from duty when their enlistment contracts expired, but a corps of men and officers remained who were properly trained for linear warfare, thanks to the training program created by Major-General von Steuben and their experience in battle. Colonel Tallmadge noted on the eve of the 1778 campaign that the Main Army began "feeling somewhat like veteran troops" (Tallmadge, p. 27.) Washington used the winter to develop a plan for militia to be used to guard specific areas, releasing Continental troops and extra militia units for mobile operations. Many historians consider the Continental Army that marched out of Valley Forge against Clinton's army the most highly trained and disciplined American force of the entire conflict. In spite of this, personnel shortfalls continued. The number of men enlisted was still well below the army's authorized strengths, which limited Washington's ability to attack Philadelphia.

A French officer of the Armagnac Regiment. (Parks Canada)

On May 8, General Clinton arrived in Philadelphia to take over command from General Howe. Clinton was ordered to withdraw from Philadelphia and decided to march overland to Sandy Hook, New Jersey. Three thousand Loyalists who feared for their safety were shipped by sea to New York, and on June 18 Clinton set off with nearly 10,000 troops and more Loyalist refugees towards New York. Private Joseph Plumb Martin remembered: "we heard the British army had left Philadelphia ... we marched immediately in pursuit" (Martin, p. 122.) The American force shadowed the withdrawing British Army, monitoring the train of supplies and men, which stretched for 12 miles (19km). Very high temperatures made for very slow going.

Major-General Charles Lee was sent with 5,000 men to harass the British rearguard, while the rest of the Main Army stayed further back. On June 28, Washington ordered Lee to attack the rearguards, although he was not certain of their size. Lee sent in the attack near Monmouth Courthouse. The fighting quickly became confused; as British officer Kemble noted: "Lee then advanced to begin the attack, but falling in with our two Grenadiers Battalions, and a Battalion of Guards, who facing about charged and pushed them above two miles" (Kemble, p. 154.) This account was confirmed by an American soldier, Jeremiah Greenman: "our division under the command of General Lee advanced towards the enemy. They formed in a solid column then fired a volley at us they being so much superior to our numbers we retreated."

The discipline imparted through the drill that the Continental Army acquired at Valley Forge provided Washington with troops that were capable of meeting the British on equal terms in the open field for the first time in the war. This image shows Baron von Steuben drilling Washington's army at Valley Forge. (Library of Congress)

Lee had smashed into the British 2nd Division, led by General Cornwallis. Washington deployed the remainder of his army to face the British counterattack, the brunt of which was borne by New England regiments. A heated verbal exchange occurred between Lee and Washington following Lee's retreat. Lee was relieved of command and would later face court martial for not obeying orders. Lee was also suspected of being a British sympathizer. An American soldier, describing the scene, said: "a sharp conflict ensued; these troops [New Englanders] maintained their ground until the whole force of the enemy that could be brought to bear had charged upon them" (Scheer and Rankin, p. 331.) Major Andre described how "this column [American] appeared to our left and rear marching very rapidly and in good order" (Andre, pp. 78-79.) The British, while successful at points along the line, launched attacks without proper orders and were unable to maintain consistent pressure. The battle was the longest of the war, beginning in early morning and lasting all day. Small pieces of land were exchanged, as were artillery duels. General Washington was able to push the British back to their original positions by the early evening. The American forces succeeded in holding the line against a British assault in the open field and retaking lost territory. The heat of the day had taken a toll, however, and neither side attempted another assault as night approached. Clinton withdrew his force when evening fell, unmolested by the Americans. He was running short of supplies and needed to reach Sandy Hook and meet the Royal Navy. The British had lost nearly 1,000 men killed, wounded, and captured, while the American forces had lost just half that.

The outcome of the battle of Monmouth was indecisive. The Americans claimed victory, but Clinton disputed "the manifest misapplication of that term [victory] to an army whose principle is retreat and which accomplishes it without affront or loss" (Clinton, p. 97.) Clinton was able to withdraw to Sandy Hook and was evacuated to New York by July 6, before the French fleet arrived, so he had

Planning the 1778 campaign at Valley Forge, Washington used the Potts House as his headquarters when the Continental Army was in winter quarters at Valley Forge, Pennsylvania, in the winter of 1777–78. (Graham Turner © Osprey Publishing)

fulfilled his orders. The British had failed to destroy or even force the Americans from the battlefield, which provided another morale boost for the Americans. More important, the Americans successfully counterattacked and seized ground in the open. As Captain Johann Ewald commented: "today the Americans showed much boldness and resolution on all sides during their attacks. Had Generals Washington and Lee not attacked so early, but waited longer, until our army had pushed deeper into the very difficult defiles in this area, it is quite possible we would have been routed" (Ewald, p.136.)

NORTHERN CAMPAIGN

On July 11 a French fleet, carrying 4,000 soldiers, arrived off Sandy Hook under the command of Admiral Charles Hector Comte d'Estaing. Clinton's successful withdrawal and redeployment meant that New York was no longer a feasible target, and the fleet shortly sailed for Newport, Rhode Island, arriving off the coast on July 29. On August 9 a second force, this one American and commanded by Major-General John Sullivan, arrived with 10,000 Continental and militia troops, to attack the British position from the north. The British had 3,000 troops at Newport under the command of General Sir Robert Pigot. The French fleet was followed closely by British Admiral Lord Howe, who arrived

CLIMAX AT MONMOUTH

Monmouth was the result of another of Washington's attempts to replicate Trenton and Princeton. Washington's original plan was to have an advance force, led by Charles Lee, pin the British rearguard while Washington's main body maneuvered on the enemy's flank. The plan miscarried when Lee panicked and precipitated a retreat. Before a disorderly withdrawal could degenerate into a precipitous rout, Washington intervened. He had General Anthony Wayne conduct a delaying action, while Washington's main body organized a new line. The climax of the battle came when the British reached this new line, formed in the open behind a low fence. The British charged the American lines three times, but they were repulsed on each occasion. The first and most critical charge, which is shown here, was made by Clinton's cavalry, primarily made up of the 16th (Queen's Own) Light Dragoons. The Continental line, which included Wayne's Pennsylvania infantry regiments, held their fire until the onrushing horsemen were a scant 40 paces from the infantrymen. Then, too close to miss, they fired their initial volley, shattering the charge. While Continental troops had fought doggedly from fortifications and had successfully ambushed British forces earlier in the war, Monmouth was the first time that American soldiers had held their own in the open field against British regulars in a toe-to-toe slugging match. (Graham Turner © Osprey Publishing)

BATTLE OF MONMOUTH. June 28, 1778.

A. Left wing of the British the night before.
B. American troops near Court house.
C. First posit.ⁿ taken by Genl. Lee in his retreat.
D. Later positions of Genl. Lee
E. Last position of Genl. Lee.
F. Disposition of the Army by Washing.
     after he met Lee.
* The spot where they met.
G. Principal Battle.
H & I. British pos.ⁿˢ after the action.

A map showing the troop position in the Battle of Monmouth, June 28, 1778. High summer temperatures resulted in both sides losing dozens of men to heat stroke. (Library of Congress)

off the coast in August to lift the siege. Evaluating the opposition, Major John Bowater noted: "the French fleet is heavier than ours, but we outnumber them." (Balderston & Syrett, p. 167.) The French fleet set out to engage the British, only to run into a storm on August 11 that damaged both. The weather forced the French to withdraw to Boston, which in turn caused problems for the American land forces, as the British continued to be resupplied, reinforced, and supported by the Royal Navy.

General Sullivan was irate with d'Estaing's withdrawal, which forced the Americans to lift the siege by August 27. This episode soured relations between the French and American commanders, as each side accused the other of lack of effort. A British relieving force under the command of Major-General Charles Grey arrived at Newport after the French withdrawal. Supported by the Royal Navy, a series of raids began along the New England coast, destroying supplies and ships and gathering stores from remote places such as Martha's Vineyard.

Coastal raiding was not all; during the summer and fall months, a series of raids led by British provincial corps, including Butler's Rangers and allied Indian tribes, struck from Fort Niagara along the frontiers of New York and Virginia. Fighting along the frontier had increased steadily throughout 1778, and raids had struck settlements as far east as Cherry Valley, 50 miles (80km) west of Albany. American efforts to counterattack were unsuccessful, and by the end of 1778 Washington and his senior officers were drawing up campaign plans for 1779.

SOUTHERN CAMPAIGN

In November, Clinton released 5,000 troops for operations in Florida and the West Indies. Meanwhile, Lieutenant-Colonel Archibald Campbell was sent with 3,000 troops, both regulars and provincials, to seize Savannah, Georgia. The Americans at Savannah, under the command of Major-General Robert Howe, were a small detachment, and were easily defeated on December 29. Savannah fell, as did the surrounding area. Campbell continued northwest and his force reached and captured Augusta, Georgia, near the end of January 1779.

OUTSIDE THE THIRTEEN COLONIES

British sailors and marines made numerous landings on enemy coastlines, either in support of the Army or to attain objects of naval significance. (Philip Haythornthwaite)

The French were the first to move in the materially important West Indies, seizing the British island of Dominica on September 7, 1778. The British went on the offensive in December; they landed on St. Lucia on December 13, after reinforcements had arrived from New York, occupying the northern side of the island. Admiral d'Estaing landed 7,000 reinforcements on the opposite end of the island, and on December 18 the French attempted to destroy the British fortifications. Their efforts were unsuccessful and they suffered heavy casualties, forcing them to withdraw on December 29 and surrender the island to the British force.

Meanwhile the British East India Company was embroiled in a war with the Maratha Confederacy in India. Word reached Bombay and Madras of the French intervention on the American side, prompting British East India Company

forces to move against French posts in India. All of these had been seized by the end of 1778, except for Mahe. In taking this action, however, the British sparked a war (also known as the Second Mysore War) with the local ruler, Hyder Ali of Mysore, who had been partially allied with the French. The war in India largely pitched the British East India Company and regular forces against the Indian princes' armies until at least 1782, when a strong French force came to the aid of Hyder Ali.

The campaigns of 1778 clearly illustrate the shift of British focus from North America to the colonial interests throughout the world threatened by the French. The Americans took advantage of the situation and proved themselves in battle at Monmouth. The Continental Army continued to have difficulties, but remained in good order as it went into winter quarters for 1778–79. The British were hemmed in at New York and Newport, and it was apparent that the focus of the war was going to shift to land campaigns in the South. Monmouth, the longest battle of the war, was also the last major battle in

Major-General Sir William Howe (1729–1814) as depicted in this painting by Richard Purcell published in 1777. (Anne S.K. Brown Collection, Brown University)

the North. From 1779, the war in northern New York and the southern colonies was to become even more bitter as Loyalists, Indians, and rebels fought fiercely for control of the interior.

THE LAND WAR: 1779

The campaigns of 1779 in North America were relatively small compared to previous years. There were minor operations at Stony Point on the Hudson River and along the Penobscot River in Massachusetts (present-day Maine). There was a successful American campaign against Indian and Loyalist raiders on the frontier. The remainder of North American operations occurred in the south. The principal reason for both the smaller-scale battles and geographical shift was that Spain entered the war against Britain in 1779, putting British interests around the world in still greater danger. The British also believed that the colonies in the south might be more loyal to the British cause.

NORTHERN CAMPAIGN

On June 16, 1779, British Brigadier Francis McLean landed at Castine, Massachusetts, on Penobscot Bay with 600 regulars. The town was strategically located to offset New England privateering efforts against British shipping. A Massachusetts militia force of 1,000 men, under the command of Brigadier Solomon Lovell, was dispatched to remove the British, landing on July 28. The Americans decided to lay siege to the fort instead of undertaking an immediate assault. A Royal Navy force arrived to lift the siege on August 13, compelling the Massachusetts militia to withdraw into the woods and the American ships in the bay to be scuttled. Washington ordered Major-General Sullivan, along with 2,500 Continentals and militia, to march from Eston, Pennsylvania, towards Fort Niagara, New York, in May. A second force of 1,500 New York militia, commanded by Brigadier James Clinton, was to meet up with Sullivan and lay waste to the Indian lands from Pennsylvania into New York. Sullivan understood how to operate in the woods and deployed small units of skirmishers to protect the flanks of his force. John Butler, the commander of the Loyalist Butler's Rangers, set out to fortify the local tribes for the onslaught.

The two American forces met on August 22 and set to work burning the crops and villages of the Indians. On August 27, Butler, with 250 Rangers, joined by 600 Indians commanded by Joseph Brant, prepared to meet the 4,000 Americans. The two forces met at Newtown on August 29–30. The Americans successfully avoided an ambush, and the Indians and Rangers were pushed out. They headed towards Fort Niagara, opening the Genesee and Mohawk valleys to the American forces. The Americans destroyed 40 villages and nearly 160,000 bushels of corn. The Indian population flooded towards Fort Niagara. The operation was successful for the Americans, but it did not signal the end of the raids along the frontier. Joseph Brant, along with his Indian warriors and Butler's Rangers, would return.

The French fleet sails into Newport, Rhode Island, on July 11, 1780 (Encyclopaedia Britannica/Getty Images)

MIDDLE ATLANTIC CAMPAIGN

Clinton advanced north from New York in late May, and seized Stony Point and Verplanck's Point on the Hudson River on June 1. He hoped by this action to force Washington to leave the defended regions of West Point and seek battle in the open, but Washington did not fall into his trap. Clinton next arranged for a series of raids along the Connecticut coast, trying to make Washington move east into New England. Washington not only failed to take the bait, but retook Stony Point on July 15 instead. As Colonel Tallmadge noted, "such was the ardour and impetuosity of the Americans, that they surmounted all difficulties ... and captured the whole garrison in a short time with bayonet alone" (Tallmadge, p. 31.)

Verplanck's Point remained in British hands. The British recalled all troops from the Connecticut coastal raids and moved towards Stony Point. The Americans withdrew, destroying defenses as they went. From this point, the fighting in the Hudson River and New York City areas deteriorated into an ongoing series of skirmishes between units foraging and undertaking reconnaissance.

French ships of the line, vessels that changed the balance of naval power in the American Revolution. (Library of Congress)

SOUTHERN CAMPAIGN

Lieutenant-Colonel Campbell had succeeded in taking Savannah and Augusta in 1778, but not all of Georgia had been subdued. Brigadier-General Augustine Prevost arrived in late January 1779 with a second British contingent from

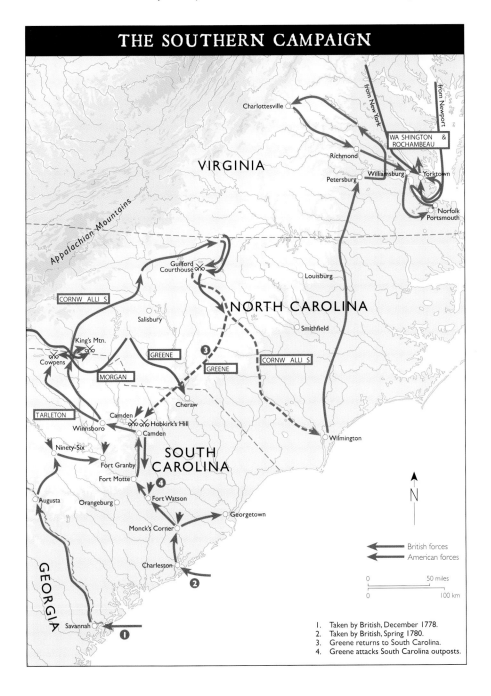

THE SOUTHERN CAMPAIGN

British forces
American forces

0   50 miles

0   100 km

1. Taken by British, December 1778.
2. Taken by British, Spring 1780.
3. Greene returns to South Carolina.
4. Greene attacks South Carolina outposts.

Florida, also taking over as the senior British commander. Major-General Benjamin Lincoln, meanwhile, replaced General Howe as commander of the American forces in the south.

The British abandoned Augusta in March, following reports of a large Carolina militia marching south, leaving Loyalists in the interior exposed to pro-independence factions. Brigadier Prevost marched to Charleston, South Carolina, and laid siege to the town. Lincoln received news of Prevost's move and turned towards Charleston

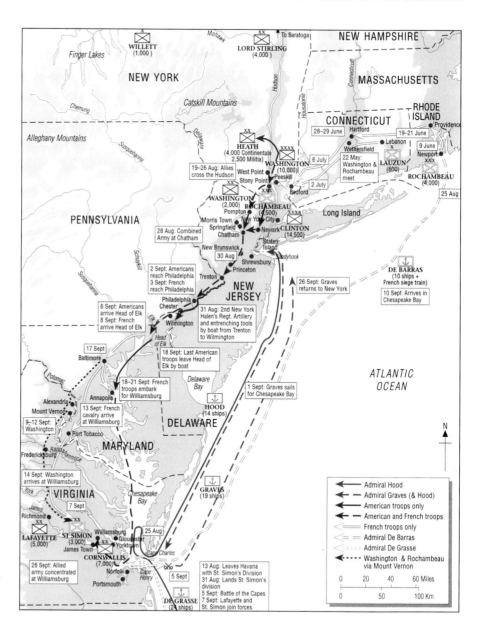

The routes taken by the separate American and French Continentals on their way south.

in pursuit. Prevost was outnumbered, and was forced to lift the siege on May 12. Lincoln followed Prevost's force as it withdrew and the two forces skirmished at Stono Ferry in late June. Prevost then moved his troops back towards Georgia, while the Americans requested support from Admiral d'Estaing.

D'Estaing arrived off Savannah on September 1 with 3,500 French troops, who landed on September 12 as Lincoln and his force were moving in from the north. Prevost was able to delay the impending French attack by asking for a few days to decide whether to surrender, although in fact he was using this time to wait for reinforcements to arrive to strengthen the defenses. By October 5, the French siege batteries were in place and American forces ringed the town. A French officer noted on October 6 that this course of action was a mistake: "we should not have constructed works. In doing so we afforded the English time to strengthen theirs. We regret that we did not attack on the first day" (Jones, p.26.)

The French command was anxious to end the siege, and on October 9 the combined French and American forces attacked. Prevost had foreknowledge of the attack from a deserter in his camp. The attack began in the early hours of the morning, described by the French officer, Count D'Estaing, as "a very lively fire of musketry and of cannon upon our troops from the trenches," (Jones, p. 30.) Men from the South Carolina Continentals and French forces were able to seize a few ramparts, but were ultimately forced back with "disorder in the

The death of the USS Randolph, *destroyed in an engagement with* HMS Yarmouth *in 1778. (Tony Bryan © Osprey Publishing)*

columns." The American and French forces lacked a coordinated attack plan, and within three hours the attack was called off.

The British forces lost about 200 men killed, wounded or missing, and the Americans and French more than 1,000 killed and wounded. On October 18, d'Estaing left, taking the French fleet with him. Lincoln, as Sullivan in Newport had been before him, was angered by this decision. So far, American–French cooperation had not proved a decisive factor in the North American campaign. The British decided to stage a combined naval/land raid to relieve pressure on Prevost and the British regulars and Loyalists in Georgia. On May 5, 1779, a fleet of 1,800 men departed from New York, landing at Hampton Roads, Virginia on May 11. The army set out to destroy all the tobacco stockpiles and shipping in the area. The operation was successful, claiming the destruction and capture of more than 140 vessels and £2 million worth of goods and property, and the fleet returned triumphantly to New York on May 24.

OUTSIDE THE THIRTEEN COLONIES

The principal problem facing the British in 1779 was Spain's decision to enter the war, and the naval balance shifted towards France and Spain as a result of this decision. Spain entered the war as an ally of the French, rather than of the Americans, on May 8; her main aim in doing so was to regain territory lost in the Seven Years' War. The British garrisons in western Florida were not aware of the Spanish entry, and so the British garrison at Baton Rouge was later seized in September 1779, an excellent performance by the Spanish regulars and Louisiana militia.

The siege of Gibraltar lasted for more than three years, the longest siege in British history. (Anne S.K. Brown Collection, Brown University)

The combined forces of the Spanish and French fleets gave the British Isles a fright during the summer of 1779. A combined force of 66 ships planned to assemble and invade Great Britain. The Royal Navy was aware of the potential threat, but had two possible invasion sites to protect, southern England and Ireland. On July 30, the combined force, under the command of Admiral d'Orvilliers, sailed from Brest, picking up troops at Le Havre and St. Malo. It appeared off Plymouth on August 16. The British fleet, under the command of Admiral Sir Charles Hardy, was out of commission, stationed off Ireland. Local militiamen were sent immediately to repel any attempted landings by the estimated 30,000 enemy soldiers.

Despite its superiority in numbers, the Franco-Spanish fleet was apparently wary of attempting a landing, even before Hardy returned. A decisive British naval victory after the troops had been landed would potentially have left 30,000 troops stranded on the coast of England. The British fleet arrived with 39 ships in early September; Hardy refused to attack, preferring to await a move by the Franco-Spanish force. The invasion force decided to withdraw by mid-September; their ships were battered, the men growing tired and ill, and relations between the French and Spanish commanders had soured. Battle had been avoided, and the threat of invasion averted. The first significant Spanish action upon entering the war was to lay siege to Gibraltar. Reinforcements were sent from Britain to support the British governor, George Augustus Elliott, although the first relief did not arrive until the beginning of 1780, under the command of Admiral Rodney. Gibraltar was under siege for the remainder of the war, with relieving fleets entering to help the garrison stay alive.

Admiral George Rodney, who by the time of the American War of Independence had already been serving in the Royal Navy for more than 40 years. (The Museum of the Revolution at Yorktown)

The entry of Spain and France into the war threatened British interests in the West Indies and Central America. Before d'Estaing sailed for the ill-fated siege of Savannah, he had had several successes in the West Indies, capturing St. Vincent in mid-June and Grenada a month later. The British badly needed troops in the area, fearing an attack on Jamaica next. Luckily for them, nothing happened for the rest of the year, for they were unprepared to face it.

In India, the French post at Mahe fell in March 1779. Of more critical importance to the British, however, was the enmity that their actions provoked in Hyder Ali and his large army. His armies directly engaged the British, and continued to do so for the rest of the war. By the end of 1779, the British military effort in North America had decidedly shifted towards the South. Prevost's

The battle between USS Hancock and HMS Fox in June 1777, as depicted by British maritime artist Thomas Buttersworth. (Naval History & Heritage Command)

defense of Savannah had sparked renewed interest in a southern campaign. General Clinton had been frustrated in his attempts to bring the Main Army to battle. The requirements of other theaters had made it clear that Clinton would not be able to rely on London for additional reinforcements. He therefore decided to abandon Newport, Rhode Island, and withdrew his force to New York. He assembled a large army in New York, and on December 26 embarked with more than 7,000 men for a campaign in South Carolina, with Charleston as his first objective. A large contingent of British troops remained in New York to protect the city, but the British post at Verplanck's Point was withdrawn.

Washington had difficulty keeping his various armies together during the stalemate in the North. The campaign in the South over the course of 1780–81 would be decisive for the future of North America.

THE LAND WAR: 1779-81

The land war in North America shifted to the southern colonies during the last phase of the war. The British generals, Clinton and Cornwallis, sought a decisive campaign in the south, believing that a large percentage of the population were Loyalists. While maintaining a presence in New York, the British shifted their principal focus southward.

General Washington was having problems with his troops. The Main Army remained in the New York area to counteract British attempts to push into the Hudson River valley or across New Jersey. The army's ability to wage war was limited by periodic mutinies, and the Southern Army bore the brunt of the fighting. The arrival of a large French contingent in 1780 enabled Washington to send the Main Army, bolstered by French reinforcements, south to Virginia. A classic siege at Yorktown followed, an incident that few foresaw might be the last major engagement of the war.

SOUTHERN CAMPAIGN

In December 1779, General Henry Clinton left New York with more than 17,000 British troops, landing south of Charleston on February 11, 1780. The American commander, General Lincoln, received word that the British were accompanied by a large contingent of Carolina Loyalist refugees. He thought that the British had another motive for their movements besides military conquest, "that of settling the country as they conquer" (*Lincoln Papers*.) The British, upon reaching Charleston, attempted to surround the town. Lincoln had 1,800 Continentals and about 2,000 militia to combat the British advance, and it was up to him to decide whether to engage in battle, withdraw, or hold out in the town. Ultimately, however, it was General Clinton who decided Charleston's fate.

By early April, British troops had crossed the northern routes of the town. A reinforcement of 700 Continentals arrived just after the town was completely

The attack on the American first line at Guildford Courthouse, 1781. The British attack on the first American militia line was delivered at 1.00pm with all the formal grace that was expected of a professional late-18th century army. (Adam Hook © Osprey Publishing)

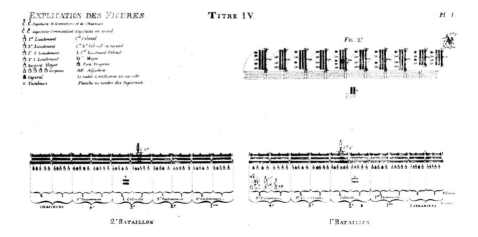

A 1776 French drill book showing 1st and 2nd Battalions drawn up for battle. (Anne S.K. Brown Collection, Brown University)

surrounded on April 14. The British began to dig siege lines and prepare artillery positions to bombard the defenders. Heavy fire was exchanged, but the British were able to dig a second line and position themselves within yards of the American lines. A Hessian officer, Captain Johann Hinrichs, reported that "the enemy stood our fire well and returned it till about noon ... but since our fire was so violent that we did not see them coming they were compelled to withdraw. At two o'clock in the afternoon the enemy hoisted a large white flag." An American observer recorded that, on May 12, "the Continental troops march out and pile their arms and the British take possession of the town" (*Journal of the Siege of Charleston.*) This was the worst single defeat for the American forces during the war. More than 2,000 Continental soldiers were captured, as well as 3,000 militia troops.

On May 29, the mixed Loyalist force known as the British Legion and commanded by Lieutenant-Colonel Banastre Tarleton, having moved north from Charleston, destroyed a Virginia Continental force at Waxhaws. The American force was almost wiped out, and there is still debate about what happened when the Americans attempted to surrender, and whether Tarleton ordered the killing of prisoners. Either way, the Legion and Tarleton became synonymous with brutal fighting methods.

This incident, which occurred in the interior, sparked a command decision to move inland to suppress any subsequent civilian rebellion. On June 8, Clinton left Charleston with 4,000 troops to head to New York. He had received word that the French fleet and expeditionary force had arrived, and feared that New York was a potential target. General Cornwallis took over command of the rest of the British forces in the south following his departure.

The British presence in South Carolina further inflamed the civil conflict already smoldering there. As the American General Moultrie noted, "large armed parties of Whigs and Tories were continually moving about and frequently falling in with each other and fighting severe battles ... the animosities between the two parties were carried to great lengths ... to enumerate the cruelties which were exercised upon each other would fill a volume" (Moultrie, p. 219.) Part of the reason for the increased hostility was a proclamation issued by Clinton before he left, demanding that all colonists must decide once and for all on whose side they were; no neutrality would be tolerated.

As the British marched into the interior, supply shortages created discipline problems, and the behavior of the British regulars won them few supporters. Cornwallis issued another proclamation, this one to the troops, regarding theft of cattle and provisions: "I do by this proclamation most strictly prohibit and forbid the same; and I do hereby give notice, that if any person offend herein ... [he] shall be further punished in a manner ... [that he] doth deserve" (Tarleton, pp. 121–122.)

General Lincoln was captured at Charleston and the hero of Saratoga, Major-General Horatio Gates, assumed command of the American forces in the south. He was able to rebuild the Southern Army with Continental soldiers from Maryland and Delaware and southern militiamen. His force consisted of only 1,500 Continentals and almost 1,000 militiamen. Gates arrived outside Camden, South Carolina, in early August. This was the main supply depot for the British forces in the interior, and Cornwallis, hearing of Gates's advance, had arrived with reinforcements from Charleston.

On the morning of August 16, the two armies clashed. The American left flank was composed of untrained militia units, with the Continentals on the right flank and in the rear of the first line. The British force moved forward and attacked the left flank first. Gates recorded that "at daylight the enemy attacked and drove in our light party in front, when I ordered the left to advance and attack the enemy; but to my astonishment, the left wing [Virginia militia] and North Carolina militia gave way" (Tarleton, pp. 146.) The Continentals fought hard. As Tarleton noted, "[Continental commander Baron de Kalbe] made a vigorous charge with a regiment of continental infantry through the left division of the British ... after this last effort of the continentals, rout and slaughter ensued in every quarter" (Tarleton, pp. 107.) A second Southern Army had been badly defeated. Baron de Kalbe was killed and Gates fell from grace in the American command structure. Following this victory, Cornwallis decided to push into North Carolina. He had failed to subdue South Carolina properly, however, and his communications and outposts were vulnerable to attack from militia forces as he advanced. Cornwallis marched into North Carolina in early September, with a second column of provincial troops under the command of Major Patrick Ferguson on his left flank. Cornwallis and

BATTLE OF CAMDEN

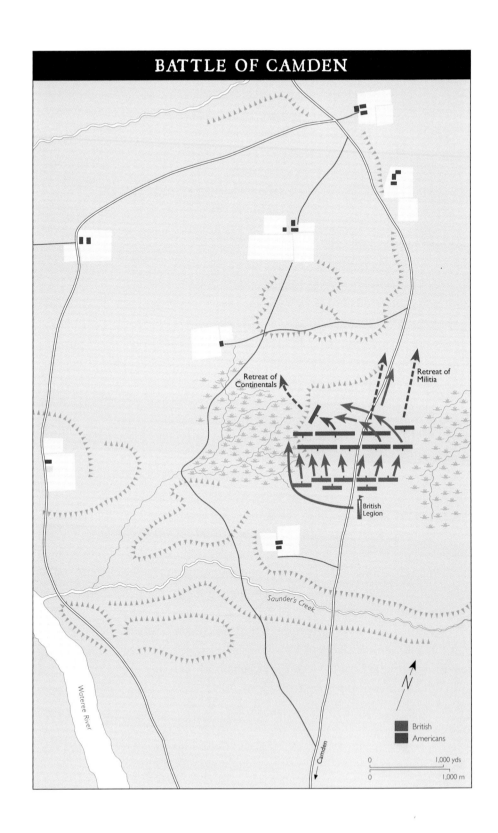

Retreat of
Continentals

Retreat of
Militia

British
Legion

Saunder's Creek

Wateree River

Camden

N

British
Americans

0   1,000 yds

0   1,000 m

the main corps reached Charlotte, North Carolina, in late September. Ferguson moved further north with his corps, but was unable to convince many Loyalists in the area to join up; his destructive actions against rebels had aroused too much hatred.

On October 7, Ferguson's force of 800 men was surrounded at King's Mountain by a militia force of 2,000 expert fighting men from the Carolina backcountry. Ferguson's force was 30 miles (48km) from Cornwallis's column, and could expect no support. Loyalist, Anthony Allaire described how "at about two o'clock in the afternoon twenty five hundred rebels ... attacked us ... the action continued an hour and five minutes; but their numbers enabled them to surround us ... we had to surrender to save lives of the brave men who were left" (Allaire, p. 31.) A North American militiaman, James Collins, commented, "after the fight was over, the situation of the poor Tories appeared to be really pitiable; the dead lay in heaps on all sides while the groans of the wounded were heard in every direction" (Wright, IE., p. 200.) The British force was completely destroyed, forcing Cornwallis to withdraw to South Carolina for winter quarters, and lowering the morale of southern Loyalists.

The American Southern Army was re-formed while Cornwallis spent the winter south of Camden, South Carolina. He was to be reinforced by a contingent under

Daniel Morgan was one of the Continental Army's most capable commanders. (The Museum of the Revolution at Yorktown)

The American 3rd line at the climax of the battle at Guildford Courthouse, March 15, 1781. The American dragoons passed clean through the British line, reaching the Marylanders behind them. But fresh British reinforcements then turned the tide, and the now-disorganized American formations were forced to retreat, along with the rest of General Greene's army. (Adam Hook © Osprey Publishing)

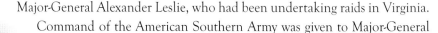

Major-General Alexander Leslie, who had been undertaking raids in Virginia. Command of the American Southern Army was given to Major-General Nathanael Greene on December 2, 1780. He had another force of 1,000 Continental troops and various militia forces at his disposal. The fighting in the backcountry between rebels and Loyalists continued unabated throughout the winter months.

In January 1781, Cornwallis decided to march back into North Carolina. General Green dispatched Brigadier Daniel Morgan and a small Continental corps to disrupt the British lines of communication and fight in the backcountry. Cornwallis dispatched a force of the British Legion and other troops, under the command of Lieutenant-Colonel Tarleton, in a mobile force to protect the left flank of the British forces and counteract Morgan's corps.

Morgan's and Tarleton's forces clashed north of Cowpens, on the border between North and South Carolina, on January 17. Morgan deployed his riflemen at the front of his force, with the militia and Continentals forming the second and third lines. The riflemen were to shoot once, then withdraw through the ranks of the other lines. The battle began at daylight, with Tarleton sending his tired troops immediately into battle. The American riflemen created holes in the British line as it advanced. The British pushed forward and the Americans, militia and riflemen, began to pull back. The British surged forward and the Americans turned and delivered a heavy volley. The British attack fell apart as the Continental troops moved forward. Tarleton and a few hundred men were able to escape, but the force had lost more than 700 men killed and captured. The reasons for Tarleton's defeat were twofold. First, Morgan had deployed well and was able to shift his forces without much disruption. Second, as Loyalist officer Alescambe Chesney noted: "we suffered a dreadful defeat by some dreadful bad management ... the rout was almost total" (*Journal of Alescambe Chesney*.) The Legion was an important asset for the British forces and, in one battle, Cornwallis had lost nearly all of it.

Cornwallis continued his advance into North Carolina after reinforcements arrived from General Leslie, and the American and British forces met again on March 15 at Guildford Courthouse in North Carolina. Cornwallis had only 2,000 troops; the Southern Army outnumbered him two to one. General Greene, however, elected to take the defensive. The Americans were drawn up as "three lines: the front line was composed of North Carolina militia ... second line of the Virginia militia ... third line, consisting of two brigades, one of Virginia, and one of Maryland continentals troops" (Tarleton, p. 314.)

Brigadier Nathanael Greene was appointed to head the Continental Army's Southern campaign in 1780. (Anne S.K. Brown Collection, Brown University)

The battle lasted for three hours. The first line of North Carolina militia fired once before breaking. The Virginia militia stood longer, delivering strong volleys. The British dealt with the first two lines of militia and turned towards the Continental troops. The British continued to press and, though suffering heavily, began to break the Maryland Continentals, causing the American right flank to falter, after British artillery fired into the confusing mass. As Greene reported: "the engagement was long and severe, and the enemy only gained their point by superior discipline" (Tarleton, p. 316.)

The British lost some 100 men killed and more than 400 wounded. The American forces lost only 78 killed and nearly 200 wounded. It was a Pyrrhic victory for Cornwallis, and afterwards he headed south to Wilmington to rendezvous with the Royal Navy and receive much-needed supplies and reinforcements. Greene turned towards South Carolina.

While in Wilmington, Cornwallis had to decide whether to move into Virginia or to return by sea to Charleston. Brigadier Greene had moved into South Carolina, while General Lord Rawdon and his troops attempted to hold parts of the interior centered around Camden and Fort Ninety-Six. Greene attacked Lord Rawdon outside Camden, at Hobkirk's Hill, on April 25; the British were able to defeat the American force. On the same day, Cornwallis and his force marched towards Virginia.

The remainder of the campaign in the Carolinas was one of gradual withdrawal for the British forces. On May 10, the British pulled out of Camden, and by June the only post in the interior still in British hands was Fort Ninety-Six. Greene laid siege to it, but was forced by a British relief column to lift the siege. The British, however, recognizing the distance from Charleston to Fort Ninety-Six, subsequently withdrew from the area, and by mid-summer they controlled only the coastal strip from Savannah to Charleston. Greene had lost many of the battles, but in the end he won the campaign in the Carolinas.

Chapter 4

THE BRITISH DEFEAT, 1781-83

VIRGINIA AND YORKTOWN

Cornwallis countermanded orders from London that his troops were to remain in the Carolinas. British troops had already been stationed in Virginia to stage raids in the area and relieve pressure on the British forces in the Carolinas. Virginia was intended to be a secondary campaign, but Cornwallis turned it into a primary operation without receiving approval from London or Clinton in New York. Cornwallis's actions clearly demonstrate the friction that had arisen among senior generals in North America. As a result of his decision, the operation in Virginia became the decisive campaign.

In January 1781, a British force of 1,500 troops was dispatched by Clinton to Virginia, commanded by Benedict Arnold, the former American general. Arnold had switched sides in 1780 because he felt that he was being sidelined by Congress and the Continental Army. He had been commander of an important American post, West Point, on the Hudson River. General Clinton had negotiated with him to turn over plans of the strategic fort to the British, but the plot was uncovered before it could be implemented. Arnold escaped to New York and was given command of a British force in the rank of major-general.

In March 1781, a second British force of 2,000 men, under the command of Major-General William Phillips, arrived in Virginia. General Phillips assumed

The cost and political unpopularity in Britain did as much to end the war than American victories. This British opposition political cartoon (1782) deplored both the cost and the use of Native American allies (fancifully depicted as tropical cannibals). (NARA)

command of all British troops in Virginia upon his arrival, and continued the raids in Virginia. Cornwallis arrived in mid-May and met with Phillips at Petersburg, Virginia. The combined British force now totaled more than 7,000 men and was under the overall command of Cornwallis, who took over after Phillips died of typhoid fever. The American commanders in the region, Major-Generals de Lafayette and von Steuben, had been focusing on trying to increase the numbers of Continental troops while contending with two earlier campaigns staged by Arnold and Phillips.

By early July, Cornwallis had received orders to establish a fortified winter base for the Royal Navy. Yorktown was chosen as a suitable site, and by the beginning of August the British had begun the work of fortifying the area and the adjoining Gloucester Point. In doing so, the British had committed themselves to a defensive position, and the American forces stationed in Virginia began to close in on Yorktown.

The year 1780 and winter in early 1781 was a difficult time for General Washington and the Main Army. In the spring of 1780, the Main Army stood at 4,000 men and was suffering from lack of supplies. Discipline was an increasing problem as the war in the north became ever more hopelessly stalemated. In May, troops from the Connecticut regiments threatened to march into New Jersey and seize stores. They were restrained from doing so by other troops, principally the Pennsylvania regiments. Ironically, in January 1781, elements of the Pennsylvania regiments themselves mutinied, this time over supplies and timely pay. The issue of delayed pay was exacerbated by the fact that the money issued by the Continental Congress was rapidly being devalued. At the end of January, elements of the New Jersey regiments also mutinied. All three revolts collapsed, and the ringleaders were found and punished, but it was clear that the Main Army was in need of a campaign.

Washington benefited at this stage from the arrival of a French expeditionary force of 5,000 troops that landed in Newport in 1780, under the command of Lieutenant-General Rochambeau. They were subsequently reinforced in Virginia with an additional 3,000 men. With Cornwallis heading towards Yorktown, the Main Army and the French expeditionary force on August 14 decided to wage a campaign against him. Proposed attacks against New York had to be rejected due to the lack of French naval support so far north, as the French Admiral de Grasse had agreed to go only as far north as the Chesapeake River. The joint American and French force, numbering more than 8,000 French and 2,000 Continentals in the summer, marched south, but in a deceptive manner. More than 4,000 Continentals and 2,000 militia remained in New York, intending to keep the pressure on Clinton while concealing from Cornwallis that Yorktown was their eventual destination.

Major-General Benedict Arnold occupies an ignominious place in American history, having switched sides to fight for the British in 1780. (Anne S.K. Brown Collection, Brown University)

The French troops provided an important dimension to the American contingent; they were regular troops, trained and disciplined to deal with the likes of the British Redcoats. With the addition of more than 5,000 Continental troops and a large artillery train, the British forces faced a solid opponent. The naval engagement at the Capes, entrance to Chesapeake Bay, in early September, although not significant in terms of ships damaged, became decisive when the British Admiral Thomas Graves withdrew to New York, isolating Cornwallis. The main American and French forces gathered in Williamsburg on September 26.

The American forces numbered more than 8,000 men, as did their French allies. The Continental Army marched towards Yorktown in three columns of troops, two French and one American. As a French officer noted, "we arrived about six o'clock that evening [September 28] before the town of Yorktown and immediately began to invest it" (Rice and Brown, p. 57.) The Siege of Yorktown followed the practices of any European-style siege: both sides embarked on raids, and fired artillery at redoubts and trenches. A French officer commented that "the day was spent in cannonading and firing bombs at each other in such profusion that we did one another much damage" (Rice and Brown, p. 59.)

The French and American engineers dug their trenches, progressing closer to the British positions, and the siege increasingly centered on the taking of two British redoubts, Nos. 9 and 10. On the evening of October 14, the French and American troops launched an attack on the redoubts. The French commander, William Comte de Deux-Ponts, detailed the attack and, although uncommunicative to a degree, noted that firing took place during the French attack. He stated that "the first 50 *les chausseurs* [light infantry] carried fascines, of the other fifty there were only eight who carried ladders, after them came the grenadiers ... [They] advanced with the greatest silence ... [and] opened fire ... we lost not a moment in reaching the abbatis. ... [It] was cleared away with brave determination ... I gave the order to fire ... the enemy kept up a sharp fire ... our fire increasing and making terrible havoc among the enemy" (Deux-Ponts, pp. 145–146.)

On October 16, a sortie of 300 men was launched from the British lines to destroy and spike the guns in two allied artillery batteries. The undertaking was considered a success, yet the guns were firing again within six hours of the attack. As Cornwallis noted,

Colonel John Graves Simcoe, the talented officer who commanded the Queen's Rangers 1777–83. (Print after J.L. Mosnier; photo by René Chartrand)

Siege of Yorktown: the American and French positions are to the south and west of Yorktown. (Antiqua Print Gallery/Alamy Stock Photo)

"the action, though extremely honourable to the officers and soldiers who executed it, proved of little public advantage" (Tarleton, p. 429.)

On October 19, Cornwallis surrendered the garrison at Yorktown. The British garrison troops marched out and laid down their arms, flanked by the American army on one side and the French Army on the other. Clinton had intended to

OVERLEAF

Siege of Savannah: French and American lines in the foreground. (Library of Congress)

send a relieving force of 7,000 men, but news arrived that Cornwallis had already surrendered before he could do so.

The battle for Yorktown was the last major engagement of the land war in North America, but the war was not yet over. The British were still fighting a war outside the North American theater and had not intended Yorktown to be the last major engagement on American soil. The Americans, for their part, had plans to drive the British garrisons out of both Charleston and New York. Other considerations for the French prevented the launch of attacks on British forces stationed on the coast of the Carolinas, or Georgia, or in New York. After Yorktown, the war shifted almost completely to the West Indies, India, Florida, and Europe.

A 19th-century depiction of Yorktown. This etching shows an almost plan-view of Yorktown and the area around it during the siege, including the British defensive line, and the York River and Gloucester Point. (Anne S.K. Brown Collection, Brown University)

LIEUTENANT-GENERAL CHARLES, EARL CORNWALLIS (1738-1805)

Cornwallis was a trusted British courtier and a former Guards officer. A Whig, he initially opposed government measures to deal with the colonists; but agreed to serve in North America, seeing action around New York and commanding a division at Brandywine and Monmouth, before being made lieutenant-general in 1778. Given command in the South after the fall of Charleston, he used Clinton's remoteness (in New York) and the vague and contradictory nature of some of his superior's orders, as an excuse to pursue his own strategy. Despite overwhelming Gates at Camden, Cornwallis was out-thought by Greene (whose strategic awareness and tactical limitations made them virtual opposites). Although he would be badly let down by the Royal Navy, his obsession with Virginia played a major part in ensuring that the surrender at Yorktown was crippling, yet he returned to England a popular figure. Cornwallis was not only personally brave, but also (except for one occasion in 1776) proved himself one of the ablest battlefield commanders on either side. Sadly, in America at least, his strategic abilities were found wanting, although he later achieved fame in India, where he eventually died. He was briefly governor-general of Ireland in 1798, but resigned over government refusal to grant Catholic emancipation.

WAR ON THE HOMEFRONT

Although the war was economically costly for all sides, it differed significantly from the Seven Years' War in that the impact on the local populations was relatively minimal. The home populations of France, Great Britain, and Spain did not suffer under foreign occupation. Large numbers of troops were raised in each country and inevitably created tension and damage by the fact of their presence, but they were not occupying forces. The large number of troops even proved an unintended boon to the British government when the Gordon Riots of 1780 broke out, and the armed forces were used to restore law and order.

The fighting in the West Indies and India undoubtedly created problems between the local populations and the various armies. The numerous and powerful cavalry of Hyder Ali set out to destroy the communications and supplies of the East India Company armies, which left civilians caught between two armies. As with all campaigns in the region, soldiers deserted from one side to the other as economic conditions dictated.

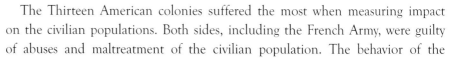

The Thirteen American colonies suffered the most when measuring impact on the civilian populations. Both sides, including the French Army, were guilty of abuses and maltreatment of the civilian population. The behavior of the French Army in 1780–81 was exemplary in its restraint from plundering and looting, but the French force that surrounded Savannah in 1779 was not so commendable. The Americans and French eventually formed a special mixed unit of French and American dragoons to police both armies.

The British and their German auxiliaries were consistently accused of pillaging, raping, and general disorder by the colonists. The British advance across New Jersey in 1776 was considered a particularly brutal episode. An American observer described how: "familys [sic] ... escape[d] from the Regular Army and left a Great Part of their goods behind them in their Houses for want of carriages to take them away, Great part of which fell into the Regular hands and they not only burnt up all the fire wood ... [but] stript shops, out houses and some dwelling houses" (Collins, p. 4.)

Many British regulars considered the conflict as a rebellion, and consequently had minimal sympathy for the civilians. The German auxiliaries' attitude was similarly contemptuous. Lieutenant-Colonel Kemble of the 60th Foot noted on October 3, 1776, that "ravages committed by the Hessians, and all the Ranks of the Army, on the poor inhabitants of the country make their case deplorable" (Kemble, p. 91.)

Kemble also succinctly described the effects of these actions: "the country all this time unmercifully Pillaged by our troops, Hessians in particular, no wonder if the Country people refuse to join us" (Kemble, p. 96.) Senior British commanders attempted to confront this issue, but it was never conclusively resolved. As previously described, a series of proclamations was written and distributed amongst the troops at the onset of the 1780–81 southern campaign, in an attempt to forestall some of the problems. The British Army's supply problems complicated the situation and more or less condoned this sort of behavior; units were sent out on foraging parties to round up cattle and other supplies. They were supposed to pay for the items, but of course abuse was common. Naval landings were carried out specifically to steal and destroy stores that could be destined for the Continental Army, with inevitable repercussions for civilians. The civilian populations of New Jersey and southern New York and New England were at the mercy of the British raiding parties.

The regions around New York and southern New England also suffered from their proximity to encampments of the Continental Army. There were cases of outright

Contemporaries were quick to condemn Native American's propensity for hanging back until an engagement was decided, but they were neither trained nor equipped for European-style warfare. In the woods it was a different matter. (Troiani, Don (b.1949)/Private Collection/Bridgeman Images/Bridgeman Images)

robbery and abuse by troops on the civilian population. As the various armies marched across New Jersey in 1776 and 1777, the countryside was stripped bare of food and supplies. The Continental Army and militia also carried out attacks on suspected Loyalist families in the area. Their properties were looted and, depending upon the local commander, certain members of the family were killed. Private Joseph Plumb Martin commented that in 1780 "there was a large number [of Loyalists] in this place and its vicinity by the name of Hetfield who were notorious rascals" (Martin, pp. 180–181.) and who escaped. Martin went on, "thus these murderous villains escaped the punishment due to their infernal deeds" (Martin, p. 180–181.) There were critics of this policy within the American high command. Major-General Israel Putnam commented in August 1777, in response to a local assembly motion from Salem, Massachusetts, to confiscate lands of suspected Loyalists: "I think such things are counter to the spirit of your resolves" (*Letter Condemning Harsh Treatment of Loyalists.*)

Most settlers lived in cabins more primitive than this replica in Gaffney, SC. Scorened by the coastal elite, they were the backbone of the militia. (Ed and Catherine Gilbert)

The southern campaign raised the level of violence within the civilian population to outright civil war. The fighting in the backcountry lasted from the official outbreak of war until well after the Siege of Yorktown. The British Army's practices and fighting tactics, as with the war in the North, turned neutrals into

Lieutenant-Colonel Banastre Tarleton, commander of the British Legion, 1782. (René Chartrand)

rebels. The American Brigadier-General William Moultrie described the march of the British regulars and "their severities against the unhappy citizens, many of whom they hung up or otherwise cruelly treated ... the war was carried with great barbarity" (Moultrie, vol. 2, p. 219.) Lieutenant-Colonel Tarleton's view of the civilian population counters this: "the foraging parties were every day harassed by the inhabitants. ... [They] generally fired from covert places, to annoy the British detachments" (Tarleton, p. 160.) The conflict turned into an irregular war in the south, and abuses were perpetrated by both sides. A Loyalist reported how "a Henry Meholm, an old man of 81 years of age, this day met us. ... [He] had walked upwards of an hundred miles [160km] ... his errand was to get some kind of assistance. He had been plundered by the Rebels, and stripped of everything" (Allaire, p. 19.)

TRADE AND ECONOMY

The economic costs of the war were heavy for Great Britain. The average yearly cost of the war was £12 million. The Royal Navy was not able to control the seas as she had done in the Seven Years' War. Taxes on the general population increased as the war dragged on, and duties on items not already being taxed were imposed to increase revenue further. The average land tax during the war was established at four shillings for every pound, and the government borrowed heavily to make up for the shortfalls. This load of debt was added to the outstanding debts amassed during the Seven Years' War.

A scene from the battle of Pensacola, showing the detonation of the British powder magazine, destroyed by Spanish troops. (Anne S.K. Brown Collection, Brown University)

Trade also suffered as a result of the war. The revenue raised from trade with the Thirteen Colonies was wiped away. The merchants who traded with the American colonies felt the pinch, especially those in the tobacco trade. The export market was also hit hard. The revenue raised from the selling of woolen and metal goods dropped sharply as the markets dried up. The incursion of France and Spain into the war increased the pressure on Britain's import and export trade as more markets shrank due to naval pressure and privateering. The need to increase shipping to get provisions and troops to North America prompted the Admiralty to lease a significant number of merchant ships. This provided additional opportunities for American privateers and Spanish and French fleet seizures, causing further disruption. It is estimated that 3,386 British merchant ships were seized during the war.

The British were able to recoup some of these losses with their own privateering efforts on Spanish and French shipping. The war did provide some benefit for a number of industries in Great Britain. The expansion of the navy and army meant an increased demand for the supplies needed to build ships, outfit troops, and supply forces in North America. Overall, however, the import and export trade fell drastically, creating significant revenue problems for the British government.

The American colonies also suffered economically as a result of the war. At first, the war increased prosperity; the trade of the Thirteen Colonies was no longer restricted to Great Britain, and merchants could trade throughout Europe and the West Indies without the interference of Royal Customs officials. American privateering activities infused additional wealth into the cause. As the fighting dragged on, however, American resources became strained as shipping was destroyed or seized by Royal Navy raids. Ironically, the Americans' biggest financial problems concerned the imposition of taxes to raise currency. Individual colonies fought to keep the right to vote on tax issues, and the Continental Congress was forced to accept that they would not be given the power to raise taxes. Coin circulation had proved insufficient to keep the war going as early as 1775. The Congress turned to the establishment of paper money or bills of credit to raise funds. The expansion of the economy during the first two years of the war allowed for paper money to be infused into the economy without any problems. As the war continued and the costs rose, however, both the Congress and the colonies continued to print money, creating enormous problems with inflation.

By 1780, the Congress and colonies combined had issued over $400 million in paper money, and inflation had skyrocketed. In an attempt to stop the inflation, the Congress tried to impose reforms, but these succeeded only in devaluing the Congress's dollars. The Congress also asked the colonies to fund, equip, and outfit their own troops in the Continental Army. The European allies also

gave the Americans nearly $10 million in loans to keep the war effort afloat, but by 1780 there was widespread disaffection within the army over issues of pay and supplies. As Colonel Tallmadge noted: "the pay to the army being entirely in continental paper, we were greatly embarrassed to procure even the necessary supplies of food and clothing" (Tallmadge, p. 33.) The inflation and debts produced by the war were to plague the newly formed United States for a number of years.

France, like Great Britain, piled debts from this war on those still outstanding from the Seven Years' War. French debt at the end of the war stood at 3,315.1 million livres, spent in developing a sizable army and navy, and providing material support to the American cause. This debt created significant economic problems after the war. In fact, many historians contend that the debt incurred during both the Seven Years' War and the American Revolution, compounded by the financial crisis of 1786, were among the principal causes of the French Revolution. Spain also suffered, but not as greatly as France. Spain nearly doubled her spending from 454 million reales in 1778 to over 700 million reales in 1779.

Then the conflict disrupted the revenue stream from South and Central America. Spain at first sought more taxes, but when this did not solve the issue, royal bonds were issued to make up the shortfall. This did not work either, and finally in 1782 the first national Bank of Spain—the Banco San Carlos—was created to centralize financial efforts. When the war finally ended, the revenue from the colonies came into the bank to help pay off the loans and bonds during the war years, enabling Spain to pay off most of her debts relatively quickly.

HOW THE WAR ENDED

As noted previously, the British Army presence in North America was drastically reduced after 1778 and received reinforcements on only a few subsequent occasions. The vast majority of the army was deployed to contend with threats elsewhere in the world. France was able to deliver a large expeditionary force to North America in 1780 that performed successfully in Virginia, but the remainder of the French forces posed an effective threat to British interests elsewhere. Most French troops earmarked for overseas duty were sent to the West Indies, but a sizable force was also sent to aid the Spanish in the Minorca and Gibraltar campaigns. Another five regiments were sent to fight in India, and the remainder of the army stayed in France, posing a continuing threat to the British Isles. The Spanish land forces, although not as well equipped or trained as their French or British counterparts, provided an additional headache for the British outposts in the Floridas and Caribbean.

THE WEST INDIES AND THE CARIBBEAN

The first major land engagements in the West Indies occurred in 1781, after a series of indecisive naval engagements during 1780. Following a declaration of war on the Dutch Republic in late December 1780, the British moved against the Dutch colony of St. Eustatius and seized it on February 3, 1781. Tensions between neutral states and the British had been exacerbated by Royal Navy seizures of neutral shipping. The Dutch had carried on trade with the Thirteen Colonies throughout the war, and Russia and the Scandinavian states had begun to form a "League of Armed Neutrality" to protect their shipping from the various belligerents. Britain feared that the powerful Dutch naval and merchant fleet would also join and decided to attack them before they could do so. British aggression put Dutch colonies throughout the world at risk.

The defeat of Cornwallis at Yorktown freed the French Admiral de Grasse to return to the West Indies in December 1781. The French land forces were led by Marquis de Bouille, governor of Martinique. The French moved against the British-occupied island of St. Lucia. On May 10, the French landed on the island, but upon deciding that the British defensive works were too strong, they re-embarked. The British force holding St. Eustatius was defeated by a French force on November 26, and St. Martin and St. Bartholomew fell in quick succession. The British island of St. Kitts became the next target, and on January 11, 1782, 6,000 men landed on the island and launched a siege. On February 13, the British surrendered the island. The French also seized Montserrat and Nevis in February 1782.

This success encouraged the French and Spanish to attempt an assault on Jamaica. Their incursion was so vigorously rebuffed by the British Admiral Rodney, however, at the Battle of the Saintes, that they decided to call off the invasion. Instead, the Spanish turned their efforts to the British islands in the Bahamas, whose small British garrisons were easily overwhelmed by 5,000 Spanish troops. Rochambeau's expeditionary force was ordered to the Caribbean in the winter of 1782–83 in preparation for another attempt on Jamaica, but the fighting in the Caribbean slowed down during 1783, when news arrived that peace negotiations had begun. The last operation was conducted by British provincial units from Florida, who seized parts of the Bahama Islands in April 1783.

Of secondary importance to the fighting in the West Indies were the campaigns in Honduras, Nicaragua, and the Floridas between British and Spanish forces. A small force of regulars, provincial troops from Jamaica, and sailors seized the

THE CARIBBEAN

WEST FLORIDA (Br)

LOUISIANA (Sp)

EAST FLORIDA (Br)

GULF OF MEXICO

Bahamas (Br)

ATLANTIC OCEAN

Cuba (Sp)

Puerto Rico (Sp)

Haiti

Anguilla

St Dominique (Fr)

St Domingo (Sp)

St Eustatius

St Kitts

Antigua

MEXICO (Sp)

Belize

Jamaica (Br)

Guadeloupe

Dominica

HONDURAS (Sp)

CARIBBEAN SEA

Martinique

St Lucia

NICARAGUA (Sp)

Mosquito Coast (Br)

St Vincent

Barbados

Lake Nicaragua

Granada

0   250 miles

VENEZUELA (Sp)

0   500 km

Spanish base at Bacalar, on the Honduran coast, on October 20, 1779. Sickness followed, soon driving the British out of the area and back to Jamaica. In 1780, the British decided to move against the Spanish establishment in Nicaragua, and a force was sent against the San Juan River area and Lake Nicaragua. The expedition, successful at first, was soon bogged down by disease and lack of supplies. As the British commander, Lieutenant-Colonel Stephen Kemble, noted: "should the sickness continue [it would] absolutely put an end to our pushing forward" (*Journal of Lieutenant Colonel Stephen Kemble*.) An officer in the Jamaica Corps also noted: "sickness is rampant." Sickness also occurred in the Spanish forces, but not sufficient enough to provoke a surrender. The British were forced to withdraw most of the troops, and the remaining small British force was easily overwhelmed before the end of the year.

The Spanish, led by Bernardo de Gálvez, had great success against the British garrisons in the Floridas. They set out to take the British garrisons at Mobile and Pensacola and took Mobile on March 14. After a year's activity, the Spanish moved towards Pensacola in early 1781. The siege of Pensacola was a joint Franco-Spanish effort of some 7,000 men, against a British garrison of only two regular regiments plus assorted provincial corps units. The Franco-Spanish force began to envelop the town in March 1781, commencing a siege that would last for close to two months.

A Spanish observer, noting the supply problems, commented: "that afternoon [May 6] the general told me of the great difficulty in which he found himself ... not enough [cannonballs] to supply the batteries ... almost all the cannonballs fired by the enemy were gathered up." Nevertheless, the British surrendered on May 9. The reason given for the surrender was that "a shell from one of our howitzers fell into the powder magazine ... the majority of the soldiers had perished in the explosion."

EUROPE

The initial threat to Britain of invasion from France had receded somewhat after the joint Franco-Spanish fleet had returned to port in France and Spain at the end of 1779, but it was still not possible for the British to release ships or soldiers for duty in other areas. The attentions of France and Spain were principally focused on Minorca and Gibraltar, but the Channel Islands were still in danger. A second French attempt to invade the islands took place in January 1781, and St. Helier was seized. However, the British retaliated and recaptured the island.

The fight for Gibraltar centered on the ability of the British to reinforce and resupply the garrison. The Spanish and French were able to lay siege effectively, but were unable to seal off the port completely or destroy all the relief fleets coming out from Britain. The British garrison was having a difficult time. A Spanish officer commented, regarding a Hanoverian deserter, "scurvy makes great ravages among the men ... [They] are extremely fatigued." The siege continued throughout the course of the war, but the British never gave in.

HMS Minerva, launched in 1781, was the Royal Navy's first 38-gun frigate intended to carry a main battery of 18lb long guns. (USNA)

Battle at St. Helier, Jersey, on January 6, 1781, as French forces attack the British garrison. The painting shows the death of British officer Major Francis Peirson. (Anne S.K. Brown Collection, Brown University)

During the summer of 1781 a Franco-Spanish fleet attempted to seize the British island of Minorca. On August 19, 1781, 8,000 troops landed and laid siege to the British Fort St. Philip. The siege dragged on until February 1782, when the British surrendered the island and the garrison.

INDIA

As noted previously, the British dispatched the French forces quickly in 1778, but then had to deal with the large armies of Hyder Ali. The British fought a series of four wars, called the Mysore Wars, with Hyder Ali and his son, Tipu Sultan. Hyder Ali and his army attacked the Carnatic in the summer of 1780, and were met by two British columns of company troops from Madras and British regulars. The British column of 4,000 men, under the command of Lieutenant-Colonel William Baillie, was defeated at the battle of Pollimore on September 6, 1780. General Sir Eyre Coote, hero of the battle of Wandiwash and commander-in-chief in India, arrived after the defeat with a significant reinforcement of troops from the Bengal Presidency. By the end of 1781, Coote had defeated Hyder Ali's army at the battles of Porto Novo on July 1, Polilur on August 27, and Sholinghur on September 27. Even so, Coote had failed to completely push Hyder Ali out of the Carnatic. The British forces lacked sufficient numbers of cavalry to drive home their advantages.

The first actions of 1782 were undertaken by the French, who landed three French regular regiments at Porto Novo in aid of Hyder Ali on February 21. The fighting for the year was primarily carried on by the French and British fleets off the coast of the Carnatic and Ceylon, although the British garrison on Ceylon surrendered in August. Hyder Ali died in late 1782 and his son, Tipu Sultan, took over command of the kingdom and army. Tipu returned to the Carnatic area, along with a second French force, which arrived at Porto Novo on March 16, 1783. The British, recognizing the danger, immediately set out to destroy the French regular forces and contingent of sepoys. The two armies met outside Cuddalore in June.

The French built a defended position, which the British attacked on June 13. The battle lasted all day, as a British observer noted: "the bloody contest continued without intermission until 5 o'clock in the evening when a cessation of firing took place ... both lines were overcome with fatigue [thus they] lay upon their arms." The French outer defenses had been breached, but they withdrew safely to the town's walls. On June 25, the French launched an unsuccessful attack on the British siege lines. Both sides withdrew upon receiving the news that peace negotiations had begun back in Europe earlier in the year. The war with Tipu continued into the following year but ended eventually because Tipu could gain no further French support, leaving the British free to concentrate on his army. The Mysore Wars did not end officially until 1799, when Tipu's capital, Seringapatam, was taken and Tipu himself killed.

PEACE

In February 1782, Lord Germain resigned as British Secretary of State for America. Lord North and his government resigned on March 20, and the new government, led by the Marquis of Rockingham, took office. Rockingham's government wanted peace with the American colonies so that it could concentrate on the Bourbon menace, and in June Lieutenant-General Haldimand, commander-in-chief of Canada, was advised that all offensive operations against the Thirteen Colonies were to cease. British and American negotiators began to meet during the summer of 1782. The negotiations lasted for five months, as the two sides

The French capture of Grenada in 1779 showed the French ability in amphibious warfare. (Roger-Viollet/ Topfoto.co.uk)

worked out the boundaries of the new country and other relevant issues, such as fishing rights. The preliminary peace was formally established between the British and the new American government on November 30, 1782. Under its terms, the British accepted the independence of the United States; all British troops stationed in the United States would withdraw. The land between the Appalachian Mountains and the Mississippi river was given to the United States, and they also received access to George's Bank, the fishing grounds off Newfoundland. The United States agreed to honor debts accrued during the war and to treat Loyalists fairly. Many Loyalists, however, chose to leave the country and move to Canada, the West Indies, or Great Britain, not trusting their new government and fearful of the future. Orders arrived on July 14, 1782, for the British to evacuate Savannah; Charleston followed on December 18, 1782. New York was not formally evacuated until November 25, 1783.

The French and Spanish had made considerable progress in eradicating the humiliations of the Seven Years' War, but the war was becoming a stalemate, and all sides were weary of it. Preliminary peace talks began among the British, French, Spanish, and Dutch in late 1782. By January 1783, an armistice had been agreed and a preliminary peace treaty signed, although fighting continued in some regions too distant to hear immediately of the agreements. The Treaty of Paris was signed on September 3, 1783. Britain handed over the Floridas (East and West) and Minorca to Spain, retaining Gibraltar and the Bahamas. France regained Senegal, St. Lucia, Tobago, and her interests in India, notably Pondicherry. The paucity of decisive naval victories for either side made it difficult to claim any major territorial gains. The British were able to retain possessions in the West Indies that they had held before the war began and lost nothing in India. They had, however, lost the United States, one of the true jewels in their imperial crown, the repercussions of which are in many ways still felt to this day.

PART 2

Armies and Navies

Washington crossing the Delaware River by Emanuel Gottlieb
Leutze. (Stocktrek Images/Getty Images)

Chapter 5

THE AMERICAN FORCES

*T*HE AMERICANS BEGAN THE WAR WITHOUT a proper army: the troops arrayed against the British in the spring of 1775 consisted of partially-trained militia. The Militia Law of 1775 designated all free men between the ages of 16 and 50 as liable for duty, and each colony formed its own militia into companies and regiments. The greatest problem with the militia organization was that there was no regular training schedule. When training was organized, the men were called to arms for a specific period of time, usually only 30–60 days, and then returned to their families. The militia was not considered fit to take on British regulars, even by their own countrymen. As General George Washington pointed out: "men just dragged from the tender scene of domestic life; unaccustomed to the din of arms; totally unaccustomed with any kind of military skill ... when opposed to troops regularly trained and disciplined and appointed supreme in arms makes them timid and ready to fly from their shadows" (Weigly, p. 5.)

The militia had some successes during the war against regular troops, but on the whole lacked sufficient discipline or training to undertake combat on a European-style battlefield. There were benefits, however, to the colonists' ability to muster a pro-independence militia. Militia could be used to offset any Loyalist attempts to provide support for the British effort; and, when used in a more irregular role, especially in raids and defense, the militia often exceeded

OPPOSITE

"The Spirit of 76." This 19th-century illustration is an idealized view of the citizen soldiers who sustained the American Army through the dark period of Washington's retreat through New Jersey. (Fine Art/Getty Images)

expectations. Following the battle of King's Mountain, 1780, the American Major-General William Moultrie noted:

> This battle as well as many others under Generals Sumter, Marion, and others, proves that militia are brave men, and will fight if you let them come to action in their own way. There are very few actions when they are drawn up in line of battle, that they could be brought to stand and reserve their fire until the enemy came near enough (Moultrie, vol. 2, p. 244.)

A Continental rifleman (left) and a regular line infantryman (right). This is a contemporary drawing made by one of the French officers who aided the American cause. (Library of Congress)

A French officer, Sub-lieutenant Jean Baptiste Antoine de Verger, observed that "they [the militia] give occasional examples of bravery when they are superior in numbers or when in possession of some defile the enemy must pass through, into which they can fire from ambush" (Rice and Brown, vol. 1, p. 152.)

The need for properly trained professional soldiers prompted the Continental Congress to sanction the formation of the Continental Army, despite widespread American bias against a standing army dating back to the English Civil Wars. The proposed structure divided American forces between the militia of the colonies and the regular Continental Army. Shortages of men available for the Continentals necessitated the use of militia in a supporting role to Continental operations and as drafts for the Continental Army. The drill master, Prussian Captain (later American Major-General) Frederick Augustus, Baron von Steuben, described the plans for militia in 1779 thus: "our business is now to find out the means of rendering that militia capable to supply the want of a well regulated standing army at least as much as lies in our power" (*Letter to Gov. Thomas Johnson.*)

The first attempts at organizing a professional army were undertaken in the summer of 1775. The "Separate Army" was formed in upstate New York in June. The Continental Congress in Philadelphia also sanctioned the formation of troops outside Boston to be listed as a Continental Force or the "New England Army." On July 2, 1775, George Washington was named commander-in-chief of all Continental and militia forces serving under the auspices of the Army of the United Colonies, both existing and to be raised. He inherited a force of some 17,000 men, mostly from the New England colonies. All of the units had different establishments, making standardization difficult. Most of the army was relieved of duty by the end of 1775, leaving Washington to muster another round of troops for the 1776 campaign. This army, again, was disbanded at the end of 1776 when its enlistment contracts ended.

Eventually the Continental Congress called for the formation of the Continental Army on September 26, 1776. The American defeats of 1776 had made Congress realize that a well-trained body of men was needed and that one-year contracts were not sufficient to prepare troops to face the British in battle. As a Hessian General noted: "General Washington and Putnam are praised by friend and foe alike but all their mastery in war will be of no avail with a mob of conscripted undisciplined troops" (Uhlendorf, *Revolution*, p. 40.) The new army was to have 88 regiments (battalions) formed from each of the Thirteen Colonies. The great difference between this force and previous musters was that the new army was to be raised for three years, or for the duration of the war, whichever was shorter. The three-year limitation on enlistment was imposed in response to recruits' unwillingness to join for an unknown duration. The Continental Army's authorized strength was 75,000 men, which it never attained. The highest level of recruitment ever reached was 18,000, in October 1778.

A reenactor peers through a spy glass during a reenactment on the two hundredth anniversary of the battle of Yorktown. (Bob Krist/ Getty Images)

The Continental Army was divided among three major armies, the Northern (Separate), Main, and Southern armies, each of which took on different numbers of battalions over the course of the war. The Continental Army consistently encountered problems in providing enough men and supplies. It was forced to compete against recruiters for the colonial militia to assemble sufficient troops, and conscription was periodically employed in an attempt to fill the army's ranks. During 1777, many commanders had difficulty clothing and arming the men in their regiments, and even in friendly territory it was difficult to supply enough food. As mentioned previously, pay was also a considerable problem, as the paper money used to pay troops and officers dropped steadily in value during the course of the war. Even facing severe shortages of supplies, men, and officers, however, the Continental Army was still able to form for battle year after year. The British were unable to destroy it completely, and on more than one occasion were defeated by the combined force of Continental and militia troops.

There is a debate among historians as to whether the Continental Army represented a levy of supporters of the independence movement, or its members had more in common with their European counterparts—men who joined the army only for payment and signing bonuses. Some contend that the militia of the time represented a more politicized element of the American forces. One historian noted that "there was little commitment among the American rank and file to the constitutional cause of Independence and very few of our patriots chose to re-enlist for a second or third time" (Duffy, p. 285.)

It is still debatable whether the Continentals were a "republican" army or a purely professional force with no concern for political issues, but ultimately they performed well in the field and proved themselves to their European allies. French officer Baron Ludwig von Closen commented: "I admire the American troops tremendously! It is indescribable that soldiers composed of men of every age, even of children of fifteen, of whites and blacks, almost naked, unpaid and rather poorly fed, can march so well and withstand fire so steadfastly" (von Closen, p. 102.)

In developing tactical training, the Continental Army had several sources of information available. Some of the senior generals appointed had seen service in British units during the Seven Years' War. Their experience was bolstered by input from a series of foreign officers who had come to advise the army and to seek adventure. They came from Prussia, Poland, France, and other European states. This infusion of officers caused confusion in the American chain of command but also provided significant expertise in organization and tactics. The Continental Army drew up its own tactical manuals, which were largely based upon contemporary British documents. Major-General von Steuben spent the winter of 1777–78 drilling the Continental Army along Prussian military lines. He also regulated the size of battalions and standardized a specific drill to be followed by all units of the Continental Army.

In 1781, there was further organizational streamlining, partially because a number of regiments were being disbanded due to lack of manpower. The fighting capabilities of the American forces remained fairly strong despite this; members of the French contingent commented on the American forces upon arrival in Newport, Rhode Island, in 1780. Sub-lieutenant de Verger noted that: "the American Continental troops are very war-wise and quite well disciplined. They are thoroughly inured to hardship, which they endure with little complaint so long as their officers set them an example, but it is imperative the officers equal their troops in firmness and resolution" (Rice and Brown, p. 152.)

Another significant asset for the Continental Army was its understanding of the need for small reforms within the organization. A French officer,

Ninteenth century prints like The First Blow for Liberty *by A.H. Ritchie color modern impressions of the militia. New England "minutemen" probably wore the clothing of townsmen and affluent farmers. (NARA)*

Lieutenant-Colonel Jean Baptiste Tennant of Pulaski's Legion, wrote an important paper examining army structure. It appears to originate after 1779, when the original commander of Pulaski's Legion was killed and succeeded by Lieutenant-Colonel Tennant. The paper, called "Uniformity Among American Troops" outlined "a scheme for establishing uniformity in the services, discipline, manoeuvre of formations of troops in the armies of the United States" (*A project to enforce uniformity.*)

Tennant proposed innovations designed to accommodate the specific needs of the Continental Army. Pointing out that the army, unlike its European counterparts, did not have the benefit of large cadres of men and officers with years of military experience, he stressed that to compensate: "the maneuvers to be introduced must be as simple as possible. The chief objectives are for the officers to know how to lead their platoons and keep their men together and for the soldiers to keep rank and file ... that all maneuvers be performed ... in greatest silence" (ibid.) He also recommended the appointment of an Inspector General to formulate training throughout the army, but stipulated that: "before introducing any new thing the Inspector General is to propose it to the Commander-in-Chief in the field ... neither the Inspector General nor inspectors of any other detached army shall be authorized to give a general order without previously communicating it with the Commander-in-Chief" (ibid.)

TRAINING

The Main and Northern armies fought from 1775 through 1777 without the benefit of consistent, formal training. Few Americans had faced French regulars during the French and Indian War, and fewer still had mastered 18th-century linear tactics, march discipline, camp sanitation, or logistics.

Militia training might at best require one training day per week. Regiments might form for mock battle and a review once each year. The officers relied on their experience in the French and Indian War or on drill manuals such as *The Manual Exercise as Ordered by His Majesty in 1764*, *A Military Guide for Young Officers*, and the *Norfolk Discipline*. Joseph Plumb Martin recorded the training he received during his first enlistment when his regiment went to defend New York in 1776: "I was called out every morning at reveille beating, which was at daybreak, to go to our regimental parade in Broad Street, and there to practice the manual exercise, which was the most that was known to our new levies, if they knew even that" (Martin, p. 18.)

The details of the manual exercise could be intricate, as in the case of preparing two ranks to fire.

Upon hearing the command "Make Ready," the Men of the Front Rank ... kneel down on their right Knees, placing the Butt-end of their Firelocks on the Ground, keeping their Thumbs on their cocks, and their fingers on the Trickets. The Center and Rear-Ranks Close forward at the same time with recover'd Arms, the Men of the Center Rank placing their left foot on the Inside of the right Feet of their File-Leaders, bringing their right Feet to the Right, but not in line with their Left, only in the same position as when they rest.

Loading and firing required officers and men to memorize 14 separate commands and 20 movements. Yet the manual exercise represented only a small portion of what a man needed to know before becoming an effective soldier. Colonial militia seldom, if ever, practiced bayonet drill. British and German regulars perfected the use of the bayonet. This asymmetry in training shaped the course of battles during the first three years of the war. When the Americans could hold their enemy at bay with musket fire, they might prevail.

When ammunition ran low or fire flagged, the bayonet won battles. A well-drilled Maryland regiment fighting under Lord Stirling on Long Island in 1776 charged superior British forces six times in succession with the bayonet, causing Washington to exclaim, "Good God! What brave fellows I must this day lose."

Overall training and performance remained patchy. John Adams justified a 1776 Congressional Resolution requiring daily drills when he wrote: "This resolution was the effect of my late journey through the Jerseys to Staten Island. I had observed such dissipation and idleness, such confusion and distraction among officers and soldiers, in various parts of the country as disturbed and alarmed me." Lack of training also exacted a price off the battlefield. On October 4, 1776, General Nathaneal Greene issued the following order: "The shameful inattention, in some camps, to decency and cleanliness in providing necessaries, and picking up the offal and filth of the camp, have been taken notice of before in general: after this time particular regiments will be pointed out by name when such practice prevails" (Duncan, p. 143.) The absence of field sanitation and basic cleanliness promoted sickness, weakening the fighting power of the army.

In terms of elevating the training of the American troops, one of the greatest contributions was actually made by a European who entered Continental service with bogus qualifications, yet made significant contributions to raising the performance of the Continental infantryman. Frederick William Augustus Henry Ferdinand Baron von Steuben met Washington at Valley Forge and presented letters of introduction from Benjamin Franklin and Silas Dean, American agents in Paris. Both men exaggerated the former Prussian captain's qualifications and rank to support his application for a commission as a major-general. His willingness to serve initially without compensation made him an attractive prospect. Washington agreed to have von Steuben join the army, unaware of Franklin and Dean's subterfuge, and von Steuben began training the Continental Army. He regarded the Continental infantry as excellent raw material and began by forming and training a platoon as an adjunct to the Commander-in-Chief's Guard. After training the demonstration platoon, he proceeded to train the army, unit by unit, at Valley Forge. Since he spoke no English at the outset, he enlisted a New York captain, Benjamin Walker, as his translator.

Von Steuben described the disagreements among the officers concerning how he should train the infantry:

> My good republicans wanted everything in the English style; our great and good allies everything in the French mode, and when I presented a plate of sauerkraut dressed in the Prussian style, they all wanted to throw it out the window, Nevertheless, by the force of proving by Goddams that my cookery was the best, I overcame the prejudices of the former; but the second liked me as little in the forests of America as they did on the plains of Rossbach. Do not therefore, be astonished if I am not painted in very bright colors in Parisian circles (Brobbrick, p. 334.)

Von Steuben's French secretary-aide described what actually transpired on the snow-covered fields of Valley Forge:

> When some movement or maneuver was not performed to his mind, he began to swear in German, then in French, and then in both languages together. When he had exhausted his artillery of foreign oaths, he would call to his aides, "My dear Walker or my dear Duponceau, come and swear for me in English – these fellows will not do what I bid them." A good natured smile then went through the ranks and at last the maneuver or movement was properly performed (Kapp, pp. 235–236.)

Each night, von Steuben dictated the lesson for the following day to his aides. They translated it into English and circulated it to the brigade headquarters. Officers at the brigade headquarters recopied it for the regimental officers. Regimental officers and literate noncommissioned officers read the lesson and then reread and explained it to those troops who could not read. When time permitted, von Steuben invited officers to his quarters in the evening to eat, and to receive informal instruction. Colonel Alexander Scammel recorded his impression of von Steuben's approach. "To see a gentleman dignified with a lieutenant general's commission from the great Prussian monarch condescend with a grace peculiar to himself to take under his direction a squad of ten or twelve men in the capacity of a drill sergeant, commands the admiration of both officers and men" (Kapp, p. 129.) Captain George Ewing recorded his feelings about training at Valley Forge in his diary.

> This forenoon, the Brigade went through the maneuvers under the direction of Baron Steuben. The step is about halfway between slow and quick time, and easy and natural step, and I think much better than the former. The manual is altered by his direction.
> There are but ten words of command which are as follows:
> 1. Poise firelock
> 2. Shoulder the Firelock
> 3. Present arms
> 4. Fix bayonet
> 5. Unfix bayonet
> 6. Load firelock
> 7. Make ready
> 8. Present
> 9. Fire
> 10. Order Firelock

When von Steuben presented his new manual to a group of officers for a critique, the only change recommended and adopted was the substitution of the command "Take Sight" for "Present."

Von Steuben's hastily written lessons evolved into a manual which went well beyond the commands for delivering a volley. Reading the manual provokes little excitement two centuries after its creation. Its style resembles that of other manuals written before or since. Its power arose from the fact that those who read it conformed their actions to its directions. The key to an army's power lies in its predictability. Consistent training, properly administered, made the Continental infantry of the Main Army reliable on the march and on the battlefield. Indeed, simplification of firing commands may appear pithy, but the simplified orders worked better on a battlefield covered in powder smoke and wracked by noise and confusion. The soldier had less to remember and a company or regiment could deliver volleys at a steady rate.

The manual covered activity on and off the battlefield. Von Steuben standardized the digging of latrines, the placement of tents and cabins in camp, and the location of the reserve ammunition wagon. Most important, he fixed the responsibility for training and he outlined the process for continued training:

> The commanding officer of each company is charged with the instruction of his recruits; and as that is a service that requires not only experience, but a patience and temper not met with in every officer, he is to make a choice of an officer, sergeant and one or two corporals of his company, who, being approved by the colonel, are to attend particularly to that business ... (Kapp, p. 201.)

Von Steuben assured that those trained at Valley Forge would deliver consistent instruction to future recruits. This process proved vital for armies whose composition changed when enlistments expired or men chose to desert. New recruits could be trained, and cooperative militia might be given a few lessons prior to battle. His program also emphasized infantry as groups arrayed in line or advancing together with the bayonet. The weapons and tactics of the time de-emphasized the individual while demanding consistent performance from the group. Some topics were omitted. It did not include instructions for meeting cavalry because Continental infantry seldom met large bodies of cavalry until the southern campaign.

Lieutenant-Colonel Alexander Hamilton (1757–1804) by A. Chappel. Originally an artillery officer, at 20 Hamilton became Washington's secretary and aide-de-camp, but argued with him in 1781, and took a field command during the Yorktown campaign. (DEA PICTURE LIBRARY/Getty Images)

TO ALL BRAVE, HEALTHY, ABLE BODIED, AND WELL
DISPOSED YOUNG MEN,
IN THIS NEIGHBOURHOOD, WHO HAVE ANY INCLINATION TO JOIN THE TROOPS,
NOW RAISING UNDER
GENERAL WASHINGTON,
FOR THE DEFENCE OF THE
LIBERTIES AND INDEPENDENCE
OF THE UNITED STATES,
Against the hostile designs of foreign enemies,

TAKE NOTICE,

Training, however, did not always guarantee victory. Some histories represent von Steuben's contribution as a magical transformation. This might be an exaggeration, but von Steuben certainly made a critical contribution to the performance of the Continental Army and to the morale of its officers and men. Washington led a collection of promising amateurs into Valley Forge, and he emerged with trained infantry.

APPEARANCE

The Continental infantryman knew that he was owed a uniform and he sometimes received his due, but very often he did not. Congress undertook to supply its army with good intentions, but the colonies' agrarian economy could not produce uniforms and equipment for a regular army. Procurement proved only a portion of the problem. Quartermasters needed wagon teams and drivers to move supplies from their place of production or import to the troops. A Congressional Committee reported from Valley Forge in 1777 that: "Almost every species of camp transportation is now performed by men, who ... patiently yoke themselves to little carriages of their own making or load their wood and provisions on their backs." When General von Steuben called on the Virginia State Quartermaster in 1781 for sufficient equipment

Americaner Soldat.

Americaner Soldat.

Accurate Vorstellung eines Americanischen Soldaten von einem Bayreuthschen Officier welcher sich dermalen in America, in Englische Dienst befindt, gezeichnet und heraus geschickt worden. Ihre Kleidung ist von Zwilch, sie habe lange Gewehr und Bayonet u. seind sehr dauerhaft u. gesund.

Ioh. Mart: Will exc: Aug. Vind.

Accurate Vorstellung eines Americanischen Soldaten von einem Bayreuthschen Officier welcher sich dermalen in America, in Englische Dienst befindt, gezeichnet und heraus geschickt worden. Ihre Kleidung ist von Zwilch, sie habe lange Gewehr und Bayonet u. seind sehr dauerhaft u. gesund.

Ioh. Mart: Will exc: Aug: V.

The most accurate contemporary depictions of Patriot military dress were by German artists. 'Amerikaner Soldat' by Johann Martin Will depicted the hunting garb, but the soldier is probably a Continental. (Anne S.K. Brown Collection, Brown University)

for 500 men along with the teams to move it, the Quartermaster wrote in reply: "To hire [horses] is impossible as no one will take the price to which we are limited, when they can get three times as much from private individuals. ... In short, sir, I have no money, no materials, no credit, and beg, while this is my situation, you will place no dependence on anything to come from the department" (Kapp, p. 396.)

Congress made its first effort to mandate uniform military dress when it designated brown as the coat color on November 4, 1775. Congress specified a uniform allowance in a September 6, 1777, resolution as:

1 coat 2 shirts
1 vest 1 hunting shirt
1 pr. buckskin & 2 pr. Overalls
2 pr. Linen breeches 2 pr. Shoes
1 hat or leather cap 1 blanket

Congress intended that soldiers pay one and two-thirds dollars out of their monthly pay of six and two-thirds dollars for their uniforms. The uniform, described as "a suit of clothes," became part of the Congressional or state bounty paid to enlistees, and the issue changed throughout the war as supply problems continued. Lafayette, still new to America, described the army in August 1777, after the brown coats of 1776 had worn out. "Eleven thousand men tolerably armed, and still worse clad, presented a singular spectacle in their parti-colored, and often naked state, the best dressed wore hunting shirts of brown linen" (Irving, p.375.)

During the spring of 1778, a shipment of blue and brown coats with red facings arrived from France. Washington distributed these among the regiments by lottery. He specified blue as the coat color in a general order dated October 2, 1779. The order also specified facing colors for groups of states: New England–white; New York and New Jersey–buff; Pennsylvania, Delaware, Maryland, and Virginia–red; North and South Carolina and Georgia–blue with thin white tape edging the button-holes. Washington ordered red facings for all regiments in 1782. Musicians wore a coat with the regimental facing and coat colors reversed. Some uniforms differed from those specified. Light infantrymen, the army's elite, modified the coat, adding cloth wings on the shoulders and shortening the tails. They wore a cap with a horsehair plume, bearskin crest, or feathers if they could get them. Alan McLane was a Marylander who raised a partisan company of scouts, and performed reconnaissance for the successful raids on Stony Point and Paulus Hook in 1779. When his light infantry company joined Lee's Legion in September of 1779, it received "Uniform light linen Jackets dyed a Purple & all their Overalls the same." The Commander-in-Chief's Guard, the best-uniformed company in the army, wore blue and buff coats, with red waistcoats and buff britches. Riflemen wore their civilian clothes and, most frequently, the rifle shirt, also known as the hunting shirt.

Soldiers received uniforms from three principal sources. Their state might provide material to make up uniforms or it might provide ready-made articles such as shirts. Congress imported uniforms, mainly from France, and it also sent uniforms and textiles captured by Continental ships to the troops. These might be issued as received, or dyed. A public subscription might, on occasion, result in the provision of a few items, such as shoes or shirts.

A fourth method of getting supplies was to take someone else's. Colonel Robert Gaskin, assigned the task of raising a Continental regiment in Virginia in May 1781, despaired when his repeated requests for supplies yielded none. He raided supplies assembled by the State of Virginia for his troops and acquired 172 pairs of shoes, 11 pairs of boots, and 20 pieces of Osnaberg cloth. Continental regiments might waylay supplies directed to other Continental units, and commanders of state troops might raid Continental stores when they could not meet their needs from other sources.

MILITIA CLOTHING AND EQUIPMENT

The standing militiaman at left (1) is armed with an expensive and elegant small-bore hunting rifle, as indicated by the delicate design and fancy brass work around the patch box built into the butt of the rifle. He wears a typical linsey-woolsey hunting shirt and narrow-legged trousers, and wide-brimmed hat. The mounted militiaman at lower right (2) is armed with a sturdy military musket, as indicated by the sling, and the cartouche (ammunition box) with prepared cartridges on his right hip. Additional weapons include a pair of heavy dragoon pistols carried in bucket holsters on the pommel of the saddle. A light bedroll is tied to the rear (cantle) of the saddle. The militia used whatever weapons could be acquired, including, from left to right, a small-bore hunting rifle (3), large-bore fowling piece (shotgun) (4), a captured British "Brown Bess" Short Land Pattern military musket (5), and a 1766 model Charleville military musket of a type provided in large numbers by the French (6). The deer hide boot was used to protect the firing mechanism of a rifle or musket from rain or damp (7). Also shown are a typical dragoon pistol, and locally manufactured swords, one in a simple hanger (8). Smaller items at lower left include the tomahawk or war hatchet (9), and locally manufactured knives of variable quality (10). The knife and drinking cup typically constituted the ordinary militiaman's only mess gear (11). The pan brush and wire vent pick were usually carried on a chain or string (12). The hinged bullet mold, powder measure cup, and ball starter were unique to the caliber of the rifleman's specific weapon (13). (Steve Noon © Osprey Publishing)

Congress initially made the states responsible for clothing the regiments they provided to the army. Some states, such as Virginia, made efforts throughout the war to provide clothing for their troops. Neither the states nor Congress ever achieved systematic supply of uniforms, although some succeeded at times. When Nathanael Greene called upon North Carolina to supply clothing and shoes for his army in 1780, it provided rifle shirts and overalls for his Continentals and seized a tannery to produce shoes. With the irregular supply of materials, men might produce shoes or moccasins if they could get a bit of hide from the butcher and had the time and the skill. The lack of both in the New Jersey campaign of 1776-77 led to the scene depicted by one of the soldiers marching toward Princeton: "Our men, too, were without shoes or comfortable clothing; and as traces of the march towards Princeton, the ground was literally marked with the blood of the soldiers' feet" (Richards, p.120.)

Men dressed as Revolutionary soldiers march during an historical reenactment of a battle at Yorktown, Virginia. (Bob Krist/Getty Images)

EQUIPMENT

Poverty and mismanagement affected equipment as well as the uniforms of Continental infantrymen. Equipment comprised what the individual soldier needed to fight and to live, together with equipment allotted to his regiment. He fared best, perhaps, with the tools of his trade, weapons. The availability of other equipment varied for the same reasons that the supply of uniforms varied.

Firearms initially ran the gamut from fowling pieces to the British Long Land Pattern musket, standard issue for British infantry. The Committees of Safety in each of the colonies had begun importing muskets and component parts from Holland and France before the outbreak of war. They also placed orders with

American gunsmiths, though in some cases the contractor assembled muskets from parts imported by the Committees. Captured weapons, such as 1,000 German muskets taken at Trenton, also found their way into the hands of the Continentals. Supply barely kept pace with losses. Untrained, retreating soldiers discarded or lost 8,000 muskets in 1776.

The situation with riflemen was slightly different. They carried unique pieces and cast their own bullets as well as solving their own supply problems. Riflemen from Pennsylvania and Northern Virginia generally carried the Pennsylvania rifle, finished in brass. Southerners carried the more austere Southern or "poor boy" rifle. Made in small batches or crafted individually, American rifles and riflemen enjoyed a reputation for accuracy and range. A musket-armed infantryman might hit something at 100yds (90m). Riflemen could hit predictably at 200yds (180m), and they might score at 400yds (370m). However, the rifleman loaded loose powder from a horn and a bullet wrapped in a greased patch each time he fired. A rifleman therefore fired at a slower rate than an infantryman firing a musket,

Shooting of British Brigadier Simon Fraser by American Sharpshooters, October 7, 1777. (National Archives of Canada)

with the end result being that a rifleman's weapon exposed him to special risks. A British officer explained for a local newspaper how to deal with riflemen:

> About twilight is found the best season for hunting the rebels in the woods, at which time their rifles are of very little use; and they are not found so serviceable in a body as musketry, a rest being requisite at all times, and before they are able to make a second discharge, it frequently happens that they find themselves run through the body by the push of a bayonet, as a rifleman is not entitled to any quarter (Peterson, p. 201.)

Von Steuben's regulations, derived from the training of the Main Army at Valley Forge in 1778, set the basis for standardizing weapons: "The arms and accouterments of the officers, noncommissioned officers, and soldiers, should be uniform throughout. ... The officers who exercise their functions on horseback, are to be armed with swords, the platoons officers with swords and espontoons, the non commissioned officers with swords, firelocks and bayonets, and the soldiers with firelocks and bayonets." French imports provided the means for standardizing muskets. American agents in Paris began importing thousands of French muskets in 1776, and these predominated as time passed. Informally referred to as the Charleville, the French musket included at least six different versions of a .69-caliber musket which proved handier, lighter, and less prone to user mistakes than its British counterpart.

Once provided with a stand of arms, the infantryman needed ammunition and either a cartridge box or a tin to hold it. A wooden block within the cartridge box would be drilled to hold from 26 to 40 rounds. Some soldiers, wary of running out of ammunition in battle, carried both. Each man also needed a bayonet and scabbard. When scabbards ran short, Washington ordered the infantry to keep the bayonet mounted on the musket. Finally, the infantryman needed a stopper for the muzzle of his musket to keep out the rain. The army could acquire or produce leather and fabric cartridge and bayonet belts. A blacksmith could produce bayonets, but he would need to forge the ring to fit a particular musket. Officers constantly had to remind men not to use their bayonets for prizing things open or as screwdrivers or spits. Constant exposure to heat made the metal brittle and prone to break when most needed.

Continental infantry fighting afloat off Boston, on Lake Champlain, and in the Delaware might use different weapons, including blunderbusses, wall pieces, grenades, boarding pikes, or cutlasses. None of these weapons found general use among the infantry because they offered no increase in firepower superior to a line of aimed muskets. The blunderbusses and wall pieces, no more than oversized muskets, were heavy, inaccurate, and slow to load.

After weapons, cooking utensils represented the most important items of personal equipment. Six or more men would share a cooking pot. Individuals might have broilers and knives, forks, and spoons. When these were in short supply, a larger number of troops might share the available utensils. They might augment their equipment from captured enemy sources or from involuntary requisitions upon civilians. A soldier also needed a pack, haversack, and blankets. The haversack could hold up to three days' supply of bread and cooked meat. Were these not available, the haversack held anything eatable that its owner could find. The pack held any spare clothing, a blanket and personal equipment or belongings such as a tinder box, book, or dice. An infantryman might receive a haversack and pack upon enlistment. Replacement came from the various states. For example, the Selectmen of Union Connecticut contracted and paid for blankets for members of the Connecticut line. In addition, the British also unwillingly provided packs, as a sergeant reported after the battle at Princeton: "In this battle, my pack, which was made fast by leather strings, was shot from my back and with it what little clothing I had. It was, however, soon replaced by one which had belonged to a British officer and was well furnished. It was not mine long, for it was stolen shortly thereafter" (Richards, p. 124.)

CONTINENTAL INFANTRYMAN, BRANDYWINE. WEAPONS, DRESS, AND EQUIPMENT

The 2nd Virginia private carries a British Brown Bess musket, weighing approximately 10lb (4.5kg), which was widely used by Continental forces until shipments of the French Charleville arrived in greater numbers. He wears a round hat turned up on the left side and held in place with a black cockade. His hair is pulled back and tied in the back. He also wears a white shirt with a black neck stock visible under his coat.

The men of the 2nd Virginia were issued new uniforms in 1777; these featured dark blue coats and facings with white worsted tape for lace. The lace pattern, unique to the 2nd Virginia, is composed of widely separated sets of two lace/button combinations on a blue facing on the cuffs and lapels and a single lace/button on the blue collar. The coat includes straps on both shoulders, attached with buttons and used to secure the cross belts. The tails of the coat are turned back and hooked together, exposing the white lining of the coat. He wears a white waistcoat and woolen pants. As the war progressed many units adopted overalls rather than pants, which were more practical and required replacement less often. Knee-high stockings protected the soldier's calves while shoes, with brass buckles, completed the uniform. Slung at his side by a woven strap is a wooden canteen, sometimes painted in various colors or adorned with a regimental designation. Also supported by whitened buff leather crossbelts are a leather bayonet scabbard containing an 18in (45.7cm) bayonet and a cartridge box, also made of leather and containing a wooden block drilled with 19 holes to hold the cartridges. He also carries a linen haversack in which he may carry additional cartridges, food, or extra clothing. The combined weight of these items was roughly 35lb (16kg). (David Bonk © Osprey Publishing)

Each regiment also needed practical and logistical equipment. Lieutenant-Colonel Gaskin included his regimental requirements along with his soldiers' equipment: "tents, Camp kettles, Axes, Hatchets, 10 wagons with four horses each and drivers, 1,000 wooden canteens, Knapsacks, Haversacks, Bags and Portmanteaus" (*von Steuben Papers.*) The regimental surgeon required a set of surgical instruments and a medicine chest. Many surgeons brought their own instruments, although Congress supplied the medicine chests and their contents as best it could. A regiment also needed drums. The regimental drums served to transmit basic commands, including Assembly, March, Reveille, Tattoo, To Arms, Parley, and the General. The regimental colors served as both a symbol of the regiment and a reference point for the regiment's location on the battlefield. In addition, regimental wagons were needed to haul tents, the officers' baggage, the sick and, if available, a small stock of construction tools employed by the sappers to improve roads or to prepare fortifications during a siege.

The uniform and equipment of a Continental infantryman depended heavily upon chance. His coat might be the same as the man next to him in line, but his pants might differ. Both might have a cocked hat, but each might drink from different canteens. His waistcoat might have come from France, Virginia, or England. He might have received a pack when he enlisted, or he might have picked one up from the battlefield. His British, German, and Loyalist counterparts all went through periodic shortages, but few endured the vagaries of a chaotic supply system as often as he did.

A print of 1780 entitled The Real American Rifleman *romaticizes the rifleman. In fact, the smoothbore musket was by far the most common American weapon of the war. (Library of Congress)*

CONDITIONS OF SERVICE

Eighteenth-century armies went into winter quarters because weather rendered them immobile. Orders to go into winter camp converted the Continental infantry to builders. Soldiers constructed cities of small cabins where they lived during the winter and spring. They also built field fortifications to protect the camp, and as fatigue duty to keep them busy.

The men employed their regimental tools or tools bought, borrowed, or stolen from nearby farmers. Washington determined the location, and quartermasters marked the sites. Washington awarded prizes to those who completed their huts first. The sooner the men got out of their tents, the less likely the danger of their freezing to death.

Log hut construction followed a uniform pattern. The officers' type usually had two or more doors and windows and a chimney and fireplace at each end. The standard size usually accommodated a maximum of four officers. The men's huts were smaller in size and were built to hold

12 men sleeping in elevated two-tier bunks. Ventilation was always a problem in these overcrowded one-room huts; windows were rarely cut in the construction, and those provided were never opened.

Oak, chestnut, and walnut were extensively used for hut construction. Suitable trees were felled by axe and pulled by sledge to the sites. Joseph Plumb Martin described the cabins built by the Continentals:

1st Continental Regiment summer–winter, New York–New Jersey Campaign (Troiani, Don (b.1949)/ Private Collection/Bridgeman Images/Bridgeman Images)

This British dragoon helmet from the late 18th century illustrates the continuing impracticality of much military uniform. (The Museum of the Revolution at Yorktown)

The next thing is the erecting of the huts. They were generally twelve by fifteen or sixteen feet [3.7 by 4.6 or 4.9m] square, all uniformly of the same dimensions. The building of them was thus: after procuring the most suitable timber for the business, it was laid up by notching them in at the four corners. When arrived at the proper height, about seven feet [2.1m], the two end sticks which held those that served for plates were made to jut out about a foot [30cm] from the sides, and a straight pole made to rest on them, parallel to the plates; the gable ends were then formed by laying on pieces with straight poles on each, which served for ribs to hold the covering, drawing in gradually to the ridgepole. Now for the covering: this was done by sawing some of the larger trees into cuts about four feet [1.2m] in length, splitting them into bolts, and riving them into shingles, or rather staves. The covering then commenced by laying on those staves, resting the lower ends on the poles by the plates; they were laid on in two thicknesses, carefully breaking joints. They were then bound on by a straight pole with withes, then another double tier with the buts resting on this pole, and bound on as before, and so on the end of the chapter. A chimney was then built at the center of the back side composed of stone as high as the eaves, and finished with sticks and clay, if clay was to be had, if not, with mud. The last thing was to hew stuff and build us up cabins or berths to sleep in, and then the buildings were fitted for the reception of gentlemen soldiers, with all their rich and gay furniture.

These log houses were usually arranged in enclaves to hold a battalion, and where possible were sited on sloping ground to ensure drainage. Laid out in rows, the men's huts came first, then the officers', then the kitchens and the supply and ammunition lines. The hospital huts were in the rear.

The men built additional cabins for soldiers with dependants. The Valley Forge camp of 1777 became the model and von Steuben's regulations standardized the details. The Continental Army built similar camps in New Jersey, Massachusetts, Connecticut, and New York, where Washington sent regiments to make subsistence easier. The Southern Army built huts and a few two-story barracks around Ticonderoga in the winter of 1776. Nathanael Greene's Southern Army campaigned through the winter of 1780 due to moderate weather and his desire to maintain the offensive. Some routines remained the same in winter as in

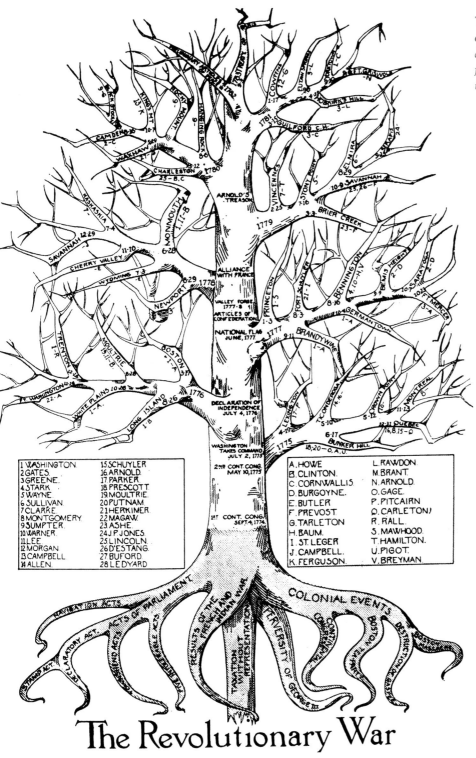

The Southern Campaign was once widely acknowledged as decisive. More actions were fought in South Carolina than in any other colony. (NARA)

The Revolutionary War

summer. Troops mounted guard, drilled, and sent detachments out to forage. Soldiers granted furloughs made their way home, hopefully to return. Officers and men organized entertainment to break up the monotony of daily duty. Major William Croghan wrote to Bernard Gratz about camp theatricals in New Jersey in the winter of 1778:

> We spend our time very sociably here; are never disturbed by the enemy, have plenty of provisions, and no want of Whiskey Grogg. We sometimes get good Spirits, Punch &c, and have Madeira sometimes. We have a variety of amusements. Last evening the Tragedy of Cato was performed at Brunswick by officers of the Army. Will the Congress be displeased? (Byers, p. 176.)

FOOD AND PAY

Work, drill, and entertainment provided distraction, but these activities did not correct an underlying problem. The infantry could shelter themselves, but they could not feed themselves. Winter weather halted wagons and delayed delivery of supplies and clothing. Congress's efforts to create a commissary system produced erratic results. More important, the lack of money, the key determinant of the Continental infantryman's condition, limited what supplies might be purchased.

Congress and the individual states printed money. None had specie (coin) reserves to back up the paper. A Massachusetts infantryman who had received his bounty in 1777 from his home state quickly learned that $3.10 of Massachusetts money equaled $1.33 in Continental currency or one Spanish milled dollar. By January 1780, the Spanish milled dollar equaled $29.30 Massachusetts or $29.40 Continental. The infantry private's annual pay of $76 Continental before stoppages equaled less than $3 in specie.

Claude Blanchard was a Commissary in the army of Rochambeau, who commanded the French army that landed in Rhode Island to cooperate with Washington. Blanchard eulogized Congress's currency during the winter of 1780: "They [the Americans] love money and hard money; it is thus they designate specie to distinguish it from paper money." After making some disbursements in American paper money, Blanchard wrote: "We were unable to make use of this paper money long, because it fell completely, and no human power could have been able to raise it again" (Balch, pp. 71–72.) The currency collapse paralleled conditions in the Main Army's winter camps. The Marquis de Lafayette described the army at Valley Forge: "The unfortunate soldiers were in want of everything; they had neither coats nor hats, nor shirts nor shoes.

Their feet and legs froze until they were black and it was often necessary to amputate them" (de Lafayette, p. 35.)

Improvement of the weather and the replacement of Thomas Mifflin by Nathanael Greene as Quartermaster at Valley Forge brought improvements. More food reached the camp in February. The troops caught thousands of shad in the Schuylkill River in March. Washington had staved off a possible smallpox epidemic by requiring the inoculation of 3,000 to 4,000 troops. However, scurvy, starvation, and other diseases required the army's doctors to use 50 barns, dwellings, meeting houses, or churches in the vicinity of the camp as hospitals. An estimated 2,500 men perished from disease or complications resulting from starvation and exposure.

Many soldiers knew that the Continental Congress set a basic ration for the army in 1775 which was recorded as:

1 lb. [500g] Of beef, or 3/4 lb. [340g] Pork, or 1 lb. Salt fish per day.

1 lb. Of bread or flour per day.

3 pints [1.4l] of pease, or beans per week, or vegetables equivalent, at one dollar per bushel for pease or beans.

1 pint [500ml] of milk per man per day, or at the rate of 1/72 of a dollar.

1 half pint [240ml] of Rice, or 1 pint of indian meal per man per week.

1 quart [1l] of spruce beer or cyder per man per day, or nine

gallons [34l] of Molasses per company of 100 men per week.

3 lb. [1.4kg] Candles to 100 men per week for guards.

Few soldiers ever received the prescribed ration at Valley Forge. Soldiers coped as best they could. Sergeant John Smith of the Rhode Islanders recorded how his regiment dealt with hunger on December 19 and 20, 1777, on the way to Valley Forge: "We found a Corn field where was Corn which we took and Eat after we Roasted it in the fire some ... towards Night we drew Some Poor Beef & one Days flower—this December 20th 1777" (John Smith Diary.) The army enjoyed a milder winter in New Jersey in 1778, but food still reached the camp irregularly, prompting Major Ebenezer Huntington to write to his brother in May 1779: "We have been without bread or rice more than five days out of seven, for these three weeks past, and the prospect remains as fair as it has been" (*Huntington Letters*.) The harsh situation led to discontent and desertion. Indeed, Washington sought permission from Congress to increase the maximum sentence for serious offenses from 50 to 100 lashes, yet at the same time he chastised Major Henry Lee for summarily executing a deserter and bringing his head back to camp as an example.

ON CAMPAIGN

The Main, Northern, and Southern armies each waged different campaigns under different conditions and leaders. The infantryman's experience therefore depended upon where, when, and under whom he served. Campaigns generally began in the spring and ended in the fall, but exceptions occurred. Common experience evolved around basic practices which each army learned or adopted.

Departure from winter camp meant the shift from log cabins to tents or borrowed housing. The firing of a gun in the morning alerted the regiments to drop tents, pack their gear, eat breakfast, and prepare to fall in for the day's march. Captain Robert Kirkwood maintained a meticulous record of his activity from April 7, 1780, when the Maryland and Delaware troops departed the Main Army for the south, to April 13, 1782, when he arrived home. He averaged 7 miles (11km) per day during two years of active campaigning, an approximate total of 5,000 miles (8,000km).

Infantry might cover 10 miles (16km) on an easy day's march. When marching to contact or retreating, troops could average 20 miles (32km). When compelled to respond to threats, as at Brandywine, they could achieve prodigies such as 5 miles (8km) in 45 minutes. Officers needed to plan carefully, however. The approach march of 14 miles (22km) before the battle of Germantown exhausted the troops before they had engaged their opponents.

Troops on campaign needed food, but the Continental infantryman could not always count on a square meal. The 1,300 men who marched into the Maine wilderness with Benedict Arnold, in 1775, faced the worst campaign of any colonial force in the Revolution. They needed to carry 400lb (180kg) bateaux for a series of portages together with their food and ammunition. They did not know that the maps of their route were wrong. They departed Fort Western, Maine, at the beginning of October and within a few days Dr. Isaac Senter recorded that:

> By this time, many of our bateaux were nothing but wrecks, some stove to pieces, &c. The carpenters were employed in repairing them, while the rest of the army was busy in carrying over the provisions, &c. A quantity of dry cod fish by this time was received, as likewise, a number of barrels of dry bread. The fish lying loose in the bateaux and being continually washed with the fresh water running into the bateaux was spoiled. The bread casks not being waterproof, admitted the water in plenty, swelled the bread, burst the casks, as well as soured the whole bread. The same fate attended a number of fine casks of peas.

Jeremiah Greenman, who was on this expedition, would describe his only meal on November 1 as "In a very misrabel situation Nothing to eat but dogs. Here we killed another and cooked I got Sum of that by good [luck] with the head of a Squirril with a parsol of Candil wicks boyled up to gether wich made very fine Supe without Salt."

The expectation of action meant that soldiers loaded up to three days' supply of cooked pork and baked bread in their knapsacks, as Joseph Plumb Martin did when he prepared to go to Long Island in 1776:

> At the lower end of the street were placed several casks of sea bread, I believe of canel and peas-meal, nearly hard enough to make for musket flints; the casks were unheaded and each man was allowed to take as much as he could as he marched by. ... We quickly embarked on board the boats. As each boat started, three cheers were given by those on board, which was returned by the numerous spectators who thronged the warves; they all wished us good luck, apparently; although it was with most of them perhaps nothing more than ceremony.

Although Martin departed for Long Island with sufficient food for the brief campaign there, Sergeant William Seymour of the Delawares went hungry as he marched under Horatio Gates to Camden in August 1780:

> At this time we were so much depressed for want of provisions that we were fourteen days and drew but one half pound of flour. Sometimes we drew half a pound of beef per man and that so miserably poor that scarce any mortal could make use of it—living on green apples and peaches which rendered our situation truly miserable, being in a weak and sickly condition, and surrounded on all sides by our enemies the Tories (Seymour, p. 4)

Infantrymen on campaign could count on being on guard duty once every three days. The army camped in the midst of a concentric ring of guards who deterred

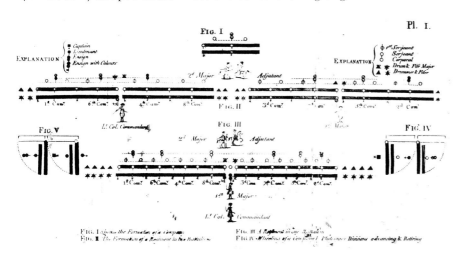

A 1779 American drill book showing formation of a company and regiment and wheeling by platoons. (Anne S.K. Brown Collection, Brown University)

desertion while attempting to prevent a surprise attack. Piquet guards secured the roads leading to camp. The camp guard comprised detachments each drawn from two battalions of a subaltern, sergeant, corporal, drummer, and 27 privates. The camp guards were deployed at least 300 paces from the camp perimeter to form a continuous sentry chain. The separate quarter guard, a sergeant and nine privates, were deployed to protect their battalion's baggage. Senior officers also received specified guard detachments according to their rank; a brigadier-general, for example, was assigned a sergeant's guard—a sergeant, a corporal, and 12 privates.

Failure to post sufficient sentinels could have deadly consequences, as Count Pulaski discovered when he took his Legion to Egg Harbor, New Jersey, in October 1778 to deter a possible raid. He billeted his cavalry and infantry separately from one another and posted a single sentry on the road leading to the infantry's billets. Captain Patrick Ferguson's 200-man raiding party captured the sentry posted to protect the infantry. Ferguson reported that:

Infantry: Continental Army, 1779–1783, IV by Henry Alexander Ogden (1856–1936), c.1897. In January 1779 Washington submitted a proposal to the Continental Congress for the standardization of uniforms, suggesting each state adopt a different color uniform, with facing colors distinguishing different units (North Carolina, South Carolina, and Georgia). (Library of Congress)

According at eleven last night, two hundred and fifty Men were embarked, and after rowing ten miles landed at four this Morning within a Mile of the Defile, which we happily secured and leaving fifty men for its Defense, pushed forward upon the infantry cantoned in three different houses, who are almost cut to pieces. We numbered among their Dead about fifty (Nelson, p. 158.)

It being a night attack little quarter, could, of course, be given.

Some infantrymen temporarily escaped the routine of marching and guard duty for service afloat. On more than one occasion, infantrymen in the Northern and Main armies found themselves pressed into service as sailors. Washington detached men to crew a small schooner squadron active in snatching supply ships bound for Boston. He called upon John Glover's Marblehead Regiment to rescue his army from Long Island and to ferry it into battle at Trenton and Princeton. Washington drafted infantrymen to reinforce the Pennsylvania Navy in his efforts to deny Howe the Delaware in 1777. Generals Schuyler, Gates, and Arnold built a squadron of small warships on Lake Champlain in 1776 to stem Guy Carleton's advance down the Champlain Valley. Continental infantrymen, dubbed by Arnold "the refuse of every regiment," served as marines at the battle of Valcour Island. They also worked as ship carpenters, riggers, sailors, and gunners.

With minimal formal command structure, militia decisions were usually reached after arguments and debates. (Steve Noon © Osprey Publishing)

Infantry regiments assigned to the Main Army had a more varied experience than those in the other armies. Since the Main Army transferred regiments and brigades to the Northern and Southern armies, some regiments compiled impressive campaign records. No regiment saw more action than that provided by Delaware. The state sent only one regiment to the Continental Army. It numbered 550 men when it went into action on Long Island in 1776 and mustered less than 100 when it fought its last battle at Eutaw Springs, South Carolina, in 1781. Henry "Light Horse Harry" Lee observed that "The State of Delaware furnished one regiment only and no regiment in the army surpassed it in soldiership" (Lee, p.185.) The Delawares' enlistments ended shortly before the battle of Princeton. Only its colonel and four men fought there. Before Princeton, the Regiment fought at Long Island, White Plains, Mamroneck, and Trenton. Once reformed after Princeton, the Delawares fought at Brandywine, Germantown, Monmouth, Camden, Cowpens, Guilford Courthouse, Ninety-Six, Eutaw Springs, and Yorktown. Detachments of the Regiment served at Paulus Hook and Stony Point and in numerous skirmishes. Maryland's regiments approached the Delawares' record, but none surpassed it.

The Delaware Regiment, until sent south, served with Washington's Main Army, but the Main Army waged no major campaigns in the middle states between the battle of Monmouth in July 1778 and its departure for Yorktown in 1781. Washington lacked the strength to storm New York, and he chose not to hazard a major battle except on his own terms. He shifted his brigades between New Jersey and the Hudson Highlands to deter a drive into New Jersey or any attempt to seize control of West Point on the Hudson. The absence of major battles did not, however, equate to an absence of action. Washington detached 4,000 men under John Sullivan in 1779 to campaign against the Indians of western New York State. This campaign featured long marches, skirmishing, and the destruction of Indian towns and crops. Nathan Davis described one of the skirmishes which punctuated the campaign. Indians, covered by trees, had opened fire on the Americans:

> We were expressly ordered not to fire until we had obtained permission from our officers but to form a line of battle as soon as possible and march forward. This we did in good order, and at the same time the Indians kept up an incessant fire upon us from behind the trees, firing and retreating back to another tree, loading and firing again, still keeping up the war woop. They continued this mode of warfare till we had driven them halfway up the hill, when we were ordered to charge bayonets and rush on. No sooner said than done. We then, in our turn, gave our war woop in the American style, which completely silenced the unearthly voice of their stentorian throats. We drove them, at once, to the opposite side of the hill, when we were ordered to halt, as the Indians were out of sight and hearing, (*The Historical Magazine.*)

However, this initial success masked the harsh realities of conflict. Lieutenant William Barton of the First New Jersey recalled a party sent to find the Indians killed in the skirmish to acquire material for leggings. He reported that they "skinned two of them from their hips down for both legs, one pair for the major and one pair for myself." Another party of 22 riflemen, sent to scout ahead, was ambushed, killed, scalped, and mutilated.

The Corps of Light Infantry did not accompany General Sullivan on his campaign against the Indians. Washington had begun grouping the best soldiers in the Main Army into a light infantry battalion during the 1777 campaign. He formed three small regiments in 1778 and a brigade of four small regiments numbering 1,300 for the 1779 campaign. The light infantry comprised chosen men, the elite infantry of the Main Army. Joseph Plumb Martin, drafted to the light infantry, described them succinctly:

> The duty of the Light Infantry is the hardest, while in the field, of any troops in the army, if there is any hardest about it. During the time the army keeps the field they are always on the lines near the enemy, and consequently always on the alert, constantly on the watch. Marching and guardkeeping with all the other duties of troops in the field fall plentifully to their share. There is never any great danger of Light Infantrymen dying of the scurvy.

One element common to all three armies was that women and children marched with the troops on campaign. British observers described the burial of 40 soldiers after the battle of Bemis Heights "after being stripped of their clothing by the women of the American camp." Washington wrote on August 4, 1777:

> In the present marching state of the army, every incumbrance proves greatly prejudicial to the service; the multitude of women in particular, especially those who are pregnant, or have children, are a clog upon every movement. The Commander in Chief therefore earnestly recommends it to the officers commanding brigades and corps, to use every reasonable method in their power to get rid of all such as are not absolutely necessary.

He went on to write more than 25 General Orders concerning women. Many enjoined the officers against permitting them to ride in supply wagons. One required that they stay out of sight when the army marched through Philadelphia in 1777 on its way to Brandywine. After staying out of sight until the soldiers passed them, they simply joined in at their accustomed place at the rear of the army.

Women undertook a variety of roles, including laundresses and nurses. Some got water for their men under fire at the battle of Brandywine. They produced soap, oil, and leather in the camp slaughterhouse. They received rations, and those with assigned jobs received pay. Doctors recruited women for the hospitals. An order of May 31, 1778, read: "Commanding Officers of Regiments will assist

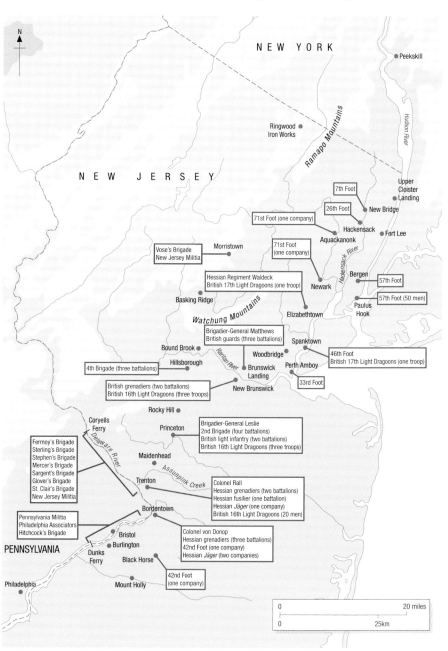

British winter quarters and American defensive dispositions, December 23, 1776

THE BATTLE OF COWPENS, JANUARY 17, 1781

Often called "the American Cannae" and "the most perfect battle ever fought in the Americas," Cowpens was one of the decisive battles of the war. Patriot commander Daniel Morgan carefully analyzed British commander Banastre Tarleton's past actions, and devised an unusual defense-in-depth. Tarleton recklessly attacked before his troops were fully deployed. As Morgan expected, upon seeing the militia withdrawing Tarleton launched a charge that disrupted British unit cohesion. The British were then confronted with a third defensive line of disciplined Continentals, who decimated the British infantry with point-blank volleys of musket fire. In the final phase of the battle, Morgan's Continentals and militia fighting on foot counterattacked the British infantry. Patriot dragoons, along with mounted militia whom Tarleton thought had fled the field, circled behind the Patriot line and unexpectedly attacked the British light infantry and Fraser's Highlanders from the left flank and rear. The British infantry surrendered en masse, and a major part of Cornwallis's army—including many of his best red-coated regulars—was lost. Major Mcarthur of the Highlanders complained bitterly, "the best troops in the service had been put under that boy [Tarleton] to be sacrificed." (Steve Noon © Osprey Publishing)

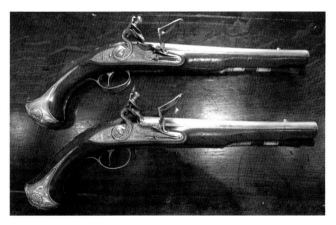

A pair of British flintlock pistols, made by Griffin & Tow of London. (The Museum of the Revolution at Yorktown)

the Regimental Surgeons in procuring as many women of the army as can be prevailed on to serve as nurses to them, who will be paid the usual price." There is only one documented case of a woman, Debra Samson, masquerading as a man to join the army. Details of her story remain sketchy, but she may have been wounded in a skirmish, leading to her discovery. Other women may have stood by their husbands in battle and shared the fate of the army. When the British Legion pursued the remnants of Horatio Gates's army after Camden, it scattered the women and children. Records do not report how many rejoined the army once it halted.

The numbers of camp followers rose and fell. At Valley Forge they may have numbered as few as 400. At Newburgh in 1781, they had grown in number to 700. They faced a difficult life under the same discipline as that governing their men. A few were tried, punished, and expelled from the camp for theft. The camp followers seldom included prostitutes in their ranks, but prostitutes nonetheless ministered to the needs of the men. When apprehended in camp, they might be flogged and expelled. Operating near a camp proved safer if less convenient.

The presence of women moderated some of the hardships of a campaign, but they could do nothing to mitigate its worst outcome—capture. Capture could prove disastrous. Sir Guy Carleton returned his prisoners to the Northern Army in hopes that tales of his kindness would weaken rebel commitment. Other British generals did not employ this tactic, and the conditions of confinement for prisoners were extremely basic. The British converted public buildings and warehouses in New York City to prisoner-of-war camps. Overcrowding, disease, and starvation quickly thinned the ranks. Once the British began using prison hulks in New York and Charleston, the death rate climbed. Peter Fayssous, the Medical Director of the Southern Department, described the situation in Charleston: "Confined in large numbers on board these vessels, and fed on salt provisions in this climate in the months of October and November, they naturally generated a putrid fever from the human miasma. This soon became highly contagious. The sick brought into the general hospital from the prison ships generally died in the course of two or three days, with all the marks of a septic state" (Gibbs, p. 118.) On a few occasions, individuals escaped, or groups were liberated before they could be sent to the ships. Capture when campaigning against Indians meant death by torture. The horrors inflicted were widely known, reflected by the Continental units in the Western Department having lower desertion rates.

The problems encountered by the Continental infantry on campaign were the result of both the enemy's activity and his conditions of service. The conditions of service became most apparent when the army ceased campaign to retire to winter quarters, and it was in winter quarters that the Continental infantryman faced the most serious threat to his existence.

CAVALRY

Cavalry was not used in large numbers by either side, the only type of horse soldier employed being the dragoon or light dragoon, trained to serve either mounted or dismounted. Heavy cavalry, cuirassiers and so on, were not employed.

Cavalry duties included scouting, raiding, patrolling, outpost and escort duties, and rounding up deserters. On the march it was the practice for the cavalry to join the light infantry as part of the advance guard; in battle they were often posted in the classic position on the wings of the line, and in retreat covered the rearguard. Due to shortage of weapons, equipment and above all horses, the new-raised American cavalry proved less mobile and far-ranging than regular horse should be, and in 1780 von Steuben tried to overcome this by mixing dragoons with special infantry to guard the dismounted forward posts from which the horsemen operated; this combination became known as a "legion."

In theory American dragoons were issued with a carbine, one or two pistols, and a sword (saber). In practice, there was a great variety of weapons ranging from hunting patterns to those captured from the British or acquired from the

Note the symbolism in this engraving from a painting of the battle of Camden by Alonzo Chappel. At left Patriot militia flee before a British bayonet charge, while a Continental officer tries to rally them. The militiamen leave the Continentals to be slaughtered (right). At center British infantrymen bayonet the German-born "Baron" de Kalbe. (NARA)

French and the Spanish. In 1778 Washington told the commanding officer of Moylan's Dragoons that swords, pistols, and carbines were unobtainable. As late as 1782, Southern cavalry were very deficient of cartridge boxes, had few pistols, and one-third of the men even lacked scabbards for their swords. The general poverty of the Continental Army led to a shortage of the basic requirement: good horses. These were costly and scarce and were often in poor condition for lack of proper forage.

Two of the best-known mounted units were Henry Lee's and William Washington's. "Light Horse Harry" Lee became famous for exploits such as the capture of Paulus Hook opposite New York in August 1779. While this was not of great tactical value it served to boost American morale, as well as showing the improving skill of the mounted arm. In December 1780 Lee's Legion was nearly 300 strong, fully uniformed and equipped, and reported to be "thoroughly disciplined scouts and raiders."

Lieutenant-Colonel William Washington's Cavalry Troop, when in Greene's Army of the South in December 1780, numbered just 90 out of a total field force of 1,600. Only half of them were equipped and a report said that their appearance was wretched beyond description. Despite this their spirit was good; a month later the troop collaborated at Hannah's Cowpen to defeat the famous Tarleton in a classic charge.

At Guilford Courthouse, March 14, 1781, General Greene had both bodies, Lee's and Washington's, in the classic position one on each wing of a curved line in a large clearing. Unwilling to risk everything on a single battle, Greene withheld most of the cavalry during the confused fighting. The British then saved their infantry by an indiscriminate bombardment of grape which hit friend and foe alike. In the confusion, the American cavalry helped to cover Greene's successful withdrawal.

At Hobkirk's Hill, Washington's Troop made an attack, sweeping round to fall on Rawdon's rear, but was held up by thick undergrowth and fallen trees. Swinging too wide to clear these, they rounded up some British stragglers. Later they were able to put in a charge and save Greene's guns from capture. Up to 1782 in the Charleston area both corps, then organized on the "legion" basis, were in skirmishes with British foraging parties.

Few though they were, and odd though many looked, the ancestors of the US Cavalry proved that they were not quite as useless as their commander-in-chief expected them to be.

ARTILLERY

Before 1775 there was little in the way of artillery in the Colonial forces; and the heavily wooded country and the guerrilla nature of the frontier fighting made it relatively ineffective. In the larger engagements of the Seven Years' War, the guns were usually provided by the Royal Artillery of the British Regular Army.

The Storming of Redoubt 10, Yorktown. The Continental attackers used cold steel and clubbed muskets in their assault; their firearms were left unloaded lest a premature shot alert the British. The resulting battle was a brutal, close-quarters, hand-to-hand action. (Graham Turner © Osprey Publishing)

One of the few non-regular artillery units in the Thirteen Colonies was the famous Ancient and Honorable Artillery Company of Massachusetts. Its beginnings lay 150 years in the past, when the early planters had been compelled to devise their own defense from Native American attacks. Some of the early settlers, members of the Honorable Artillery Company of London, formed a new military association on the same lines in Boston. Throughout the years leading local figures served in and supported it, providing funds for the purchase of arms, an armory, and the construction of "gun-firing" platforms. Moreover, for many years the Company emulated its London parent by providing most of the officers of the New England militia regiments.

In September 1774, during the period leading up to the outbreak of hostilities, the gathering now known as the First Continental Congress was held in Philadelphia. It included such men as John Hancock, Samuel Adams, and Paul Revere, who with other Massachusetts Patriots began to plan and organize the collection of military stores, including a few guns, at the town of Concord. This was the first attempt by the revolutionary colonists to organize artillery, and British efforts to seize these guns frustrated it then, but also led to the outbreak of war.

What body of knowledge the colonists had, had been acquired in the British Army, and at the outset they were equipped mainly with British guns. Later they acquired French guns with French volunteers to serve them, and so some of the latter's methods of operating came into American usage. Among the guns used by the British in the campaign, some of which came into American hands, were: light 12-pdrs; light 6-pdrs; 5in howitzers; light 24-pdrs; light 3-pdrs; mortars; medium and heavy 12-pdrs; medium and heavy 18-pdrs; heavy 32-pdrs.

Generally speaking, the main difference between "light" and "medium" (or "heavy") guns of the same caliber was the type of carriage. The light type was mounted on two large wheels, which gave it greater mobility in the field; the latter was on a heavier carriage which had four small wheels, giving limited mobility in a fort. (These were the same type of mountings as used on board ship in that period.)

The howitzer—the high-trajectory weapon—was, in effect, the field version of the mortar of the period. Like the light gun, the howitzer had large wheels, but the mortar was usually mounted on a solid wooden bed without wheels. The normal projectile for the flat-trajectory guns was solid roundshot for long range, sometimes heated red-hot for firing at ships or wooden fortifications. When the range closed to 350yds (320m), grape or canister shot would be used if available. Exploding bombs were fired from the howitzers and mortars.

The generally bad roads and rough open ground made the movement of a train of artillery a slow and laborious business. Up to 12 horses would be required to draw a light 12-pdr gun, attached to a wagon (to which the trail of the gun was lashed) or to the evolving "travelling wheels" which finally emerged under French development into what we now call the limber. The perpetual shortage of horses caused the Americans to resort to the British practice of hiring (or impressing) civilian drivers and their animals, who were understandably reluctant to get too near the scene of action. This usually meant that the last part of the approach to action was done by manhandling the guns forward, the crew members hauling their piece with drag-ropes attached to hooks on the axle outside, and a handspike for maneuvering the trail.

If the position was a prepared one, the guns would be sited in redoubts, the size and strength of which depended on the time and labor force available. The American artillery used to call upon black slave labor to dig their redoubts for them. These earthworks would be chosen to protect an inlet from the sea, or the approach to a ford or bridge, or the heights above a town. If the action was what could be described as eyeball-to-eyeball between field forces, the cannon were usually positioned in pairs between regiments in the line. Sometimes, if the ground dictated it, they might be placed in advance of the line.

The firing sequence was lengthy. A bag of powder was rammed down the barrel, followed by a ball or bag of "grape" or a shot. A brass pick was then thrust down the vent to break the powder bag, and this vent hole was then primed from the measured powder-horn. When the order to fire was given, the "slow match" on the pole linstock was put to the vent and the powder ignited. The resultant combustion propelled the shot out of the cannon's mouth in the general direction of the enemy. Although there was a quadrant to check on elevation, and the artillery soldier could adjust the line of fire by moving the trail, the aim can only be described as random. After firing, members of the gun crew had to run to the front of the gun, insert a metal worm, on a pole, to scrape away any embers; and then insert a wet sponge, also on a pole, down the barrel to mop up any sparks or small pieces of smoldering material.

The uniform devised for the artillery did not come into general use much before 1779. It included the tricorne hat and the normal single-breasted coat of blue, faced and lined with scarlet. The coat edging and button-holes were bound with tape or lace according to rank. White overalls were prescribed with buttons down the sides, and black shoes. The general appearance was much the same as that of the Royal Regiment of Artillery in the British service.

Among the actions in which American artillery played a prominent part was the action at Fort Sullivan near Charleston in June 1776. Here, thanks to Moultrie's fortifications, the 100 or so guns defending the entrance not only withstood the fire of some 300 ships' guns, but returned it with deadly effect. The gun duel lasted ten hours and most of the British ships were severely damaged. The flagship

The battle of Assunpink Creek was fought around Trenton January 2, 1777. Repeated British assaults on American defensive positions were defeated in turn. (Graham Turner © Osprey Publishing)

suffered most, one American writer recording that "the admiral experienced the climactic indignity of having his breeches blown off" (Peckham, p. 34.) Though this was probably an invention, it argues a certain amount of imagination.

When Manhattan Island had to be abandoned, the batteries erected to guard the Hudson River were skillfully evacuated in boats manned by the Massachusetts Regiment of fishermen. Those installed at Fort Lee were lost, however, when the inexperienced Lee escaped with his men. A little later, three of the guns from Manhattan Island were used to repel British troops landing at New Rochelle.

In October the aggressive Benedict Arnold launched a home-made armada of river craft on Lake Champlain. They carried cannon on their rough unpainted decks, and slugged it out with General Carleton's flotilla, which included three warships brought overland in sections. At the end of the second day's battle the Americans had to abandon their "greenwood navy," which they either set on fire or scuttled, but Carleton called off his proposed junction with Howe at New York and returned to Canada.

In the attack on Trenton, Knox was in charge of the shipping of cannon across the blizzard-torn Delaware River, and then of dragging them along the rutted roads covered in frost and snow. In the dawn Knox's guns raked the streets and prevented the Hessians (who had been celebrating Christmas) from forming up to defend the town. Losses and wear of guns and carriages were more than made good by the booty acquired when Burgoyne surrendered at Saratoga in October 1777.

In the South, especially in 1779, there was not much scope for use of artillery. The Loyalists' strength in the area turned the fighting into a series of small local actions and raids between rival bands of rebels and "Tories." Likewise, the frontier fighting of that year saw little opportunity for the use of guns except in occasional attacks on British-held posts.

In August Paul Revere was in charge of the artillery shipped out on the Massachusetts State fleet for the attack on the British-held town of Castine in Penobscot Bay. The expedition was ignominiously routed by a superior British fleet that suddenly appeared from New York, though the militia and guns had already been landed. Paul Revere was among those court-martialed by the Americans for the defeat.

The British revenge for Saratoga came at Charleston in 1780. After the British failure of four years earlier, the forts on Sullivan's and James's Islands had been allowed to crumble. In April, the British ran a squadron of ships past them into the bay and their land forces began bombarding the city from batteries set up across the river and on the Charleston peninsula. The investing troops included a curious unit called the "Volunteers of Ireland," a corps made up of Irish deserters from American units, commanded by an English peer, Lord Rawdon, known (most unjustly) as "the ugliest man in England." The city was called on to surrender to a total of 10,000 British. While the American general, Lincoln, temporized, British horsemen rode around to the north and cut off the one escape route. Deciding to fight on, Charleston held out for a month during which the American defending artillery more than held its own under the British

The Crossing, *December 1776 by Lloyd Garrison. This painting provides a more realistic representation of the conditions under which Gen. Washington crossed the Delaware on December 25, 1776. (X3A Collection/ Alamy Stock Photo)*

JAMES LAFAYETTE: AN UNLIKELY HERO

It is fascinating to think that an enslaved man could have influenced the outcome of the American Revolution but that's exactly what James Armistead did during the siege of Yorktown in 1781. Owned by William Armistead, Jr. of New Kent County, James learned how to read and write, and eventually met the Marquis de Lafayette, likely while assisting Armistead on business in Williamsburg or Richmond. "Impelled by a most earnest desire of gaining liberty which is so dear to all mankind," and with his owner's permission, James became a spy for the Marquis.

Under the direction of Lafayette in the summer of 1781 James, about 32 years old, infiltrated the British camp, possibly in disguise as a forager bringing food to Cornwallis' headquarters—with Lafayette

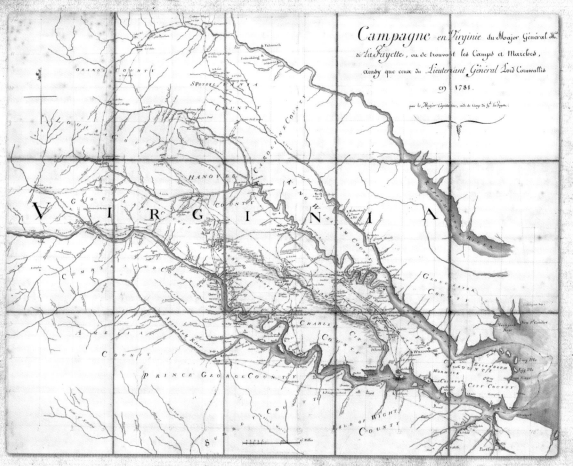

A close up of "Campagne en Virginie du Major Général M'is de LaFayette: ou se trouvent les camps et marches, ainsy que ceux du Lieutenant Général Lord Cornwallis en 1781," this map shows the British and American troop movements in New Kent County.(Library of Congress).

and the Continentals nearby but just out of reach. Almost certainly concealing his literacy, James gradually became a familiar face in the British camp and gained access to areas that otherwise would have been off-limits. As later recorded, James, "at the risk of his life, entered into the enemy's camp, and collected such intelligence as he supposed of importance, and which he conveyed in the utmost expeditious manner to the Marquis de la Fayette."

Lafayette wrote to General George Washington that Cornwallis guarded his documents so zealously that Lafayette's "honest friend," possibly James, was unable to access them. However, because of James' actions, Lafayette conveyed important information to Washington, such as troop movements and the number of British naval vessels in Hampton Roads. One month later, Lafayette wrote that the British were fortifying Yorktown and that "should a French fleet Now Come in Hampton Road(s), the British army would, I think, Be ours."

After the victory at Yorktown, James returned to his master. In 1783, Virginia's General Assembly granted freedom to slaves who served in the military

The Marquis de Lafayette directing American troops during the battle of Yorktown. James can also be seen here holding Lafayette's horse. (Anne S.K. Brown Collection. Brown University)

but James, as a spy, was ineligible. Hearing this, Lafayette wrote an affidavit in 1784, asserting that James' "intelligences from the enemy's camp were industriously collected and faithfully delivered [...] and (James) appears to me entitled to every reward his situation can admit of." With this, James petitioned for his freedom. He stated that he repeatedly risked his life on behalf of the Marquis de Lafayette by conveying messages "of the most secret & important kind" through enemy lines.

Finally in 1786, the General Assembly granted James his freedom. James adopted the surname "Lafayette" in honor of the Marquis. Surviving documents show that he returned to New Kent County and paid taxes on himself and several enslaved household members, including "Silvia," who was probably his wife, and by 1816 James owned 40 acres of land. Two years later, 70-year-old James Lafayette successfully petitioned the General Assembly for a state military pension. When the Marquis de Lafayette returned to Virginia in 1824, James met his old friend once more. The *Richmond Enquirer* reported that during a parade, James "was recognized by (Lafayette) in the crowd, called to him by name, and taken into his embrace." James collected his final pension payment in March 1830, only five months before his death in Baltimore, Maryland.

bombardment. But on May 12 Lincoln capitulated, and in their biggest victory of the war the British took over 300 cannon.

Sixteen months later came the astonishing reversal of fortune at Yorktown which Cornwallis had occupied after failing to overtake Lafayette. About to attack New York, Washington suddenly decided that he was better placed to deal with Cornwallis. The Franco-American force of more than 15,000 included a large train of artillery brought down overland from the Hudson, and a number of guns landed from their fleet. Washington personally supervised the building of redoubts, and the bombardment of Yorktown began in the classic style of an 18th-century siege. After five days the British outworks were assaulted and taken. Some of the American guns were temporarily spiked in a British sortie on the 16th, but in a few hours they were recovered and in action again in the 100-gun bombardment which pounded the British force into surrender. Although they did not know it then, this was to be the last big action of the war in which the American artillery was to play a major part.

ENGINEERS

A lack of engineers was among the first things noted by George Washington when in July 1775 he became commander-in-chief and visited the main force at Cambridge. Among the natural engineers to emerge was William Moultrie, whose construction of fortifications on Sullivan's Island was to make all the difference, accounting for the British failure to take Charleston in I 776. These fortifications were made of earth faced with palmetto—a spongy wood which just absorbed cannonballs.

Among the first of the foreign volunteers to come to America's assistance was a young Polish engineer, Colonel Tadeusz Kościuszko. In 1777 he was responsible for strengthening, with a lot of stone, the defenses of Fort Ticonderoga, as well as making earthen outworks around it and on nearby Mount Independence. This able foreigner served in the Saratoga campaign and throughout the rest of the war. His name is remembered in towns and counties across the country.

When the French entered the war, they provided a group of their engineers, then among the most scientific in the military world, grounded in the traditions of Vauban. They were led by Colonel Louis Duportail, who so impressed Washington that he recommended him for early promotion to major-general. These talented men did much for the American Army thanks to their expert knowledge in defense works, sapping, and mining.

Defenses such as breastworks were constructed to a recognized pattern. Brushwood was first cut by the troops with billhooks or tomahawks and then made up into fascines—bundles bound together varying in lengths up to 10ft (3m).

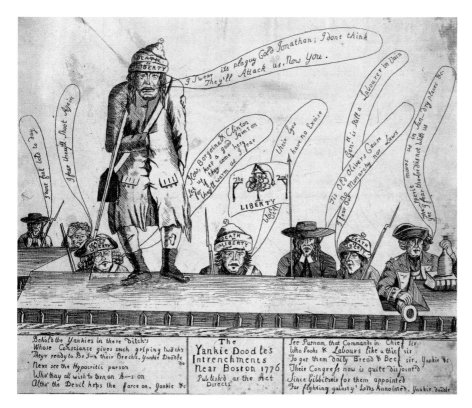

The figure shows a caricature with speech bubbles and the following captions at the bottom:

Behold the Yankies in there Ditch's
Whose Conscience gives such griping twitch's
Theyr ready to Be s—t their Breech's. Yankie Doodle
Next see the Hypocritic parson
Who they all wish to turn on A—s on
Altho' the Devil keps the farce on. Yankie &c

The Yankie Doodles Intrenchments near Boston 1776
Publish'd as the Act Directs

See Putnam that Commands in Chief Sir
Who looks & Labours like a thief sir
To get them daily Bread & Beef sir. Yankie &c
Their Congrefs now is quite disjointed
Since Gibbitsets for them appointed
For fighting gainst ye Lords Annointed. Yankie Doodle

Speech bubbles include: "I don't feel bold to day", "If our throats shoot Again", "I Swear They'll Attack us. Now You.", "I Swear its plaguy cold Jonathan; I don't think", "Now, Borgoine & Clinton Jamison Let uf for if they come here I fear for if they'll warm us", "Their Gen: have no Excise", "Their Gen: is Butt a Laborer in Vain", "'Tis Old Oliver's Caure I fear Our Monarchy nor Laws", "Their Spirit moves us in Ion-dry places &c yet I fear the Lord ain't with us"

The flag reads: The LIBERTY

British caricature of American soldiers at Boston—not an accurate depiction. (Topfoto.co.uk)

Another preliminary move was the making of gabions, cylinders of woven brush up to 3ft (0.9m) in diameter, in which the newly cut brushwood was interwoven to form a circular basket.

Entrenchments were begun by spitlocking, i.e. digging a trace of the outline, or by staking it out on the ground. As a rule these works were angular, although more sophisticated designs were introduced by the French. The first lines of gabion baskets were placed along the outlines and more rows added according to the width of the defenses. The trench would then be dug behind and the soil thrown into the gabions. When these were filled and covered over with earth, the fascines were laid on the sloping sides and secured by long stakes driven through them into the earth-packed gabions. When time permitted these breastworks would be covered with sods.

In winter quarters areas such as Valley Forge, a great deal of hut construction was carried out under engineer supervision. The log house "city" at Morristown had more than 1,000 buildings, whilst Valley Forge had 900 for which Washington himself supervised the plans and layout. Field trench latrines were also dug, usually in sites downwind and 100yds (91m) from the nearest tent or hut. When it became necessary to change them they would be covered in by the soil of their successor dug close by.

The battle of King's Mountain (1780) was fought on these steep, tree-clad slopes. The "over-the-mountain men" climbed the hill, and despite repeated bayonet charges by the loyalist defenders, they managed to gain the summit and overrun the defenders' position. (Angus Konstam)

NEW WORLD ARMY

By the standards of today, or indeed by those of the more sophisticated European powers of 1775, the army of George Washington was administered in a fashion so haphazard as to be almost reckless. The French and Prussian generals of the period would have been shocked indeed to find themselves at the head of such poorly-found troops. But we must remember that very few of the Continentals had ever been soldiers before the Revolution. They were far from being dismayed at the lack of administrative conveniences whose existence they had never suspected. The best of them were frontiersmen, rugged, hardy individuals, used to living rough and traveling light. Men such as these did not expect to be issued with tents and camp kettles. They were well able to live off the forests in which they lurked. Even the less self-sufficient of Washington's troops belonged to a pioneering generation in a new country. Only the Bostonians and New Yorkers lived in cities which could be compared with those of the comfort-loving Old World. In any case an army can be over-administered, as was Burgoyne's in the Saratoga campaign. One could make out a case for attributing the American victory not to their good organization, but in some ways to their truly horrible administration. With no quartermaster's delights to look for, they just got on with their fighting, while the British commanders often lumbered around with a great train of logistics, came to a foundering halt, and could not pluck up the energy to attempt a retreat.

Washington did not like pitched battles against the Redcoats and their German allies. And no wonder. These regulars, drilled to the standards of Malplaquet,

Washington at Valley Forge, December 1777. (Photo12/ UIG via Getty Images)

The battle of King's Mountain, October 7, 1780. Militiamen of Colonel Thomas Brandon's 2nd Spartan Regiment fight their way into the main loyalist camp near the close of the brief battle. (Steve Noon © Osprey Publishing)

Dettingen, and Minden, were formidable when it came to a firefight on a piece of terrain that resembled a European parade ground. It is no reflection upon the newly-formed Continentals to say that in the conditions prevailing at Long Island, Brandywine, or Camden, it is impressive that they held out for as long as they did. Even when things were not going so well at Bunker Hill, Monmouth, or Cowpens, the British at unit level fought always with tenacity, often with real dash—though not always with intelligence. Here one of Lafayette's ADCs, Major le Chevalier de Pontgibaud, gives us a glimpse of them at the battle of Monmouth: "The English had a deep ravine to cross before they could reach us: their brave infantry did not hesitate an instant, but charged us with the bayonet, and was crushed by our artillery. The fine regiment of the guards lost half its men, and its colonel was fatally wounded" (Moré, pp. 55–56.) An army such as we have described is essentially a tactical machine. It was not at the tactical level that the British lost the American war.

In the field of grand strategy, it must be remembered that after 1778, when the French entered the conflict, Great Britain was not merely fighting to put down a colonial rebellion, but was engaged in one more of her long series of wars with France. When Spain and Holland were added to the hostile array, she was practically engaged in a world war.

At the level of campaign strategy, it is no use trying to conceal the shortcomings of the British commanders behind the alleged incompetence of the much-maligned Lord George Germain. This is not the place to discuss the merits of Burgoyne, Cornwallis, Clinton, and Howe. Suffice it to say that, with the exception of the second, they were a mediocre lot. As strategists the realistic and practical George Washington had them outclassed. And though some of his generals, notably Greene, showed talent, he really had no rival who was a credible alternative as commander-in-chief. Indeed, the best American officers were the guerrillas, Marion "the Swamp Fox," Ethan Allen, and the rest. Which leads one to wonder whether dear old Baron Steuben was not really rather counter-productive. By instilling the rudiments of a Frederician style of discipline he was trying to meet the British on their own ground—the drill-ground.

The finest hours of the American revolutionary army were at King's Mountain, Freeman's Farm, and Bemis Heights. But these were not victories of the Continental line so much as of the frontiersman in his deerskin "battle-dress" and the homespun New England farmer, fighting for hearth and home. As General Sir Frederick Haldimand said in 1782, when explaining the impossibility of invading New England from Canada: "It is not the number of troops Mr Washington can spare from his army that is to be apprehended, it is the multitude of militia and men in arms ready to turn out at an hour's notice at the shew of a single regiment of Continental Troops that will oppose this attempt."

CHAPTER 6

THE BRITISH AND LOYALIST FORCES

*O*N THE EVE OF WAR IN 1775, the British Army stood at nearly 49,000 officers and men, distributed throughout the garrisons of North America, Ireland, Great Britain, Minorca, Gibraltar, Africa, and the West Indies. Eight thousand of these were stationed in North America. The numbers of the overall British establishment did not increase significantly between 1775 and 1778, when only one line regiment was raised. Only the entry of the French into the war in 1778 prompted the British government to raise more regiments nearly 30 from 1778 to 1783. This increased establishment totals to 110,000 officers and men, plus additional numbers of militia and volunteers raised to defend Great Britain.

The British Army had been successful in the Seven Years' War, but the American Revolution presented a different set of challenges. The British faced the prospect of fighting a war in hostile territory thousands of miles from their home base. Strategic planning that focused on how to end the uprising seemed to be lacking, especially during the early years of the war. British generals were unable to capitalize on tactical advantages gained after the battles of Bunker Hill and Long Island, which could potentially have crippled the military capabilities of the Americans early in the war. Infighting among British commanders on land and sea created more problems, compounded by the arrogance of a number of British officers and

OPPOSITE

The British retreat from Concord at the outset of the American Revolution. (North Wind Picture Archives/ Alamy Stock Photo)

Light Infantryman, 63rd
Regiment of Foot, 1777.
Starting as early as 1776,
this uniform was typical
of lights during the summer
campaigning season and in
years where the supply of
clothing was interrupted.
(Gerry Embleton © Osprey
Publishing)

government officials who considered the American forces a rabble, easily dealt with by a small force. Even if they had been capable of defeating the Americans militarily, it is questionable whether the British would have grasped how to deal with the political implications of the conflict. It is likely that they would have found themselves in the position of a garrison force attempting to contain an obstreperous political element—an unsavory prospect for any army.

The British Army consistently lacked sufficient troops to contain the insurrection, a situation made considerably worse from 1778 by the entry of first France and later Spain into the hostilities, forcing the British to disperse their forces throughout the world. The percentage of the British Army stationed in North America dropped from 65 percent in 1778 to only 29 percent in 1780.

Despite these obstacles, the British Army itself was a formidable machine of war, a fact that was especially apparent during the conflict's early years. Its discipline and firepower generally outstripped those of the American forces, and its junior officers were reliably capable under fire. These strengths were undermined, however, by the considerable problems of supply. Troops could not expect to receive adequate supplies from the local populations, which dictated dependence upon a 3,000-mile (4,800km) supply line vulnerable to the effects of weather, privateering, and, eventually, the attentions of the French and Spanish navies. Supply shortages meant that the British Army and its German allies engaged in frequent plunder and theft in the countryside surrounding marches or positions, behavior that galvanized support for the independence cause from previously neutral colonists. A French officer who was present in North America as an observer noted the following causes for British defeats up to 1777: "the present military success of the Americans can be ascribed to certain handicaps the English generals have faced: their unfamiliarity with the area of hostilities; their difficulties in obtaining reinforcements and supplies once the armies have advanced inland" (Recicourt, p. 206.)

The British raised a series of Loyalist Provincial Corps over the course of the war, and also fought alongside Native American allies (see the discussions below.) Further afield, the British East India Company continued to expand and train its native forces (sepoys) in the use of traditional linear tactics following the end of the Seven Years' War. By 1775, there were about 100,000 troops in the three presidency armies of Bombay, Bengal, and Madras. Between 1778 and 1782, two Hanoverian and eight British regiments were sent to India to reinforce the East India Company forces.

The fighting qualities of the sepoys were considered to be superior. A lieutenant of the 71st Regiment of Foot noted, upon his arrival in Madras in 1780, "the Company's officers have acquired much praise by their steady adherence to the duties of their profession, which the excellent order of the sepoys clearly confirms and which strikes every stranger with surprise ... the frequent opportunities of seeing service gives them [Company troops] [a] great fund of professional knowledge" (Munro, *Narrative*, pp.26–28.) The British and Company forces, however, lacked sufficient numbers of cavalry to contend with Hyder Ali's armies for most of this period.

Historical re-enactors as British soldiers 1776. (Neil Holmes/Getty Images)

The shortfall in British regular forces also compelled the British to seek a loan of troops from Russia. The Russians refused to loan troops for service in North America, and Britain was forced to look elsewhere. Having used troops from the German princely states before, she made use of this resource again, and troops from Hanover were sent to Minorca and Gibraltar to release British troops for North American service. (Troops from Hanover were not considered mercenaries, since one of George III's titles was Elector of Hanover.) By early 1776, the British had

The title of this Hessian unit during the Revolution was the Infanterie Regiment von Donop; in 1784, when the watercolor was painted, it had been redesignated Regiment von Knyphausen. In the Prussian tradition, the Hessians were known for their steadiness under fire. (Private Collection/Photo © Don Troiani/Bridgeman Images)

negotiated treaties with Brunswick, Hesse-Cassel, Hesse-Hanau, Anspach, Waldeck, and Anhalt for troops for the war in America. Since the largest contingent came from Hesse-Cassel, all German auxiliaries were commonly referred to as Hessians.

Over the course of the war, 29,166 German auxiliaries served in North America. Most of the German troops were organized in traditional Continental

Recruiting for the 80th Foot, 1780. This scene, based upon a rather convincing looking sketch by Bunbury, must have been a familiar one throughout the British Isles in the 18th century. (Richard Hook © Osprey Publishing)

style. The grenadier companies were often formed into independent units, and there was also a *Jäger* corps, which was in great demand after the battle of Long Island. The *Jäger* corps averaged 700 men throughout the war.

The German auxiliaries caused considerable problems for the British, principally with discipline and public relations. The German troops became known for pillaging and destroying farms and houses in 1776. While all factions were guilty of this, the Americans used the German abuses as propaganda, and the French officer Baron Ludwig von Closen noted "the ravages of the Hessians who made themselves hated by their lack of discipline and inconsideration for the peaceful inhabitants during the winter quarters in New Jersey" (Closen, p. 115.)

The fighting qualities of the German contingents, like those of the Provincial Corps, ranged from excellent to poor. A French officer commented that "the English, Hessian, and Anspach troops, [were] the elite of those who had been in Carolina" (Rice and Brown, p. 151.) The Hessian troops were considered the equal of the Prussian Army, and the *Jäger* corps was held in high esteem by the American and French forces arrayed against it. The Brunswick contingent, on the other hand, which served in Burgoyne's campaign of 1777, was not so highly regarded; although well disciplined, their fighting abilities were considered mediocre. Troops from Hesse-Hanau were criticized by Lieutenant-General Frederick Haldimand, the British commander in Canada in 1778, as being unfit for the American war.

The fact that German troops were used as part of the British Army in North America caused great consternation amongst the American colonial population and like-minded individuals in Great Britain. Their presence has historically been given as a reason why the American people dislike and distrust mercenaries. This is a simplistic and somewhat hypocritical argument, especially considering that the American commanders apparently had no qualms about accepting the services of various soldiers of fortune from Europe.

THE REDCOATS

When the Seven Years' War ended in 1763, Great Britain proceeded to decimate the army which had done so much to win her an empire. All infantry of the line were disbanded above the 70th Foot, and all cavalry above the 18th Light Dragoons. The establishment was therefore a miserable 17,500, 3,000 of whom were the emergency force so aptly known as the "Corps of Invalids." There were also 1,800 gunners and sappers, and 12,000 men on the Irish establishment.

A grenadier of the Hessen-Kassel Leib-Regiment; this regiment's grenadiers served with Grenadier-Bataillon Linsing at Brandywine, and later participated in the siege of Charleston. Anne S.K.Brown Collection, Brown University)

The colonies were allowed 10,000 men, excluding 4,000 for Minorca and Gibraltar, and, though the East India Company had its own forces, this meant that the rest of the empire was pitifully under-policed. Hatred of standing armies at home and abroad could hardly be taken further.

The brutal and ruthless "green dragoons" of Tarleton's loyalist British legion were recruited from the northern colonies. they were the militia's most feared foes. Note the fur flaps on the pistol holsters to protect against rain or snow. (Don Troiani (b.1949)/Private Collection/Bridgeman Images)

The events leading up to the American Revolution are not the concern of this chapter, but several points must be stressed where the Redcoats were concerned. Firstly, though many Britons were not convinced that Canada was worth possessing, none doubted the importance of the American colonies and the sugar-rich West Indies. The government's methods in this period were blundering in the extreme. True, Britain had spent a fortune to win Canada from the French and to make the 13 American colonies safe, so therefore felt obliged to extract money from Americans to help pay the cost of keeping troops in America, and also to ease the national debt. But to use sledge-hammer tactics instead of tact to get the money from the independent-minded Americans was fatuous. Yet only the most far-sighted could foresee an actual war breaking out between the mother country and her own people in America so soon after the bells had been ringing for the destruction of New France.

But the government, even if it could not foresee a revolution, should have realized the folly of cutting down the army because of what happened the very year the war ended. Pontiac's dramatic rebellion, the last real chance the Indians ever had of driving the whites back to the Atlantic, should have made ministers at once aware of the folly of cuts as the better of two white evils, not least because Pontiac was pro-French. After sensational successes elsewhere, his main campaign against Detroit just failed, and perhaps because of this, the British did not grasp the lessons of his rebellion.

So when the Revolution started in 1775, the British Army was only 48,647 strong, with 39,294 infantry, 6,869 cavalry and 2,484 artillery. Six years after this, as already noted, when the military war was over in America except for skirmishes and the formalities, the army had reached the 110,000 mark, 57,000 of them stationed in America and the West Indies. This does not include the 70 or so Loyalist regiments and formations, the 30,000 German mercenaries and the fluctuating number of Indians who fought on the British side.

Recruiting had never been more difficult than for this war. Apart from the unpopularity of the conflict, the 1770s were the last years before the Industrial Revolution introduced a large number of the working classes to a fate worse than taking the King's Shilling: the nightmare world of prison-like factories. They were the last years when Britain was more an agricultural than an industrial nation, when even the poorest countrymen could expect to eat well, and when enclosures had not yet wrecked the rural way of life.

So the temptation to join up was minimal: poor pay, savage discipline, and bad food, combined with the prospect of fighting fellow Britons, was enough to put off all but born fighters and adventurers.

The pay of a private soldier was eight pence a day, but most of it was promptly taken away from him. Sixpence allegedly went for subsistence, though some of the precious pennies were put aside to pay for clothing, medicine, and the repair of arms. Much of the remaining two pence was deducted to pay the Paymaster-General, the Chelsea Hospital (a place a recruit was so unlikely to reach), the regimental agent, etc. The system of pay and stoppages was unbelievably complicated, but the result was the same: the soldier got next to nothing.

Barracks were few in Britain in the 1770s, so the recruit was likely to be under canvas, or, more probably, in lodgings where his presence was greatly resented.

British camp in southern England. (Anne S.K. Brown Collection, Brown University Library)

Discipline was 18th-century traditional, the only difference from earlier times being that the lash was the universal penalty for most crimes. Other tortures like the "horse" and "running the gauntlet" were not being phased out for humanitarian reasons, but simply because flogging was simpler: 1,000 or more lashes was still a frequent sentence.

Food was generally appalling and continued to be so when the soldier reached America. Legend has it that the Redcoats lived comfortably off the land; legend is wrong. Recruits in Britain were often so underfed in their dingy billets that they were scarcely able to endure the drill that turned them into remarkably good soldiers.

Most of the major battles of the Revolution were fought on European patterns, so the uniform red coats of the men were not in themselves a menace to safety, even though the Americans from the start picked off the officers. As the war progressed dress regulations were relaxed, making it easier for the soldier to fight. The stock was not yet a tortuous high leather collar, but was more often made of velvet or horsehair, and gaiters had been black since 1768. But it still took the average soldier up to three hours to get himself ready for a parade, where a slight movement or a badly arranged head of hair (covered in unhygienic grease and powder according to regulations) could get him 100 lashes or more.

The Royal Artillery at Freeman's Farm, September 19, 1777. (Adam Hook © Osprey Publishing)

As for equipment, it might weigh as much as 60lb (27kg), though some have claimed probably wrongly that it sometimes weighed almost twice as much. Burgoyne considered 60lb too much, and the following revealing report about equipment, dated June 15, 1784, soon after the war was over, shows that notice was taken of complaints if senior officers made them. It is a *Report of the Proceedings of a Committee of General Officers Regarding the Equipment of Soldiers*, and the listed recommendations received approval:

1 Ordnance Cartridge Box at present in use found to be inconvenient.
2 Powder-Horns and Bullet-Bags of Light Infantry were never used during the late war.
3 Matches & Match-Cases of Grenadiers are becoming obsolete.
4 Grenadiers' swords were never used during the last war.
[It was proposed that all these articles be abandoned.]
5 The whole battalion to be accoutred alike, with the addition of two articles for the Light Infantry, e.g., Hatchet & Priming Horn, which may be carried either with the knapsack or as the Commanding Officer shall think most convenient.
6 Shoulder-belts to be of equal breadth, and to have the Ammunition divided; to carry the Pouch on the right side, and the Magazine on the left.
7 Pouch & Bayonet-Belts to be of Buff Leather & both to be 2 inches broad, the Bayonet-Carriage [frog] to slip on & off the belt with two loops.
8 A Leather cap worn by some of the Light Infantry during the late war is strongly recommended.
9 Propose a black woollen cloth gaiter with white metal buttons & without stiff tops in place of the black linen gaiters at present in use.

So something had been learnt from the campaign in America. Back in 1775, it must have seemed to some that there would be no campaigns from which to learn, for recruiting was practically stationary. In December, Edward Harvey, the Adjutant-General, lamented: "Sad work everywhere in recruiting. In these damned times we must exert zeal."

Personnel of the 43rd Foot, easily identified by their white facings, are depicted in camp during the 1750s in this modern work by the Canadian artist Lewis Parker. (Courtesy Fort Beauséjour National Historic Park, Parks Canada; photo René Chartrand)

WEAPONS, DRESS AND EQUIPMENT, 1759

This private of the 43rd Foot is armed with a .75-calibre Land Pattern musket with buff leather sling. Like all British regular infantry he wears a red woolen coat, cuffed, lapelled, and lined in the regimental facing color, although the distinctive lace edgings have been stripped off. Under it he has a red woolen waistcoat and red woolen knee breeches. His gaiters are of black linen, but the tops above the strap are stiffened with leather for additional protection when kneeling down, and on his feet is a stout pair of black leather shoes. Topping off the ensemble is a black wool felt hat, trimmed with white lace, which was supposed to be folded and blocked into a tricorne shape but was often slouched on service. His equipment comprises a black leather cartridge box containing 24 rounds of ammunition in the form of paper cartridges containing 70 grains of powder and a lead ball, as well as spare flints and tools for his musket. On his back is a cowhide knapsack normally containing spare clothing and any other possessions, but most of its contents have been left on the ship, tied up in his blanket which would normally be rolled under the top flap. On his left side is a linen haversack for rations together with a 2-pint tin canteen for water. His buff leather waist-belt has been slung over his shoulder for comfort, and like his French counterpart he has discarded his sword and uses the belt to carry only his bayonet. (Peter Dennis © Osprey Publishing)

RAISING THE REDCOATS

Harvey was right, for apart from the many reasons for not joining the army, there were other disadvantages. Service was normally for life and postings abroad could go on for decades. Notoriously, the 38th Foot was trapped in the West Indies for 60 years. And the deep unpopularity of soldiers was as rampant as at any time in the century. At least the sailor, pressed, flogged, and wretched, could—and often did, even at this dismal time in naval history—comfort himself with the thought that he was the nation's pride.

Volunteers joined up for three years or the duration, but, except for in Scotland, there were pitifully few of them in 1776. Some recruiting parties in their despair levied invalids and pensioners, and even Roman Catholics, unwelcome before 1775, were recruited.

Less successful was an attempt to enlist 20,000 Russian mercenaries, or to entice a Scotch brigade back from service with the Dutch. This led, as we have seen, to the hiring of Germans from Hesse-Cassel and elsewhere. The Highlands, however, proved good ground for recruiting parties, many clansmen coming forward to get away from grim conditions at home, or to seek glory, or both. Lowlanders also came forward, some even refusing bounty, and in certain towns, the families of those who went were supported by those who stayed behind. The English, Irish, and Welsh showed no such ardor.

Until 1778, volunteers received one-and-a-half guineas, but as there were far too few of them, pardoned criminals and deserters were welcomed. The required height was 5ft 6in (1.67m), though youngsters who looked as if they might grow were enlisted, whereas the lame, the ruptured, and those prone to fits were not.

After 1778, when Saratoga brought the French into the war, recruiting became more urgent. Volunteers got three pounds and, as in 1775, a discharge in three years or at the end of the war; and in Scotland and the London area, the "able-bodied idle and disorderly" were pressed for at least five years or until the end of hostilities. The age limits were 17 to 45. The "idle" persons elsewhere in Britain were left to work the land.

This scheme, too, failed, so in 1779 volunteers got three-and-a-half guineas and the right to set up in business after service wherever they chose, whatever local corporations might say. The wounded were to get similar privileges. The pressed men, meanwhile, could now be as short as 5ft 4in (1.62m) and as old as 50. New sorts of rogues could be taken, and the whole country could be scoured for them. The only escape was to join the militia, a fair ploy as Britain seemed to be in danger of invasion.

Despite desertions, self-maimings, and fights with the press-gangs, just enough men were found—1,463 in southern Britain between March and October 1779—

British Army, 33rd Regiment of Foot, Grenadier Company 1776 (Troiani, Don (b.1949)/ Private Collection/Bridgeman Images)

but what saved the army was the fact that many now came forward to volunteer to avoid being pressed and to benefit from the very fair terms.

In 1778, 12 new regiments of foot were raised and 17 more had been raised by 1780. Four regiments of light dragoons were raised between 1778 and 1781. Old regiments were enlarged, a system the king preferred as he suspected (rightly in many cases) that colonels of the new regiments would place too many relatives in them. Towns, too, raised regiments—the 80th (Royal Edinburgh Volunteers) was one—and also gave generous bounties. Less happily, the system of drafting was much in evidence, a badly mauled regiment being forced to send its officers, NCOs, and drummers home to recruit while its surviving privates transferred to another regiment also in need of men, but not destitute. This seriously interfered with esprit de corps. Some draftees of the Black Watch mutinied rather than join the 83rd and be forced to abandon their kilts, and 30 were killed in a pitched battle.

The recruit to the infantry found himself in a regiment of some 477 men divided into ten companies forming a single battalion. One company consisted of grenadiers, who no longer hurled grenades, but were the tallest and strongest men in the regiment. Another was made up of light infantrymen, wiry troops who were the regiment's crack shots. These chosen men were placed on the flanks.

Recruits were subjected to endless arms drill, often a rugged ordeal on inadequate rations. The basic infantry weapon was the "Brown Bess" musket, with a carbine for the cavalry, while fusiliers carried a fusil (a light musket). The finest British firearm of the war, the Ferguson breech-loader invented by the dashing Major Patrick Ferguson, was only used by 100 or so picked marksmen in America.

Regimental doctors, as recruits found, varied from good to ghastly. And as for the consolations of religion, it was an irreligious age, and though each regiment officially had a chaplain, few ever appeared. Sergeant Lamb, the diarist and surgeon's mate of the 9th Foot, claimed he knew many pious soldiers, and there was no reason for him to lie.

Despite the origins of many men, and the brutish lives they had endured, the average Redcoat cannot have been so very different from his successors a century or more later. William Cobbett, the great radical politician and writer, thought highly of soldiers. He joined the army in 1784 and became a sergeant-major. He once wrote: "I like soldiers, as a class

172 IMPROBABLE VICTORY

in life, better than any other description of men. Their conversation is more pleasing to me; they have generally seen more than other men; they have less vulgar prejudice about them. Among soldiers, less than amongst any other description of men, have I observed the vices of lying and hypocrisy." Written permission from an officer was needed for Cobbett's admired private soldiers to marry. In barracks at home—though true barracks only date from the 1790s—husbands and wives were entitled to screened-off beds in barrack rooms.

As for the standard of officers, it was perhaps higher than it had been in the Seven Years' War, in which so many of them had previously fought. There was no general in the Revolution quite so ineffective as Abercromby of Fort Ticonderoga (1758), but nor was there a Wolfe. And Sir William Howe, regardless of his feelings about the war, was not the equal of his incomparable elder brother, Lord George Augustus Howe, killed at Ticonderoga just before Abercromby did his worst, which included allowing the Black Watch to be massacred. Ironically, Howe, Burgoyne, and Clinton were all Members of Parliament and it was not considered wrong for a general-politician to return to London in the winter and speak in the House.

One often fortunate factor at this time was that no officer was forced to serve overseas. This not only meant that lunatics and infants were not obliged to take the field, but that the ambitious might rise faster because many officers preferred to stay at home on half-pay rather than serve. To reach the top in the 1770s it was best to be in the Guards or the cavalry, but that was to hold good for many years to come.

The real stumbling block was the number of serving soldiers who simply did not wish to fight Americans. Lord Percy, later Duke of Northumberland, whose conduct on the first day of the Revolution helped save the retreating British Army, was one of many officers who could not stomach the war. After distinguished service in 1776, he returned home.

Fortunately for British arms, there were plenty who could; plenty of career officers who got on with the job along with a hard core of fine NCOs. And under them was that much-abused, sorely tried, usually valiant, and humorous man of war, the Redcoat.

Brass shoulder belt plate, Butler's Rangers, c.1778–1783. (Parks Canada)

THE REDCOAT'S WAR

When the "shot heard round the world" rang out on Lexington Green on April 19, 1775, some Redcoats at least must have sighed with relief. For most of the previous seven or so years, life in Boston for unwelcome British troops had been not unlike their successors' life in Ulster in the late 20th century, though even more unpleasant. The food in the 1770s was worse, billets were worse, restrictions on any sort of action were worse, to say nothing of the harsher discipline and the distance from home.

The flood of troops needed to fight in America, once the scope of the war was realized after Bunker (Breed's) Hill, created a major transport problem. Cork was then the main embarkation port for North America, and ships used as transports varied from fine East Indiamen to old and unseaworthy hulks. Convoys of up to 12 ships, sometimes more, crossed the Atlantic, and there was an endless flow of victualers as well. Officers seem to have made real efforts to keep their men happy on the transports, but it was uphill work. The situation was candidly summed up by a Guards officer on his way to join Howe in New York, who wrote, "There was continued destruction in the foretops, the pox above-board, the plague between decks, hell in the forecastle, the devil at the helm."

The loss of horses could be terrible if a voyage went on longer than expected, and their destruction undoubtedly affected the results of certain battles. Howe could have turned his victory at Brandywine in 1777 into a total rout if he had commanded a well-mounted corps of light cavalry, and as for Clinton, on his expedition from New York to Charleston in 1779–80, he lost every single horse.

Sailors were in short supply to man the transports and victualers, and there was usually a shortage of ships, too, made worse because the authorities in America failed to turn the transports round and send them home quickly enough. Add bribery, corruption, gross inefficiency in many quarters, and inter-departmental quarreling, and it is hardly surprising that the Redcoats were usually short of food and equipment.

The transport situation in America was slightly better than in the French and Indian War when Braddock and other British commanders sometimes despaired of getting hold of wagons. Everything from four-horse wagons to sledges were usually hired during the Revolution. Special vehicles were used as ammunition carts, others as hospital wagons and forge carts "compleat with anvils and bellows." Horses, too, were bought or captured. The drivers of the vehicles were hired civilians. A single statistic will show the scope of the problem: from December 1776 to March 1780, Howe and Clinton continually used an average of 739 wagons, 1,958 horses, and 760 drivers.

Rivers and lakes were a vital form of transport in the war, especially as good roads were in almost as short supply as they had been in Wolfe's day, and fleets of flatboats, bateaux, sloops, and other vessels were in constant use, some from Britain, many more bought, hired or seized locally.

The organization, 3,000 miles (4,800km) from home, needed for such enterprises was so vast that the wonder is that the system worked as well as it did. There was so much incompetence in the administration of the army at home that honest, efficient men often despaired, yet even a good administrative machine would have been hard put to organize the conquest of the Americans in a country of such vast distances, and where so little food could be obtained usually by fair money from the land. The Redcoats often starved and sometimes froze in their ragged uniforms. Washington's valiant men at Valley Forge may have been the champions in the misery stakes, but there were plenty of British challengers.

Starvation could sometimes be warded off by plunder. Howe, Burgoyne, and others demanded high standards of conduct, which naturally could not always be maintained. But it was regarded as vital that thieves, rapists, and marauders should be discouraged. Private Thomas MacMahan of the 43rd got 1,000 lashes for receiving stolen goods in Boston in 1776 and his wife got 100 lashes and three months in prison; and two privates of the 59th were hanged for robbing a store.

There was no stopping crime, of course, especially with so many criminals in the ranks. The German mercenaries naturally had no great interest in the sensibilities of the local population and, though not entirely the monsters of legend, were notorious for their plundering in New York and on Long Island and around Trenton. Howe simply could not stop this, nor could he control some of his newly arrived and more bloodthirsty officers. The Hessians had a reputation as butchers of surrendered troops in 1776, but they were sometimes put up to it by the British. One officer wrote: "We took care to tell the Hessians that the Rebels had resolved to give no quarters to them in particular, which made them fight desperately and put all to death that fell into their hands. You know all stratagems are lawful in war, especially against such vile enemies to their King and country" (Force, Peter, *American Archives*.)

Both sides tried to use Native Americans, but few sided with the land-hungry colonists. The British authorities utilized the services of some 10,000 Indians, chiefly from the Iroquois and Algonquin nations. They were principally employed as scouts and raiders, in recognition of their formidable knowledge of forest warfare. Their deployment sparked controversy in both America and Great Britain, and created further support for the independence movement among neutral colonists. Indians operated along the frontier regions of New York, Pennsylvania, and Virginia.

As allies they varied in usefulness and quality, but they would have said the same about the British as allies. Their use inflamed public opinion in America and in Britain, but they could never have remained neutral. The fabulous, well-educated Joseph Brant, a Mohawk who knew Boswell, George III, and the Prince of Wales, was their finest leader.

Redcoats often fought alongside Native Americans and continually with the 70 or so Loyalist regiments. Being Britons and ordinary humans, they had mixed views on their allies. Some soldiers who detested scalping encouraged by whites as evidence of death were quite prepared to view or administer 1,500 lashes. Even discounting rebel propaganda, there were plenty of instances of rape, for which Redcoats could be court-martialed. The Hessians were less subject to military punishment for the crime.

The most famous quotation on the subject, and one thoroughly grotesque to modern ears, was penned by Lord Francis Rawdon in a letter to his uncle in 1776. It defies comment except to note that for once the Redcoats were being properly fed:

The fair nymphs of this isle [Staten Island] are in wonderful tribulation, as the fresh meat our men have got here has made them riotous as satyrs. A girl cannot step into the bushes to pluck a rose without running the most imminent risk of being ravished, and they are so little accustomed to these vigorous methods they don't bear them with the proper resignation, and of consequence we have the most entertaining court-martials every day (Historic Manuscripts Commission.)

Women followed the flag in disputed numbers. Howe allowed six to every company in 1776 and 1777, while Burgoyne had three per company for his expedition. He always denied that there were 2,000 women on that campaign. Like Howe, he had a mistress to console him and, according to the wife of the Hessian commander, Baroness von Riedesel, in her marvelous account of the ill-fated march that ended at Saratoga, he had the bottle as well towards the end. But few 18th-century commanders were more loved by their men than "Gentleman Johnny," not least, perhaps, because he was no great flogger and was known to mention common soldiers in dispatches.

Women acted as laundry maids and sometimes as nurses on campaign. They and their children were fed from the public stores, and clothed as well. There was at least one near mutiny at Cork when a ship without women did not set out because the Redcoats aboard threatened to desert unless the matter was put right.

Sadly, little is known of the ordinary women who went to America. Ironically, the best-known woman of the Revolution on the British side was the unfortunate Jane McCrae, famous because she was murdered by some of Burgoyne's Indians, who neither knew nor cared that she was a Loyalist, due to marry a Loyalist officer. Her cruel death was turned to maximum advantage by the Americans, with justification; yet the worst incident of the entire Revolutionary period was committed by American frontier militia who, systematically and in cold blood, butchered some 100 Christian Delawares, men, women, and children.

As noted, a worse fate than being butchered awaited many prisoners on both sides. Just as in the Civil War one is confronted by the nobility of Robert E. Lee and the horror of Andersonville prison camp, so in the Revolution the decency of many British leaders is in striking contrast to the terrible prison hulks off New York, where perhaps 7,000 Americans perished in utter squalor and misery. And the Redcoats (and especially the Loyalists) suffered almost as badly. The Americans imprisoned some of the British in the nightmarish Simsbury copper mines. Generally, the Redcoats suffered less because the Americans had fewer prison facilities.

Not that that can excuse the shameful treatment accorded to Burgoyne's surrendered army. His victor's very generous terms were quashed by Congress, but it has since come to light that Howe was eager to use the men again rather than, as the treaty specified, have them sent back to Britain, which puts both sides in the wrong. But Congress did not know of Howe's secret letter to Burgoyne. Burgoyne's men first endured harsh treatment in New England, were then marched south, partly to make the men desert which many Hessians did

This soldier is from the 2nd Company, Hessen-Kassel Feldjäger Korps, in that unit's green uniform faced with dark red. (Troiani, Don (b.1949)/ Private Collection/Bridgeman Images)

and were finally quartered in Virginia. Many, like Sergeant Lamb, escaped, a few Redcoats deserted, and the rest remained loyal until, in 1781, they were separated from their officers and vanished from history. How many of the original 3,000 Redcoats disappeared is uncertain.

Many of the Hessians and some of the Redcoats who did desert, no doubt settled down to a new life in America. The war saw hundreds of deserters, only a small percentage of them Redcoats, but not so many traitors in the conventional sense. Naturally, the Loyalists regarded all rebels as traitors, and vice versa. But in the full sense of the word, of men who betrayed their side as opposed to changing sides in the manner inevitable in a civil war, there were few, the most notable being the rebels' best general, Benedict Arnold.

Hospitals on the American side were much worse than British ones. Not all can have been as bad as Ticonderoga's in 1776, which "beggars description and shocks humanity," as Anthony Wayne wrote. But the general standard must have been in stark contrast to the British ones. Dr. Rush, a signatory of the Declaration of Independence, paid a fulsome tribute in a letter to John Adams about Howe's hospitals and his doctors, even stressing that wounded American prisoners were much better looked after by the British than the wounded in American hospitals.

The British "pay a supreme regard to the cleanliness and health of their men," wrote the doctor after his inspection, and contrasted American hospitals most unfavorably.

Of course, temporary hospitals on campaign must have been akin to butchers' shops, and it must not be supposed that the chances of recovery from serious wounds could ever be high in the 1770s and 1780s; but this tribute is significant, not least because it shows Howe's concern for his men, which made him such a popular commander. Rush even paid a tribute to the British for filling their men with vegetables. Regimental doctors, many of whom were most dedicated, were paid so badly that some bought an extra commission and fought as well as healed.

Disease was a greater killer in the war than battle, though, strangely, British casualties are not known. The American figures are mere guesswork, perhaps 12,000 killed, which may be not so different to the number of British deaths in action. It was not a very sanguine war.

British soldiers shown dispatching the fallen Baron de Kalb at the battle of Camden, 1780. (Granger, NYC/Topfoto.co.uk)

When the war finally ended the Redcoats had the rare and unpleasant experience of sailing away defeated despite many victories, in contrast to the more usual British technique of ultimate victories after disastrous early campaigns. Their record was good, for honors could have included Long Island, White Plains, Fort Washington, Brandywine, Germantown, Savannah, Charleston, Camden, and Guilford. Saratoga and Yorktown, those crucial defeats, were lost because strategy, communications, and liaison were at fault. Though the war was frequently fought on the European pattern, rigid formations often gave way to looser, more open tactics.

PROVINCIAL/LOYALIST FORCES

The American War of Independence was, in some respects, a civil war. From the very first engagements in 1775, there were Americans who supported the actions of the British government in its American colonies, and who were opposed to any unilateral measures by their fellow citizens that would result in independence from the mother country. These Americans became known as the "Loyalists," from their loyalty to Great Britain, its king, and its government.

The British raised a series of Loyalist Provincial Corps over the course of the war. Most of these units were trained and used as regular line infantry, with light infantry and grenadier companies. Some were used as garrison troops in outposts as remote as Charleston, in the south, or Québec and Halifax, in Canada. Selected units were used in a more irregular role, among them Butler's Rangers, who fought alongside Indian tribes in the upstate New York and middle Atlantic regions; the majority fought in traditional Continental style.

Relatively early in the war, the British attempted to establish a centralized system for recruiting, training, and equipping the corps with the establishment of a dedicated Inspector General, Lieutenant-Colonel Alexander Innes, in January 1777. Despite this, the British authorities demonstrated little faith in the capability of the Provincial Corps, and did not actively promote their raising and employment until the defeats of 1777 and the entry of the French into the conflict

The retreat from Concord: This action is widely held to illustrate how ill-equipped the British army was to deal with light troops, but in the circumstances Colonel Smith and his men did remarkably well. (Interim Archives/ Getty Images)

made the need for them apparent. The fighting qualities of the corps ranged from excellent to poor. The British Army regulars initially disdained provincial units, but revised their opinions when reports from the field indicated competence, and in some cases excellence. An American Establishment, not including all Loyalist formations, was formed in 1779 (and formally listed in 1782), in an attempt to recognize the more successful units of Loyalists and to repair damage caused by British regulars in their evaluation of Loyalists as second-rate. The American Establishment compromised five regiments, Volunteers of Ireland, King's American Regiment, the Queen's Rangers, New York Volunteers, and British Legion. The major areas of operation for the Provincial Corps were in New York in 1778–79 and the southern campaigns of 1780–81. It is estimated that about 19,000 men served in the various Provincial Corps throughout the war.

Open supporters of the Loyalist cause were in a minority, but not a negligible one; it may be estimated at about 20 percent of the population living in the original Thirteen Colonies at the time of the American Declaration of Independence in 1776. They came from all walks of life and origins; most were of British descent, but some were Native Americans, and others were African Americans. Furthermore, there were many individuals who took the side of the British Crown outside the borders of the original colonies. These were inhabitants of the provinces of Nova Scotia, Prince Edward Island, Newfoundland, East and West Florida, and—most of all—the province of Québec (which encompassed much of present-day central Canada, and was often simply called "Canada" at that time). Further away, Jamaica in the British West Indies received Loyalist units from North America to fight the Spanish in Central America.

An important point to note was the division of North America into two separate command areas, ordered by the Earl of Dartmouth on August 2, 1775,

This watercolor of the "Encampment of the Loyalists at Johnstown, a New Settlement ..." made on June 6, 1784, by James Peachy, symbolizes the fate of more than 40,000 Loyalist Americans who fled the United States after the war. (Library and Archives Canada)

and probably effective by the fall of that year. One command (essentially present-day Québec and Ontario) was under the governor of Canada, Sir Guy Carleton; the other, under General Gage and his successors, embraced the present Canadian Atlantic provinces and the American colonies on the seaboard. This division had an important impact on Loyalist corps: each of these commands represented a different troop establishment and supply system, which has understandably confused some historians unaware of this administrative detail. Orders and supplies destined for a corps serving in the Canadian command came under a different authority from those for a corps in New York. Thus a corps such as the King's Royal Regiment of New York was in fact, in spite of its name, part of the Canadian establishment. As the supply network was also different, assumptions that uniforms and arms sent to New York would be issued to units in Canada cannot be sustained. Furthermore, due to distance and the slow and limited means of communication, colonies such as Newfoundland or West Florida tended to be semi-autonomous commands. Finally, some American Loyalist corps were sent to serve further afield, in Bermuda, the Bahamas, Jamaica, and Central America, all areas that fell under other commands.

Rifleman of the Queen's Rangers, c.1780, after a James Murray watercolor. (Library and Archives Canada)

To define exactly who was a Loyalist, and if a provincial unit raised on the American continent falls into that category, thus becomes a hazardous and somewhat futile exercise. The fundamental factor common to all was that they rallied to fight for the British Crown. Their reasons were extremely varied: some were part of the British government's social and political establishment in America, others had strong business ties with Britain, and still others felt that their rights would be better protected by the Crown than by the rampaging advocates of "Liberty," who in practice often turned violently upon anyone who disagreed with their arguments.

Indeed, quite early in the conflict, the more passionate promoters of independence brutally persecuted their loyal or "Tory" neighbors, and seized their property. This treatment created sizable groups of bitter refugees, who demanded arms and the means to create corps to fight for the Crown in the American colonies; and as early as the middle of 1775 the first units of Loyalist volunteers started to appear in Boston, Nova Scotia, and Québec. For their part, the British authorities gladly sanctioned these units of "Royal Provincial" troops, created specific provincial military establishments for them, and supplied money, arms, uniforms, and logistical assistance. Soon, every North American province would have them. As the conflict expanded, the movement to create provincial units loyal

ORISKANY, 1777

During the battle of Oriskany, August 6, 1777, Loyalists tried to penetrate the American lines by pretending to be reinforcements from Fort Stanwix, reversing their drab-faced green coats and marching towards their enemies as if on parade. Captain Gardenier of Visscher's regiment (the American rearguard) spotted the ruse when one of his men went out to greet these 'friends' and was promptly captured. Gardenier, armed only with a spontoon and sword, rushed forward and killed his man's captor: he then killed a second Loyalist and wounded a third, before three more knocked him down, two of them bayoneting him through the thighs. The third, a Lieutenant McDonald, went to bayonet him in the chest, but Gardenier caught the bayonet with his left hand, which cut him badly, but brought McDonald down on top of him. As a militiaman distracted the other two attackers, Gardenier grabbed his spontoon and killed McDonald with a single thrust, then shouted, "They are not our men—they are the enemy! Fire away!" (Adam Hook © Osprey Publishing)

to the Crown also spread. Most Indian nations opted to ally themselves with the British. One could say that the Loyalist movement even exported itself, when such units raised in North America were sent to the West Indies and Central America.

LOYALIST CONTRIBUTION

In most cases, the Loyalist corps in North America could provide excellent information on terrain and enemy strength when operating in familiar parts of the country. British senior officers were thus just as well informed in such matters as their American opponents. In tactical terms, many Loyalist corps were meant to be light troops that would maneuver swiftly and in loose formation, strike quickly, and keep moving. The most famous Loyalist corps such as the Queen's Rangers, the British Legion, and Butler's Rangers were made up of units of both light infantry and light cavalry. In the case of the Queen's Rangers and the British Legion, they provided a sizable and very effective light cavalry and light infantry to a main British army operating in settled American heartlands such as New Jersey, South Carolina, or Virginia. Butler's Rangers represented a very different application of light infantry tactics; this corps specialized in raids on wilderness frontier communities in partnership with Indian allies.

In this case, the Loyalist frontiersmen replicated almost exactly the practices that had made the settlers of New France and their Indian allies so feared and effective until the surrender of Canada to the British forces in 1760. However, not all Loyalist light corps achieved such fame and success, and many spent much of their time in garrisons. Most Loyalist units in the American seaboard provinces were meant to act as line infantry; some, such as the Loyal American Regiment or De Lancey's Brigade, were often deployed on campaign or participated in sieges, and gave distinguished service; but others attracted too few recruits for campaign service, and usually served in large garrisons such as the city of New York.

At the end of 1778, some 6,300 Loyalist soldiers were spread among 31 units, thus giving an average of 204 men per unit on the Atlantic seaboard. A few corps such as the Queen's Rangers, the Volunteers of Ireland or the Royal Highland Emigrants had between 300 and 400 men each, and were considered very effective. The strength of most of the other units hovered between 100 and 200 men, sometimes fewer, and these were thus unable to make any serious contribution. In Canada the smaller Loyalist corps were merged into one unit, Jessup's Loyal Rangers, in late 1781; but no such measures were taken on the Atlantic seaboard, so that most Loyalist corps in that region remained under-strength and thus less effective than if they had been amalgamated.

BRITISH TRAINING AND TACTICS

On joining his regiment, the British Redcoat recruit was issued with a basic suit of clothing and embarked upon basic training. First the recruit was taught to be the "master of his person," that is to carry himself properly "chin up, shoulders back and stomach in." Having thus started off the process of smartening himself up, he proceeded to learn the intricacies of foot drill and marching.

Once he had mastered, or at least proved himself to be reasonably proficient in, foot drill and marching, he was finally introduced to his "fire lock." As today, the very first lesson was the naming of the parts. That done, he then learned the "manual exercise" or weapon handling: first without ammunition, then with blank charges, and finally with ball.

He then moved on to learn the platoon exercise or, more precisely, to learning and practicing the actions required of him. This basically entailed getting used to loading and firing in three ranks.

During the War of Independence, British infantry fighting doctrines were heavily influenced by the 1728 Regulations, which had in turn been cribbed from Humphrey Bland's elegantly written *Treatise of Military Discipline*, first published in 1727. The importance of Bland's drill-book may be gauged by the fact that it went through no fewer than nine editions, the last being published in 1762, and it is important to understand this system to contrast it with that eventually adopted in North America.

According to Bland's system, the battalion was divided into four grand divisions for the purposes of maneuver, and a much larger number of platoons for fire-control purposes. In the forming of these divisions and platoons (the two bore little or no relationship to each other), the various companies were divided up as required and only the grenadiers survived as an independent unit.

Bland's treatise outlined in exhaustive detail the intricacies of a coordinated platoon maneuver and firing system, but it was over-complicated and sometimes simply did not work. There were essentially two reasons for this. First, by dividing a battalion up into evenly-sized platoons, the normal company-based command structure was necessarily disrupted. It is perhaps too easy to overestimate the effects of this, since proper training—or, more accurately, rehearsal—should have overcome the worst of them. The second and real reason why the platoon firing system tended to break down was that all too often such training and rehearsal was lacking. This, in turn, can be attributed to a number of factors, chiefly that it was rarely possible to assemble enough officers and men in one place at one time to practice platooning properly. Except for the footguards, concentrated in London and near to Hyde Park, and the regiments of the Dublin garrison, close to Phoenix Park, most units were too widely scattered to carry out the necessary training.

The result, perhaps predictably, was an utter shambles when the British army had its first real opportunity to put Bland's teaching into practice, at Dettingen in 1743. Doubtless drawing upon wartime experience, the 1748 Regulations simplified Band's platoon exercise. Under the 1748 Regulations, there were now to be four platoons in each of the four grand divisions. The 1756/7 Regulations essentially retained the simplified platooning of the 1748 Regulations, but took a major step forward in closing up the distances between files. Bland advocated an interval of half a pace between each file, or in effect a frontage of about 30in (0.75m) per man when firing. The 1756/7 Regulations closed this frontage up to 24in (0.6m) per man.

At the same time, close order (one pace of about 30in/76cm) became pretty much the standard distance between ranks for firing as well as maneuvering. This speeded up the locking of ranks and hence the rate of fire. In the early days when three ranks fired at once, the front rank went down on one knee, the second crouched a little, and only the rear rank remained upright. This created two problems: first, if the center rank did not crouch low enough, it was difficult for the rear rank to do other than fire in the air; second, the distance between ranks

British troops fire during a reenactment of the battle of Brandywine. (Dave G.Houser/Getty Images)

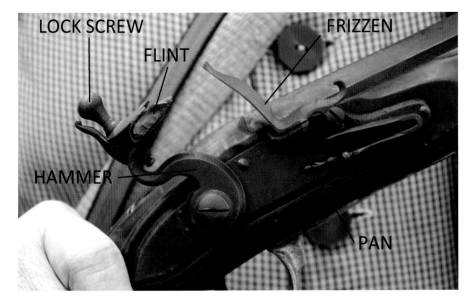

LOCK SCREW

FLINT

FRIZZEN

HAMMER

PAN

Components of a typical flintlock firearm. In continued firing the flint had to be reseated using the knob at upper left, and the vent cleared using the vent pick. (Ed Gilbert and Catherine Gilbert)

placed the muzzles of the rear rank firelocks uncomfortably close to the heads of the men in the front rank. Bland's drill-book solved this problem by advocating the locking of ranks immediately before firing.

All the loading and reloading was done at the proper intervals. When ordered to "lock," the front rank went down on one knee as before, but otherwise did not move. The center rank closed up hard on the first and took half a pace to the right, while the third rank similarly stepped forward and took a full pace to the right. By this means the file was now ranged in echelon with the center man firing down the gap between the front rank man and his neighbor on the right. The rear rank man was firing over the head of that neighbor, but was sufficiently close to him to obviate any danger of blowing his head off.

Notwithstanding these improvements, the 1748 and 1756/7 Regulations essentially did little more than tinker with Bland's system. In the meantime, a number of regiments were engaged in the quite unauthorized development of the "alternate" system of firing, which would eventually replace Bland's platooning in the 1764 Regulations. By comparison with Bland's platooning, the alternate system was simplicity itself. Proceeding on active service, a battalion would first equalize its companies—that is, transfer men from one to

Short land pattern firelock: lock detail–flash pan open. (Stuart Reid)

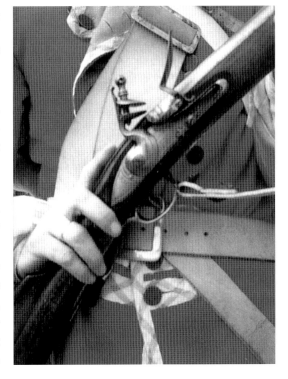

another until they were all roughly the same size. Each company then acted as a platoon, commanded in action by its own officers. As a further refinement, the eight battalion companies (the Establishment was reduced from nine to eight at the end of the Seven Years' War) were also paired off to form the sub-divisions of the four grand divisions required for maneuvering. The sequence of firing was also considerably simplified. The platoons prescribed by Bland, and the later 1748 Regulations, were numbered off both as to the three or four firings and in a straightforward numerical sequence so that volleys could be delivered in one of two ways. Either all the platoons of the first firing could blaze away at once and at the same time, followed by the platoons of the second firing and so on, or each individual platoon could fire one after the other according to their numerical sequence.

The 1764 Regulations were undoubtedly a great improvement. There still remained a danger that the longer firing went on the more likely it was that platoons would begin firing out of sequence and that ultimately the firefight might degenerate into each individual soldier loading and firing as fast as he could. However, close attention paid to the manual exercise led to the average British soldier being able to load and fire his weapon faster than his Continental counterpart. This, rather than the overrated platoon firing system taught by Bland, may in part explain the noted British superiority in firing.

GRENADIER AND LIGHT INFANTRY UNITS

Common to both platoon and alternate firing was the practice of treating the grenadier company as an entirely separate unit. This was done for two reasons. In the first place, it was sometimes helpful to have a reserve of experienced men specifically charged with guarding the battalion's flanks in battle. Second, it became increasingly common for the grenadier company to be detached from its parent unit.

The grenadier's role in the 18th century was an interesting one. Grenade throwing had from the beginning been only incidental to their real role as fast-moving assault troops. It was a role which they retained, despite the effective abandonment of the hand grenade, which was only of any real use in assaulting or defending

A typical British grenadier on active service. (Anne S.K. Brown Collection, Brown University)

fortifications. Indeed, under the alternate fire system, the grenadiers were soon paired off with the newly-introduced light company. When a battalion was drawn up as a single organic unit, the grenadiers would often be tasked with skirmishing on the right of the battalion, while the light company skirmished on the left.

It became increasingly common, however, for both flank companies to be drawn off from their parent units and formed with other similar companies into provisional assault battalions. Although the practice seems to have been pioneered during the Seven Years' War, both in Germany and in North America, the most notable example of it was to be seen during the American War of Independence. All the grenadier companies serving in that theater were formed into four semi-permanent battalions of grenadiers, and the light companies into four light infantry battalions. These provisional units appear to have built up a considerable esprit de corps, and within a short time their officers, and presumably by extension their men, were taking to describing themselves as serving in the British Grenadiers rather than belonging to their parent battalions.

"Present ... fire." Note how the soldier is taught to lean into his shot; contrast this with the much stiffer posture in the 1764 manual exercise. (Stuart Reid)

The extent to which their roles differed is difficult to gauge, since both grenadiers and light infantry were expected to serve either as skirmishers or as shock troops as the occasion demanded. Indeed, where it was impractical to form separate battalions of grenadiers and light infantry, as on San Domingo in 1794, a single composite "flank battalion" would be formed from grenadier and light companies. This linkage may at first appear surprising, but it was entirely in accordance with Continental thinking on the employment of light troops.

In North America, the locally-raised ranger companies were supplemented by the formation of a light infantry company in each regular battalion. These companies, and the 80th Light Infantry who followed, were tasked with scouting and skirmishing in the woods.

Those who saw action were shipped overseas as quickly as they were raised, without proper training in the platoon exercise or much else in the way of drill. Their role, however, was not to stand shoulder to shoulder in the line of battle or to skirmish from behind cover, but to serve as lightly equipped formations capable of undertaking rapid marches and heavy raids deep into enemy territory. Once in contact with the enemy, they almost

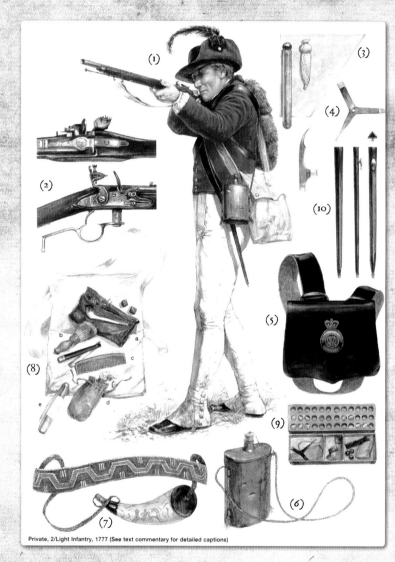

Private, 2/Light Infantry, 1777 (See text commentary for detailed captions)

PRIVATE, 2/LIGHT INFANTRY, 1777

1: This soldier belongs to one of eight provisional battalions formed by General Howe in 1776, in preparation for the invasion of Long Island. 2: The Ferguson breech-loader. The rifle's subsequent demise is popularly attributed to the conservatism of British generals, but modern tests have revealed that the breech screw mechanism is susceptible to fouling, and under battlefield conditions it is likely to have become inoperable after a relatively short time. 3: Cartridge making: a piece of "cartridge paper," a .75-caliber ball, and 70 grains of black powder, all tied together with thread. 4: Combination tool. 5: Cartridge box with regimental badge. 6: Tin canteen. 7: Powder-horn attached to a moose-hair tumpline. 8: Duck haversack—in theory to be used for carrying rations, but occasionally used in place of a knapsack, and typical small items of personal kit: (a) whale bone pipe; (b) shaving kit; (c) comb; (d) purse; and (e) folded blade. 9. Cutaway of cartridge box emphasizing the hidden compartment holding cleaning equipment and spare cartridge-making materials. 10. Front, back and side-views of bayonet scabbard. (Richard Hook © Osprey Publishing)

invariably went straight in with the bayonet. In effect, their role was not unlike that of the modern air-mobile brigade.

At the end of the Seven Years' War, both the regimental light companies and the light infantry regiments were disbanded. (It was a common misconception, both in Britain and on the Continent, that all light troops were a rascally set of *banditti* who were of some use in wartime, but had no role to play in a peacetime army.) Sufficient interest remained to see the official formation of light companies in all regiments on the British Establishment in 1771 and in the Irish Establishment in 1772. It was one thing to order that these light companies be formed; quite another to produce a competent body of light infantry. So in 1774 Major-General Howe, who had gained some very useful experience of light infantry work in North America, devised a "discipline" for the new companies and managed to exercise some of them in it just before the outbreak of the War of Independence. This "discipline" was in some respects rather limited. Although marksmanship was stressed, together with considerable practice in "irregular & bush fighting," the real meat of the training was to enable them to maneuver and fire in accordance with the 1764 Regulations while dispersed in open, or even extended, order.

Once appointed commander-in-chief in North America, Howe then took the whole process a stage further by effectively training all his regular infantry as light troops. In the 1750s, the intervals between ranks and files had been tightened up quite considerably in order to speed up maneuvering. But Howe trained his battalions to march and fight in two ranks rather than three and to do it in open order, that is, with a full arm's distance between each file.

The result may not have been very pretty, but this "loose file and American scramble" served the army well throughout the war, and is usefully described in a set of standing orders issued by Major-General Phillips:

> It is the Major General's wish, that the troops under his command may practice forming from two to three and four deep; and that they should be accustomed to charge in all those orders. In the latter orders, of the three and four deep, the files will, in course, be closer, so as to render a charge of the greatest force. The Major General also recommends to regiments the practice of dividing the battalions, by wings or otherwise, so that one line may support the other when an attack is supposed; and, when a retreat is supposed, that the first line may retreat through the intervals of the second, the second doubling up its divisions for that purpose, and forming again in order to check the enemy who may be supposed to have pressed the first line. The Major General would approve also of one division of a battalion attacking in the common open order of two deep, to be supported by the

other compact division as a second line, in a charging order of three or four deep. The gaining the flanks also of a supposed enemy, by the quick movements of a division in common open order, while the compact division advances to a charge; and such other evolutions, as may lead the regiments to a custom of depending on and mutually supporting each other; so that should one part be pressed or broken, it may be accustomed to form again without confusion, under the protection of a second line, or any regular formed division, (Simcoe, *Military Journal* pp. 187–188.)

From this and from other similar descriptions, it is clear that the tactics employed by the British army during the American War of Independence were radically

A correct musket-firing position. Note how the soldier's weight is transferred to his left foot, and how the firelock is supported at the swell of the stock. This provides for excellent balance and allows the soldier to take proper aim. (Stuart Reid)

Cornwallis rejected the use of a conventional artillery train during the campaign, due to the appalling transportation problems the guns would have encountered in the Carolina backcountry. Instead, he relied on light "galloper guns" for support. This image shows a typical canon at the Yorktown battlefields. (Kelly Light/ Alamy Stock Photo)

different from those practiced in Europe. Gone was the solid firing line; instead there were, to all intents and purposes, a heavy screen of light infantry backed up by soldier assault columns ready to exploit any weakness in the enemy lines. The frequency with which "charging" (presumably with the bayonet) was stressed is also significant. The troops ranged in these loose files were not intended to act as skirmishers per se; although the regimental light companies (and to a certain extent the grenadiers as well) were trained in that role, particularly in broken ground, it generally remained the prerogative of specialist units of riflemen and marksmen.

As is evident from the analysis above, the War of Independence was as formative for the established British Army as it was for the emerging American forces. The war showed both the strengths and weaknesses of the British way of war in stark relief. The common soldiery remained as tough and obstinate in battle as ever, but such men, as always, were players on a much larger stage in which political will, military governance, and age-old logistical problems could determine their fate.

CHAPTER 7

THE FRENCH, SPANISH, AND AMERICAN-ALLIED FORCES

WITHIN THE UNITED STATES TODAY, IT is often forgotten how important a military contribution outsiders made to the formation of the United States, especially the French. The French Army had emerged from the Seven Years' War at a low point, having been defeated in North America, Europe, and India. Evaluation of its performance had brought about a number of reforms from 1763 to 1775. Artillery units were revamped and standardized into seven large regiments, and infantry regiments were regularized as well. By 1776 all regiments comprised two battalions, with each battalion composed of one grenadier, one chasseur (light infantry), and four fusilier companies.

The training of the infantry and cavalry was standardized and revamped to include summer training camps. The Crown undertook to supply the regiments directly with clothing and muskets to counteract the officers' practice of profiting on military supply contracts. Military enlistment was fixed at eight years, to provide a large corps of properly trained soldiers. By 1778 there were more than 200,000 men in the French Army.

The French Army had no continental commitments during the war, as it had in the Seven Years' War, and was therefore able to direct most of its energies against British interests throughout the world. The performances

of the French Army at Yorktown and in the West Indies demonstrated the successes of the reforms and presented a different army from the one that the British had fought in the Seven Years' War. A French expeditionary force arrived at Newport in 1780, under the command of Lieutenant-General Jean de Vimeur, Comte de Rochambeau. Thomas McKean of the Continental Congress reviewed the troops in Philadelphia and afterwards wrote to Rochambeau: "the brilliant appearance and exact discipline of the several Corps do the highest honor to their officers, and to afford a happy presage of the most distinguished services in a cause which they have so zealously espoused," (Rice and Brown, p. 46.)

A French soldier of the period, after Charles Parrocel (1688–1752). (Anne S.K. Brown Collection, Brown University)

THE LEGACY OF THE SEVEN YEARS' WAR

The French forces that fought during the American War of Independence were, to a very large extent, a product of the disasters that the Seven Years' War brought to the armies of France. During that war, just about everything that could have gone wrong did so: the fleet had been swept off the oceans, especially after Quiberon in 1759–the "Year of Victories" for the British–and nearly all colonies had been lost. In Europe, the war had started off fairly well with the capture of Minorca and some minor successes in Germany. Then came a series of disastrous defeats to the combined forces of France, Austria, and Russia, struck by the military genius of Frederick the Great of Prussia and his army. By 1762, fellow Bourbon King Carlos III of Spain tried to rescue his French cousin Louis XV only to see his colonial capitals of Havana and Manila fall to the British. The Treaty of Paris in 1763 confirmed the loss of North America, of India (except for a few posts), of valuable West Indian islands, of most of Senegal, and humiliating clauses such as the destruction of the fortifications of Dunkirk.

Well before the end of the war, the court of France was getting desperate; a rapid succession of ministers was briefly responsible for the army and the navy.

There was increasing discontent among the French public and, at the news of defeat after defeat, sweeping reforms were demanded. The man who initiated these reforms was the Duc de Choiseul, a man of considerable ability and tenacity who had been foreign minister until 1761. By then it was obvious that the war was lost, and he was appointed by the king to be minister of both the army and the navy—all military forces on land and sea. Choiseul inherited a demoralized army still basically functioning as in the days of Louis XIV. As late as the 1740s, Marshal de Saxe was writing of his "dreams" that it should one day march in step!

Etienne-Francois de Choiseul, the leading force in French military reforms prior to the American War of Independence (INTERFOTO/Alamy Stock Photo

The fleet was all but lost and equally disgraced—"a corps which must be totally reformed if it is to be of any use," the Duc d'Aiguillon wrote sternly. Public pressure and the humiliations to France's glory, however, gave Choiseul more liberty than had been the case for some of his predecessors, who had been fighting strongly held vested interests.

REFORMS IN THE ARMY

Choiseul went to work with determination, making sure that he made himself available for a suitable number of consultations, including putting up with a review board of some 80 generals. From the end of 1762, a series of royal orders dictated by common sense and good planning were signed by the king, and a vast reorganization was started. From then on, regiments would all be organized the same way, have the same training, be supplied by the Crown, and attend large summer training camps for brigade and division maneuvers. Weapons were improved, and uniforms standardized down to stamping the regiment's number on the buttons. Regimental officers were held accountable at their various levels, thus abolishing the percentage system on clothing and other items; recruiting was centralized, abolishing yet another officer's perk. All this was not achieved without grumbling from the officer corps, but within a couple of years the

A French drummer. Drummers were a battalion's signallers, and had a vital role in combat. (Anne S.K. Brown Collection, Brown University)

new ways were accepted. Riding schools were established for the cavalry, and from 1765 the artillery system devised by General Gribeauval was adopted. For all his good sense and sound reforms Choiseul made many enemies at court; he managed to elude them until 1771 when the devious courtesan Madame du Barry finally convinced an aged Louis XV, no doubt in the comfort of his bed, that Choiseul had to go.

By then, however, the work of the skilled minister had convinced many, and Choiseul's successors followed his course of reforms in spite of accusations of "Prussianizing" the army. Of these, the Comte de Saint-Germain, minister from 1775, caused the most uproar by trying to introduce corporal punishment, abolishing part of the King's Guards including the Musketeers and the Horse Grenadiers as too expensive, abolishing the purchase system for officers' commissions, and retiring some of the 865 colonels. He reorganized, mainly for the better, everything from the supply system to the militia, and introduced a rather strange infantry uniform in 1776. Louis XVI, king since May 10, 1774, supported his minister, but while most of Saint-Germain's reforms are now seen as good, the controversies in his own day were such that he resigned in 1777. The Prince de Montbarrey, a smoother courtier, carried on until 1780, and Marshal de Segur until 1787. It was during Segur's ministry that the infamous royal order of May 22, 1781, was issued, requiring henceforth that only noblemen would qualify for officers' commissions. Segur was against it but had to comply with the wishes of the king's brother (the future Louis XVIII) and his clique. Cruelly ironic, considering that the French Army was then fighting for the liberty of Americans, the order was bitterly resented by talented NCOs and enlisted men, who did not forget this injustice when their hour came eight years later.

King Louis XVI saw assisting the Americans as an opportunity to weaken the British Empire and to regain territory lost in the Seven Years' War. (The Museum of the Revolution at Yorktown)

From 1776, all infantry regiments except the Guards and the *Régiment du Roi* (King's Regiment) were ordered to have two battalions. For the older four-battalion regiments this meant that their 2nd and 4th battalions became new regiments. At peak strength, each battalion had 963 officers and men, plus 26 officers and other ranks attached to an auxiliary recruit company, plus the regimental staff for an establishment of 990 all ranks for the two battalions of each regiment. The actual average battalion strength was about 500, and this was the number used for the battalions sent to the United States and Minorca. The French Army's Royal Corps of Artillery saw considerable reforms during this period which saw the introduction, against many objections, of the excellent Gribeauval system.

By these various reforms, the Army establishment was brought up from 90,000 to nearly 170,000 infantry and from 25,000 to 46,000 cavalry at the eve of the war. To support the infantry and artillery even further, provincial militia battalions were ordered activated on January 30, 1778.

From these, 13 regiments of *Grenadiers Royaux* were formed with the grenadier companies, 13 regiments attached to the seven regular artillery regiments, five regiments attached to the engineers, and the Paris and Corsica provincial regiments for those areas. Some 79 battalions were each attached to a regular regiment to serve as a third battalion. These 75,000 embodied militiamen did garrison and coast guard duty in France during the war and all provided volunteer recruits to their regiment.

WEAPONS, DRESS, AND EQUIPMENT

This fusilier, *Régiment de Guyenne,* is armed with a .69-caliber Modèle 1728 musket with iron furniture and russet leather sling and also a bayonet, but the sword which would ordinarily be carried in the lower frog on the left of his belt was not much used in Canada and a hatchet normally substituted instead. Like all French regular soldiers serving in Canada he wears a white woolen coat with large cuffs displaying his regiment's facing color and a unique arrangement of pocket flaps. Underneath is a long-skirted waistcoat of the facing color, white wool knee breeches, white linen gaiters, and stout leather shoes. On his head is a wool felt tricorne hat bound with false gold lace and decorated with a white cockade. His fighting equipment comprises a buff leather belt fastened around the waist and a russet leather giberne or cartridge box containing a wooden block holding 20 rounds of ammunition in the form of paper cartridges, each containing approximately 70 grains of powder and a lead ball. Attached to the bracing strap of the buff leather sling for the giberne is a rolled-up forage cap. (Peter Dennis © Osprey Publishing)

The French Army that the British Army would face from 1778 was completely different from that of 20 years earlier. By all accounts it was impeccably drilled, well armed, well equipped, capable of fearsome firepower, and led by a competent officer corps that had done a lot of hard work and study. Trained mainly to face the Prussian or Austrian armies in a continental war, it performed extremely well in the various overseas operations, usually holding the British forces at bay when not compelling the enemy to surrender. It could be added that the work of the

Left: Hussar, Lauzun's Legion, USA, 1780–83. Center: Gunner, Royal-Artillerie, c.1780–83. Right: Infantry corporal, Lauzun's Legion, USA, 1780–82. It is often overlooked that half of Lauzun's 600 men consisted of infantry. (Francis Back © Osprey Publishing)

staff officers and the engineers was disciplined and impressive, and that most general officers were of a bold, yet crisp and measured temper.

REFORMS IN THE COLONIAL ARMY

Colonial troops were a separate entity from the metropolitan army and the marines. The various army orders on uniforms, weapons, composition of units, pay, awards, etc., did not apply to colonial troops, who had their own regulations on such matters. For instance, a colonial officer did not need to have blue blood (although being the son of a colonial officer was a considerable advantage), so that the hated 1781 *noblesse* regulation in the metropolitan army did not apply.

During the *Ancien Régime* the Minister of the Navy was also responsible for the colonies that were administered by the Crown. From the end of 1762, Choiseul designated a number of army regiments to serve as garrisons in the colonies. Apart from being rather unpopular with the army, this led to administrative difficulties, with paper battles between the bureaucracies of the army and the colonial side of the Ministry of the Navy. Colonists did not like it either; they had been used to seeing troops belonging to their colony, with officers often coming from the colonial gentry rather than the somewhat disdainful nobility of France. By 1766 it was resolved to raise a "Legion" per colony, but only those of Île-de-France and Saint-Domingue came into being. The Leeward Islands of Martinique and Guadeloupe continued to have army troops, while Guyana and Senegal each had a colonial battalion. With the *Compagnie des Indes* (French East India Company) closing its books in 1770 the Crown took over its responsibilities, which included keeping garrisons in southern India.

On August 18, 1772, the colonial army was considerably reorganized. The regiments of Du Cap and Port-au-Prince were created to serve in Saint-Domingue, those of Martinique and Guadeloupe to serve in the Leeward Islands, and those of Île-de-France, Port-Louis, and Île-de-Bourbon to serve in the French islands of the Indian Ocean. On December 30 the regiment of Pondicherry was raised to serve in India.

The new regiments were to be of two battalions, incorporating whatever troops were in the colony and boosted by some recruits. While this worked in the West Indies, the East Indian regiments were very weak. On January 21, 1775, the regiments of Port-Louis and Île-de-Bourbon were abolished and incorporated into the Île-de-France regiment, which was boosted to four battalions. The Pondichery regiment's 2nd Battalion was never raised, but it was compensated for by a battalion of sepoys. Also raised on December 30, 1772, was the three-company Volontaires de Benyowski to serve in Madagascar, and a company of invalids to be stationed in Île-de-France.

Benyowski's volunteers, named after a Polish adventurer who had convinced the court (and himself) that a vast new colony could be established in Madagascar, withered away, becoming an independent company in 1778, and its sickly survivors were evacuated and incorporated in the Île-de-France regiment in 1782. The battalion of *Troupes nationales de Cayenne* in French Guyana had eight companies from 1775 raised to ten in 1779. In Gorée, Senegal, was a "half company" (50 men) of the *Volontaires d'Afrique*; while the islands of Saint-Pierre-et-Miquelon in the North Atlantic, south of Newfoundland, also had 50 men for a complete "company." There were also colonial artillery companies, called *Canonniers-Bombardiers*, in most colonies.

In spite of a lack of complete uniformity in organization (this was achieved after the war), there were 15 battalions plus a number of companies of white troops with a battalion of sepoys on duty in the colonies at the outbreak of the war. The colonial army had an establishment of more than 12,000, although the actual strength was probably about 8,000–9,000 white officers and men in 1778.

A number of other units were raised during the war. The most famous is probably the Duc de Lauzun's Legion, which served in the United States (notably in the cavalry fight near Yorktown where Lauzun's Legion hussars routed Tarleton's British Legion light dragoons). The unit was formed from the 2nd Legion of the *Volontaires étrangers de la Marine*. Like other corps, such as the *Volontaires de Nassau* or the *Volontaires du Luxembourg*, nearly all units raised in France for colonial service during the war were largely composed of foreigners, usually Germans.

WAR WITH BRITAIN

From the outset, the increasing disputes between Britain and her North American colonies roused interest and sympathy in France. From 1775, when it became an armed conflict, it was felt prudent to send five metropolitan army battalions to reinforce the colonial troops in the West Indies. The United States of America proclaimed their independence on July 4, 1776, but there was no way to tell which way the struggle would go. French intellectuals delighted at the wording of the American Declaration of Independence; businessmen were starting to wonder about a possible new market; and the general public started to hope for revenge against "perfidious Albion." At court, ministers and officials were cautious and wished to see the resolve of the Americans tested before embarking on a war with Britain. However, Foreign Minister Comte de Vergennes was arranging secretly via the playwright Beaumarchais for artillery, small arms, uniforms, and other supplies to be sent to the Americans. Vergennes was also using every device he could to isolate Britain from her traditional allies. Then came the news of the British disaster at Saratoga in October 1777.

Left: Sepoy, Île-de-France Regiment, India, 1782–83
Center: Fusilier, Île-de-France Regiment, India, 1782–83.
Right: Sepoy, Austrasie Regiment, India, 1782–83.
(Francis Back © Osprey Publishing)

Thereafter it was only a matter of time before the persuasive American ambassador to the French court, Benjamin Franklin, convinced France to recognize the United States, which was done by a treaty of friendship and commerce on February 6, 1778.

The news was received coldly in London, which recalled its ambassador from France. War had not been declared yet, but Admiral d'Estaing's squadron was sent to reinforce the West Indies in April. On June 17, off Brittany, several British ships attacked the French frigate *Belle-Poule*, but she fought them off and got away to a triumphant return in Brest. On July 10, Louis XVI ordered his warships to "give chase" to those of the Royal Navy.

The real war was now on. It was a gamble for France, which had 52 ships of the line against Britain's 66. Fellow Bourbons in Spain hesitated for nearly a year before coming into the conflict on May 8, 1779, after which date the 58 Spanish ships of the line joined France's 63 against Britain's 90. In November 1780, Britain, which could find no allies, also declared war on Holland. In 1781 the lesser naval powers such as Denmark, Portugal, Sweden, and Russia formed themselves into an "Armed Neutrality," while Austria and Prussia would have nothing to do with the conflict. Comte de Vergenne's diplomatic skills left Britain completely isolated. The war would be fought at sea and overseas.

THE WEST INDIES

In Martinique, the news of war arrived on August 17, and the energetic 38-year-old Governor-General Marquis de Bouillé set the tone. He gathered a mixed force of regulars and colonial volunteers and militias on a few frigates, and captured Dominica—the British island between Martinique and Guadeloupe on September 7. Reinforcements poured in from France and Britain, but the French kept the initiative in the smaller islands while the Spanish concentrated on Louisiana and West Florida. By 1782 the only British islands left were Barbados, Antigua, St. Lucia, and Jamaica. Some 27 French metropolitan infantry battalions, beside smaller detachments and artillery, had joined the eight colonial infantry battalions plus the colonial artillery and volunteers in the West Indies.

THE UNITED STATES

The first actions by French troops on American soil were at the siege of Savannah during September and October of 1779, which ended in failure. But 5,000 officers and men the equivalent of about nine battalions of infantry and artillery with 300 of Lauzun's Legion hussars under the command of Rochambeau arrived at Newport, Rhode Island, in July 1780. This force, placed under the supreme command of Washington, considerably impressed the Americans as it marched south in 1781, slowly isolating Lord Cornwallis in Yorktown by September. They were joined by 3,000 more troops who had come up from the West Indies in Admiral de Grasse's fleet, making the besieging Franco-American army some 16,000 strong. The 7,000 British and mercenary Hessian troops marched out to the sound of drums and music on October 19. Thereafter military operations in the United States almost stopped. The British evacuated Savannah in July and Charleston in December 1782, while most of the French expeditionary corps (except for Lauzun's Legion) left from Boston bound for the West Indies on 23 December. Only New York remained to the British.

THE EAST INDIES

From August to October 1778, the French posts in India were all captured and the Pondicherry regiment was sent to France. The four battalions of colonial troops in Île-de-France were joined in July 1780 by the 2nd Battalion of the Austrasie regiment. The 1st Battalion with the 3rd Legion of the *Volontaires étrangers de la Marine* arrived in October 1781. On February 25, 1782, Austrasie, the 3rd Legion, 1,500 men of the Île-de-France regiment, the *Volontaires de Bourbon*, and artillery landed at Porto Novo in India and joined the forces of Hyder Ali, which attached

sepoys to each French battalion. These troops were also used by Admiral Suffren as marines and for the capture of Trincomalee in Ceylon during August 1782.

The Marquis de Bussy, an aged veteran of India from the Seven Years' War, was in command of four more infantry battalions and an artillery brigade (2,300 men) sent from France. They landed in India on March 19, 1783, and sepoys were likewise attached to them. Tipu Sultan, son of Hyder Ali, was also there with his army. The British force of 15,000 men, including 3,500 European troops, under General Stuart was losing control of the military situation in southern India and tried to contain the French in Cuddelore on June 13; but much of the 102nd Foot was destroyed in the process. Admiral Hughes was beaten off by Suffren, which made Stuart's position critical; but luckily for him a British frigate arrived on June 29 with news that the preliminaries for peace had been signed in Europe on 20 January. Most historians contend that, without naval power, Stuart's demoralized force could have been beaten by the Franco-Indian forces and southern India lost to Britain.

The French contribution to the eventual American victory cannot be underestimated. Indeed, the Americans had far more allies fighting the British

The surrender of Lord Cornwallis to General George Washington at Yorktown, Virginia 1781 (Niday Picture Library/Alamy Stock Photo)

around the globe than are generally remembered today. The majority of these allies were French, and the independence of the United States owes much to the vast deployment of troops and ships across the world by France between 1778 and 1783.

SPAIN

By 1700, more than 200 years after the story of the vast Spanish overseas empire began with Columbus making landfall in what is now the Bahamas archipelago, a string of lost wars in Europe had brought Spain to its knees, both economically and diplomatically. This situation was then aggravated by a dynastic crisis, as two contenders claimed the throne: Prince Charles of Austria, and Philippe, Duc d'Anjou and grandson of France's King Louis XIV. The War of the Spanish Succession that ensued in 1702 did not end until 1713–14, by which time the rivals were exhausted. France had lost some of its prestige as a world power to Britain, but it had secured the confirmation of Philippe as Felipe V, King of Spain and "the Indies."

Spain, however, was not to become a French puppet state, as was quickly demonstrated by the rather ludicrous and half-hearted war that it waged in 1718–20 against France, Britain, and several other countries. Thereafter, Spain's government had to confront the most pressing issue: the need to halt the nation's decline and to restore its prestige as a viable power.

In the years that followed the armed forces were thoroughly modernized, soon coming to employ standardized French-style tactics, maneuvers, weapons, and uniforms. As the years passed, much of Spain's infrastructure, its cultural institutions, and its government organization adopted French models, and these reforms proved very beneficial. The reign of Carlos III (1759–88) was the period of *La Illustración* (the Enlightenment) during which time Spain was again a major power.

From 1702, all of Spain's overseas territories rallied to Felipe V as king, and they would expand greatly in North America during the 18th century. New outposts appeared in Texas and Arizona, and a massive addition of territory occurred after 1763 with the transfer of Louisiana from France to Spain. Simultaneously, "Upper" California was planted with missions and forts to counter any Russian adventures; by 1790, Spanish coastal explorations had reached as far north as Alaska, and the fort of Nootka had been built on present-day Vancouver Island in British Columbia, Canada. In defense terms, the result of this expansion was a gradual shift of new responsibilities from the Caribbean Sea basin north of the equator to the North American mainland.

METROPOLITAN REGIMENTS IN NORTH AMERICA, 1764-93

Following the end of the Seven Years' War, King Carlos III and his ministers started preparing the armed services for the next war against Britain that would inevitably break out within a few years. The army was reorganized and modernized, while the navy was rebuilt with capital ships, the size of which had never been seen before in Spain. Huge sums were expended to make Havana, San Juan (Puerto Rico), and Cartagena de Indias almost impregnable fortress cities.

Left: Officer, French Navy, 1778–83. Center left: Bombardier, Bombardiers de la Marine, 1778–83. Center right: Fusilier, Corps Royal de l'infanterie de la Marine, 1778-83. Right: Fusilier, Barrois Regiment, 1776–82.(Francis Back © Osprey Publishing)

Cuba, especially its capital Havana, became the main military base in North America. Besides the local regular colonial garrison, many metropolitan battalions were now posted to Havana. In April 1763 the Cordoba Regiment was shipped to Havana, where it helped to reorganize the Fijo de Habana Regiment before returning to Spain in 1765. It was replaced by the Lisboa Regiment until 1769, followed by Sevilla and Irlanda in 1770–71, by Aragon and Guadalajara from 1771 to 1774, by Principe from 1771 until 1782, by Espana in 1776, Navarra in 1779, Napoles in 1780–82, and subsequently by other units.

The transfer of Louisiana from France to Spain was a gradual process between 1766 and 1769 when, following some resistance from the French settlers, a large force was sent to New Orleans. This included the Lisboa, Aragon, and Guadalajara metropolitan infantry regiments, the Havana colonial regiment, and companies of Havana's Moreno and Pardo Militia (both these Spanish terms for "brown," "dark," or "swarthy" indicated the racial make-up of this militia).

Detachments from the garrison in Cuba were sent to Louisiana and used with great success by the young and energetic Governor Galvez in 1779 and 1780, when he conquered most of British West Florida. In March 1781, a Spanish force of about 8,000 men from metropolitan and colonial regiments undertook the siege of Pensacola. This was the largest operation by the Spanish forces during the American War of Independence, and Pensacola's British garrison surrendered on May 9. Spanish operations in Florida ceased thereafter, as there was no strategic value to conquering British East Florida.

Spanish forces did take Nassau in the Bahamas in 1782, but most metropolitan units assembled in the French colony of Saint-Domingue (now Haiti) for a projected Franco-Spanish invasion of British Jamaica. This was never attempted, however, due to the defeat of Admiral de Grasse's French fleet at the Battle of The Saints by Admiral Rodney's Royal Navy squadron. Nevertheless, most British islands and all of West Florida were now occupied by Spanish or French forces, and the intensity of operations diminished as peace negotiations got under way in Europe. New Spain, too, was reinforced with metropolitan regiments.

The process began with the transfer there of the America Regiment from 1764 to 1768, when it was relieved in Mexico City by Ultonia, Flandes, and Saboya until 1771, 1772, and 1773 respectively. The Grenada Regiment was also in Vera Cruz from 1771 to 1784. The Asturias Regiment was stationed in Mexico City from 1777 to 1784, and Zamora in Vera Cruz from 1783 to 1789.

In Puerto Rico, the Leon Regiment served mostly at San Juan from 1766 until 1768, when it was relieved by Toledo until 1770. The Vitoria Regiment arrived in 1770, being joined by Bruselas in 1776, both regiments going back to Spain in

1783. Napoles arrived in 1784 and stayed until 1789-90, helping to form the new Fijo de Puerto Rico Regiment; thereafter Cantabria served in Puerto Rico from 1790 to 1798. The 2nd Battalion of the metropolitan Toledo Regiment, part of which acted as marines on warships, was posted to Santo Domingo in 1781-82. In the latter year some 10,000 Spanish troops (Hibernia, Flandes, Aragon, 2nd Cataluna, Leon, Castillo de Campeche, Corona, Estramadura, Zamora, Soria, Guadalajara, Flandes, detachments of Santo Domingo and Havana, with artillery) gathered in various parts of the island for the intended invasion of Jamaica, but dispersed following the defeat of the French fleet at The Saints. The Leon Regiment remained at Guarico until 1783.

In Central America, elements of the Navarra and Hibernia regiments were in Honduras during 1782-83, while Corona was in Darien fighting local Indians. Units from Spain were also sent to Caracas and elsewhere in northern South America, but these postings must fall outside our study.

Up to the 1760s, the Spanish fought their European enemies largely in the Caribbean, but during the American War of Independence battles were fought mostly in Louisiana and Florida. By then, the Spanish metropolitan army

The provincial battalions of Pardos Libres of Puebla and Mexico City, organized in 1776 and 1777 respectively, both had the same uniform (at left). (Archivo General de la Nacion, Mexico City, courtesy of René Chartrand)

numbered some 89,000 men and the regular colonial troops overseas about 15,000 men. Disciplined militiamen in North America may have amounted to about another 25,000, most of them in New Spain (Mexico). The strategic aims decided by King Carlos III had been to drive the British out of Florida, the Gulf of Mexico, and the east bank of the Mississippi in North America, and, in

Colonial troops, Louisiana, 1769–1780s. Left: Private, Louisiana Regiment, c.1780. Center: Officer, St. Louis militia cavalry, 1779. Right: Officer, New Orleans militia battalion, c. 1780. Organized in 1770, the five city companies were formed into a battalion that included a grenadier company in 1775. (David Rickman © Osprey Publishing)

Europe, to retake Gibraltar and Minorca. Except for stubborn Gibraltar, all these objectives were successfully achieved by 1783.

The contribution of the French and the Spanish in terms of land warfare was significant, even critical, to the outcome of individual battles and even the entire war. Yet one of the greatest contributions these imperial powers made to the British defeat was actually at sea, a theater in which the Continental Americans were pitted against the most powerful navy on Earth.

CHAPTER 8

NAVAL FORCES

*T*HE MAIN NAVAL ENGAGEMENTS OF THE American Revolution were between France and Great Britain, although the Spanish fleet entered the fray in 1779, tipping the balance in France's favor. The Royal Navy spent most of the war period on the defensive, and the French Navy, though able to grapple with the Royal Navy, was unable to cripple the opposition decisively and bring the naval conflict to a close. The naval war was characterized by local victories, undermined by the failure of the commanders to capitalize on their successes. Only a few engagements influenced the land campaigns in any way, although the naval forces were instrumental in transporting and landing ground forces in North America, the West Indies, and India.

The most important, and militarily majestic, component of each navy was its ships of the line. The naval term "ship of the line" refers to a three-masted, square-rigged vessel carrying 60 or more cannon on board (the minimum firepower to be able to stand in the "line" of battle against an enemy.) Ships with fewer than 60 cannon were referred to as cruisers and frigates. First-rate ships carried 90–100 guns; second-rate usually fielded 80–90 guns; third-rate ships had 64–74 guns. Fourth-rate ships (frigates) usually carried 50 guns, and fifth- and sixth-rate ships (cruisers) carried 24–40 guns.

The Royal Navy's North American Squadron, under the command of Admiral Lord Howe, spent 1775–78 concentrating on three major naval efforts: supply and reinforcement of the British Army; blockade of the American coast; and raids on strategic points along the coastline. The entry of the French into the hostilities in 1778 committed the Royal Navy to a world war destined to stretch its resources very thin. The Royal Navy did not follow the strategy successfully employed in the Seven Years' War and attempt to blockade the French Navy in its chief ports of Toulon and Brest. Instead, efforts were principally focused on protecting the West Indies and British home waters, with smaller deployments in North America and the Indian Ocean. In 1778, there were 41 ships stationed in North America, and eight ships in the West Indies. By 1780, the numbers had been effectively reversed, with 13 ships in North America and 41 in the West Indies.

As with the British Army, the Royal Navy was not committed to a serious building program until the threat of French opposition became a reality. As of July 1, 1778, the Royal Navy stood as follows: 66 ships of the line: 30 in European waters, 14 in North America, 13 en route to North America, and the rest serving in or en route to Minorca and India. By 1782 the Royal Navy's strength had increased to 94 ships of the line, but did not outnumber the combined strength of the Spanish and French fleets, at 54 and 73 ships respectively.

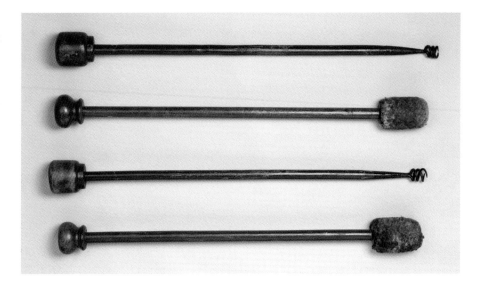

Here we see essential cannon tools. Top and 3rd down: Shot rammers with worm (screw) ends, the latter for extracting debris from the barrel; 2nd and 4th down: Barrel sponges, for swabbing out burning embers before reloading. (The Museum of the Revolution at Yorktown)

Tactics also remained largely unchanged; Royal Navy commanders had been given "Fighting Instructions" that tied them rigidly to "line-ahead" tactics. The line-ahead was similar to linear formations of the land armies. The idea was for a squadron to form in line and attack the enemy fleet with broadside fire along a continuous line, hoping for a break in the enemy's lines of ships. Many commanders did not follow this system, however, choosing instead to attempt the "mêlée." The mêlée, or penetration of the enemy's line of ships, was intended to inflict damage by more aggressive means. Some commanders were brought before court martial for deliberate use of the mêlée, but most were exonerated, reflecting the opinion of the courts martial that battle tactics should be decided by the commander at sea.

The French Navy had emerged from the Seven Years' War with a poor reputation and immediately set to work to reform the service. New ships were

A naval cannon priming horn, used to apply gunpowder to the cannon's priming pan and vent hole. (The Museum of the Revolution at Yorktown)

built, naval officers considered unfit to command were relieved of duty, naval artillery was improved, and, most important, training was established as a priority. Two major naval works devised and implemented were the *Tactique Nava* and *Les Manoeuvres*, both of which were considered to be superior to the British "Fighting Instructions." The absence of a Continental threat to France led to the decision to combat the Royal Navy on the high seas from the European theater to India and the West Indies. On July 1, 1778, the French Navy stood at 52 ships of the line; 32 ships were stationed in European waters, with 12 ships en route to North America and the rest in the Mediterranean and Indian oceans.

The Spanish fleet also played an important role in the war on the high seas. On July 1, 1779, the Spanish fleet stood at 58 ships of the line. The vast majority of the Spanish ships were stationed in European waters and Gibraltar, with smaller squadrons in the New World. The Spanish ships were very well designed and some naval historians consider them superior to both their French and British counterparts. Unfortunately, the Spanish Navy lacked a well-trained officer and ratings corps to man the ships, and neither the tactics nor the professionalism of the Spanish Navy was equivalent to those of the French and British.

In the fall of 1775, the Continental Congress authorized the construction of a small American fleet, consisting of only five ships. The Continental Navy and the recently-raised Continental Marines captured the Bahamas Islands from the British in 1776, marking the first combined American naval-marine operations. The Continental Navy was successful in raiding parts of Nova Scotia and even

Shortly after the alliance between France and the United States was concluded, France recognized the United States as an independent nation when the French Navy formally saluted the Continental sloop-of-war Ranger *in Quiberon Bay on February 14, 1778. (GL Archive/Alamy Stock Photo)*

parts of the British coast, but was never strong enough to cause real damage to the Royal Navy. The serious threat to the British came from the privateering activities of the Continental Navy and commercial fleets. Development of an American Navy ceased after the French joined the American effort.

The first significant engagement between the French and British navies took place on July 27, 1778, off the coast of Brittany. The British squadron, under the command of Admiral Lord Augustus Keppel, engaged a French squadron under the command of Admiral Comte d'Orvilliers. The French force was able to slip back to Brest. Both sides suffered damage but the battle decided nothing. The rest of the engagements recounted here were those considered locally decisive.

In January 1780, Admiral Sir George Brydges Rodney and a squadron of ships left Great Britain with provisions and stores for Gibraltar. On January 16, his squadron fought an engagement with a Spanish squadron under the command of Don Juan de Langara. One of the Spanish ships was destroyed and another six were captured. The Spanish squadron blockading Gibraltar was easily dispersed, and Rodney was able to lift the siege. Rodney and his squadron sailed for the West Indies, where they engaged a French squadron commanded by Comte de Guichen on April 17 and May 15, 1780. The French ships were damaged, but Rodney was unable to destroy the squadron completely, only to delay its landing in the West Indies. In September 1781, squadrons under the command of Rear Admiral Thomas Graves and Comte de Grasse met off Chesapeake Bay Capes. De Grasse had sailed from the West Indies with reinforcements for the French forces in North America and 24 ships of the line. He was able to land his troops unmolested. Admiral Graves sailed with 19 ships of the line, drawing from the West Indies and North American squadrons. The two squadrons engaged for more than two hours, with both sides suffering heavy damage. For the next two days each side watched the other warily, but following reports of a larger French squadron on the way, the British naval high command decided to withdraw to New York. This decision meant, incidentally, that British troops at Yorktown could not be reinforced, which sealed their fate. This is discussed in more detail later.

In April 1782, the main West Indies squadrons of the British and French navies met off the coast of Dominica and Guadeloupe. The French flotilla, under the command of de Grasse, had sailed for Jamaica with an invasion force of 10,000 troops. The British combined squadrons, under the command of Rodney and Rear Admiral Samuel Hood, chased de Grasse. During the engagement, Rodney was able to smash through the French lines with a mêlée attack. Five French ships were taken in the Battle of the Saintes, but Rodney failed to pursue the remainder of the French line. Admiral Hood criticized him for this action, but it did stave off the invasion of Jamaica and so is considered a decisive engagement.

The Royal Navy was uncontested in the East Indies between 1778 and 1781. The French admiralty did not wish to engage the Royal Navy until 1782. From then the British commander, Rear Admiral Sir Edward Hughes, engaged a French squadron under the command of Admiral Pierre-Andre Suffren de Saint-Tropez five times in two years. The French were victors in all the engagements, but like the Royal Navy they were unable to capitalize on their advantage. The British were therefore able to hold on to their gains in India and the Indian Ocean.

Building on this overview of the naval war, we now turn to explore the individual navies in more detail. First is the American navy, a strengthening David compared to the British Goliath.

BUILDING AN AMERICAN NAVY

The first American warships commissioned in the American Revolution predated the Continental Navy. George Washington had been given a general's commission and, in July 1774, command of the forces besieging the British garrison in Boston. Short of everything except problems, he decided that two of these problems his lack of supplies and the British surfeit of the same could best be solved using a naval force. He obtained and armed small sloops and schooners, manning them with soldiers recruited from American seaport communities.

The experiment proved a success. Washington's squadron of five warships was soon bringing in British prizes. Many of the vessels taken as they approached Boston were carrying supplies for the British garrison, and Washington was soon feeding, clothing, and arming the Continental Army using material from these captures. Before the squadron was disbanded in 1777, it contributed to the capture of Boston and also served to train many Continental Navy officers, including John Manley.

The colonies in rebellion were doing likewise. Starting with Rhode Island in June 1775 and Massachusetts in August, they began commissioning ships for state navies. Eventually, 11 of the 13 colonies had such navies. Only New Jersey and Delaware abstained. Some states, like Georgia, commissioned only small forces. Others, like South Carolina and Massachusetts, established state navies that rivaled the Continental Navy in size and strength. Initially these ships were purchased merchantmen, usually small sloops or schooners, such as the Rhode Island Navy's 12-gun sloop *Providence*, which was later transferred to the Continental Navy. Soon individual states were authorizing construction of warships up to frigate size. South Carolina even purchased the 40-gun *L'Indien* from France, renaming it *South Carolina*. By October 1775 it was becoming apparent that the Colonies needed a national navy. On October 13, 1775, the

Continental Congress authorized the purchase of two small warships, to be fitted out to search for British transports.

By the end of 1775, the Congress authorized the purchase of six additional ships, authorized construction of 13 frigates, and set about organizing a navy. On November 2, Congress also began developing an officer corps, which would be critical to leading the new navy. Esek Hopkins, brother of one of the naval commissioners and an old, experienced merchant captain, was named senior captain on November 5. Four other captains and 13 lieutenants were commissioned. The captains' list included Dudley Saltonstall, Abraham Whipple, Nicholas Biddle, and John Hopkins. Senior lieutenant on the list was the then-unknown John Paul Jones. Some of these men became famous; others notorious. On November 10, Congress created the Marine Corps, and by the end of November it issued a set of regulations governing the Navy. Drawn up by John Adams of Massachusetts, these rules borrowed heavily from Royal Navy regulations. By New Year's Day, 1776, the United States not yet an independent nation had a navy.

EARLY YEARS

The year 1776 proved to be the year of the purchased warship. It had to be construction of the authorized ships proceeded slowly. Even after launch, shortages of supplies and weapons delayed completion. Even once ships were fitted out, finding a crew delayed commissioning. Of the 13 frigates authorized, just two were commissioned before year's end, entering service in December. In January 1777, Hopkins received orders to raid New Providence in the Bahamas. The objective was to seize gunpowder stored at forts there—a commodity the Revolutionary cause needed. At that time the eight ships of the Continental Navy were icebound in Philadelphia harbor, but by February 17 the flotilla departed.

The raid was a partial success. On March 3, the American force successfully landed on New Providence, and took a major fort guarding the harbor, including a sizable number of guns. However, most of the powder had been spirited inland before capture, foiling that objective. After loading whatever stores they had captured, Hopkins' fleet departed, sailing back to the mainland on March 17. By April they reached the New England coast. They cruised in search of British ships, and on April 4 captured the six-gun schooner HMS *Hawk* off Rhode Island.

On April 6, the flotilla fell in with HMS *Glasgow*, a 20-gun sloop-of-war. The battle that followed highlighted all the weaknesses of the Continental Navy. Despite a clear superiority *Alfred* alone outgunned *Glasgow*, and had *Andrew*

Whether the ship was a small warship, like USS Lexington shown here, or a three-deck ship of the line, the hull dimensions had roughly the same ratio of length to breadth to draft. (Naval History & Heritage Command)

Doria, Cabot, Columbus, and three sloops in company—*Glasgow* escaped. The flotilla's attack was completely uncoordinated. Several American captains held back. The sloops got in the way of the aggressive ship commanders, keeping them from reaching *Glasgow*. Ships within range withdrew after taking minor casualties. The Continental Navy was still just a collection of armed ships—not a navy.

The flotilla arrived in New London, Connecticut, on April 8. Except for a few day cruises in April, it never sailed again as a unit. Individual ships were sent out cruising, with any success dependent upon the captain. *Providence*, under the newly promoted John Paul Jones, conducted an aggressive cruise against the Newfoundland fishery. *Alfred* under Nicholas Biddle (and later Jones) also had successful cruises. Despite numerous successes against British merchant vessels, however, even the successful cruises were little different from privateering. Furthermore, since privateering paid better, the Continental Navy experienced difficulties recruiting crews. Yet 1776 was a productive year. The navy had gained experience, and more importantly, learned which officers were good and bad. Men like Jones, Biddle, and Manley would play an important role in future events.

By year's end, the Continental Navy's popularity was high. Without losing a single ship, it had captured 60 vessels. Congress authorized more construction, and purchased six more ships three brigs and three sloops. It also sent representatives to Europe, seeking to purchase or build warships in European yards.

This European venture achieved mixed success. The American commissioners in Europe failed in a bid to purchase or borrow eight ships of the line from France. The French, still neutral but with one eye to the future, insisted that every French ship would be needed in any war against Britain. The commissioners did succeed, however, in having a 32-gun frigate, *Deane*, built at Nantes, purchased the 28-gun *Queen of France*, and made arrangements for the Dutch to build a 40-gun ship, *L'Indien*, for the United States. However, British diplomatic pressure forced *L'Indien*'s transfer to France, which eventually sold it to the South Carolina Navy.

By January 1777, the first new frigates were in commission. *Randolph* sailed for the first time in February, but this fruitless cruise ended in Charleston in March. There the ship remained until August, recruiting a crew. After another short cruise during which *Randolph* took a privateer and three other ships, it returned to Charleston, remaining there for the rest of the year. In May, *Hancock*, under John Manley, and *Boston*, commanded by Hector McNeill, sailed together from Boston, accompanied by nine privateers. Once at sea, the privateers scattered on individual cruises. *Boston* and *Hancock* encountered a British convoy, then on June 7 fell in with HMS *Fox*, a 28-gun frigate, which they took after a one-hour battle.

This good start was soon erased. In July, the three frigates encountered three British warships the 44-gun HMS *Rainbow*, the 32-gun HMS *Flora*, and the

The Continental Navy sloop Providence *began life as* Katy, *a vessel typical of the numerous merchant and commercial ships built in the American colonies prior to the Revolution. (Naval History & Heritage Command)*

ten-gun brig HMS *Victor*. As a group the Yankee force was a match for the British, but *Boston* fled, followed by *Fox*. *Flora* and *Victor* pursued and recaptured *Fox*. Manley, on *Hancock*, believing *Rainbow* to be a 64-gun vessel, also fled, but was overtaken by *Rainbow* after a long stern chase, and surrendered. McNeill was later court-martialed, and suspended from service. *Raleigh*, whose commissioning had been delayed due to a search for guns, sailed for France in August. In company with *Alfred*, it found a British convoy. However, a stout defense by the escort, the 20-gun *Druid*, drove off the Americans.

In October, the British moved against Philadelphia, the American capital. The enemy expedition proved disastrous to the Continental Navy. *Delaware* was captured at the onset of the invasion. *Andrew Doria* and five other small warships were trapped in the Delaware River and burned to prevent capture. The unfinished hulls of *Washington* and *Effingham* were towed up the Delaware and sunk near Bordentown, New Jersey.

Other losses in 1777 included *Cabot*, taken by HMS *Milford* (32 guns) in March; *Reprisal*, lost at sea in October; and *Montgomery* and *Congress*, the two New York frigates, which were burned on the stocks in October when British forces advanced towards their building yard.

At the end of 1777, the Continental Navy had nine frigates, three shiprigged sloops-of-war, and four smaller ships. The sloops-of-war included the 18-gun *Ranger*, authorized in 1776 and ready for sea by November 1777. More importantly

Alfred was the first flagship of the Continental Navy. It is shown here at Philadelphia in December 1775. (Naval History & Heritage Command)

for the navy, the US gained a powerful European ally in 1778. The American victory at Saratoga had convinced France that the Americans had staying power. France had been providing covert aid to the United States and agreed to enter the war as an active participant, effective February 5, 1778. The war had changed from a local insurrection to a global conflict.

THE FRENCH ALLIANCE

Raleigh and *Alfred*, which had sailed to France in 1777, left from there together on December 29, 1777. In the mid-Atlantic en route to the West Indies they encountered British merchantmen escorted by HMS *Ariadne* (20 guns) and HMS *Ceres* (16 guns). In a mismanaged action, *Alfred* tackled *Ariadne* without waiting for *Raleigh*, then fled but was quickly captured. *Raleigh* also fled after witnessing *Alfred*'s capture, despite having a heavier broadside than both British ships. *Raleigh*'s captain was later relieved of his command.

Meanwhile, *Randolph* sailed for the West Indies as part of a flotilla containing a South Carolina Navy ship and three South Carolina privateers. On March 7, 1778, near Barbados, the flotilla encountered the 64-gun HMS *Yarmouth*. *Yarmouth* ran down the Yankee ships by nightfall. *Randolph*, commanded by Nicholas Biddle, attacked, ineffectually supported by only one of its companions which accidentally fired into *Randolph*, wounding Biddle. Biddle's furious attack took

The poop was the highest deck in a warship, on the after end of the quarterdeck. It was usually too light to take the weight of long guns although it offered Marines an elevated platform from which to fire their muskets. (Mark Lardas)

Yarmouth aback, but as *Randolph* attempted to wear around *Yarmouth*'s stern, the American ship exploded. Only four of its crew survived. The rest of the American squadron scattered. On March 31, *Virginia*, commanded by James Nicholson, joined the ranks of former Continental ships. Sailing from Annapolis, Maryland, where *Virginia* had been blockaded for nearly a year, the ship promptly ran onto a shoal. Found still aground the next morning by two British warships, it was forced to surrender, and later taken into the Royal Navy as a 32-gun frigate. Better luck attended the Continental Navy in European waters. *Ranger*, commanded by John Paul Jones, reached France in December 1777. After refitting, Jones left Brest on April 10, 1778. In just 28 days, he conducted a cruise that made his reputation. Sailing into the Irish Sea, Jones captured several merchant vessels, led two raids on British soil, and fought and captured the 20-gun HMS *Drake*. While the victory over *Drake* was minor, the two raids resulted in panic in Britain and a reallocation of military resources to prevent future raids.

Back in the United States, *Washington* and *Effingham* had been refloated during the spring of 1778, and were being refitted under the command of Thomas Read and John Barry. They were trapped, with the British between the American frigates and the sea. When the British pushed up the Delaware, the frigates were stripped of their crews, who were sent under Barry's command to harass the British. Barry had some success, but the British forced their way upriver, and on May 7 both frigates were burned to prevent their capture. Barry was sent to Boston, where he took command of *Raleigh* on May 30. The aggressive Barry suffered the delays usual to outfitting a Continental Navy ship, finally sailing on September 25. The next day *Raleigh* encountered the British warships HMS *Experiment*, a 50-gun two-decker, and HMS *Unicorn*, a 22-gun sloop-of-war. A 60-hour chase ensued which ended with *Raleigh* trapped against the Maine coast. After an eight-hour night-time battle, Barry ran *Raleigh* aground and took its crew ashore to prevent capture. The British pulled the American frigate off the rocks before Barry could send a crew back to burn it. Barry and his crew walked back to Boston.

Boston had sailed for France in February and arrived on March 31, carrying a diplomatic contingent including John Adams. After refitting, *Boston* made some short European cruises during which it captured a few ships. It was joined in June by the frigate *Providence*, which had slipped through the British blockade of Narragansett Bay. On August 22, the two frigates, along with *Ranger*, now commanded by Thomas Simpson, sailed to Portsmouth, New Hampshire. (Jones had been detached from *Ranger* and promised *L'Indien*.) By the end of 1778, the Continental Navy was down to six frigates, two sloops-of-war, and one sloop. Two new frigates would appear in 1779, as well as a few more purchased ships, but the arrival of a French fleet in American waters in the summer of 1778 reduced the need for the Continental Navy. The new year, 1779, opened with a series of minor cruises by the frigates in American waters. They captured a number of British merchant vessels, without loss to the Continental Navy. However, the navy was finding it increasingly difficult to recruit sailors, mainly due to competition with privateers.

In July an expedition consisting of *Warren*, the sloop *Providence*, the Continental brig *Diligent* (captured from the British earlier in 1779, and purchased as a warship), three ships from the Massachusetts Navy, one from New Hampshire's navy, and 12 privateers were sent to Penobscot Bay to capture a British base. Arriving July 25, the American fleet under the indecisive command of Dudley Saltonstall spent several days sparring with three small British warships, before settling in for a siege. While the Americans dithered, the Royal Navy took action, sending a 64-gun ship of the line, three large frigates, and three sloops-of-war. The American flotilla trapped in Penobscot Bay was captured by the British or destroyed by the Americans to prevent capture. *Warren*, *Providence*, and *Diligent* were burned.

Across the Atlantic, John Paul Jones took a squadron to sea from France on August 14, 1779. This consisted of *Bonhomme Richard*, *Alliance*, *Pallas*, *Cerf*, *Vengeance*, and two French privateers. *Bonhomme Richard* was Jones's poor reward for victory over *Drake*. A superannuated East Indiaman, it was slow and decrepit. Jones had never received the promised *L'Indien*. Having spent almost a year ashore by the time he was offered *Bonhomme Richard*, Jones accepted. *Alliance* was a fine new American frigate which sailed to France in January 1779. It was commanded by Pierre Landais: a former French naval officer, given command of *Alliance* as a mark of gratitude for the French alliance. Landais, however, was decidedly eccentric, possibly even insane. The final three vessels were French warships "loaned" to the United States. While flagged as American warships, they had French officers and crews.

The cruise proved as important as Jones's 1778 *Ranger* expedition, and as frustrating as it was important. The privateers left almost immediately, the American-flagged French warships came and went as they pleased, and Landais, with *Alliance*, proved mutinously insubordinate. Regardless, Jones sailed around the British Isles into the North Sea, capturing ships along the way. On September 21, off Flamborough Head, they encountered a British Baltic convoy escorted by HMS *Serapis* (44 guns) and HMS *Countess of Scarborough* (22 guns).

Jones in *Bonhomme Richard* still had *Alliance* and *Pallas* in company. *Bonhomme Richard* went straight for *Serapis*. *Pallas* swept down on *Countess of Scarborough* and took it after a long fight. *Alliance* remained disengaged, cruising between the

convoy and the battling *Bonhomme Richard* and *Serapis*. A battle it was. The latter two ships blazed away yardarm to yardarm for most of the night. Casualties were heavy on both sides. One of *Bonhomme Richard*'s 18-pdrs overheated and exploded. *Serapis* suffered heavy quarterdeck casualties when a grenade lobbed by an American marine exploded in an arms chest. *Bonhomme Richard* began sinking. *Serapis*'s captain, Richard Pearson, called on Jones to surrender. Jones curtly refused, pressing the fight.

Then *Alliance* intervened, firing several broadsides into *Bonhomme Richard*. Landais hoped to sink *Bonhomme Richard* and then take *Serapis* himself. Jones continued fighting. Pearson, unaware of Landais' target, surrendered *Serapis* to Jones. *Bonhomme Richard* sank that night, after Jones had transferred his survivors to *Serapis*. Jones took *Serapis* into the neutral Dutch island of Texel, where it was interned. The convoy escaped the Americans due to its escorts' stout defense, and Pearson was afterwards knighted. Jones was given *Alliance*, but Landais stole it, sailing it to America. The battle of Flamborough Head proved to be the high point for the Continental Navy during the American Revolution. By cementing first French, then Dutch and Spanish intervention in the war, it obviated the necessity for an independent American navy. The United States' maritime needs could be served by its European allies.

HMS *SERAPIS*

Serapis was one of 19 Roebuck-class 44-gun two-deckers ordered and built during the American Revolutionary Wars. Based on a 1769 design by Sir Thomas Slade, these ships were low-draft ships intended for use on the shallow North and Baltic Seas and for coastal defense. *Serapis* had only a brief career with the Royal Navy, as it had been in commission less than six months prior to the battle of Flamborough Head, when it was captured. At the time—as intended by its design—it was escorting a Baltic convoy, returning to London. Following its capture by the Continental Navy, diplomatic efforts by Britain led to its transfer to the French Navy. Recommissioned, it was sent to reinforce French naval forces in India. In July 1781, while off Madagascar en route to India, an overturned lantern in the spirit room started a fire that destroyed the ship. (Peter Bull © Osprey Publishing)

No further construction was authorized after 1777, and construction of previously authorized ships slowed. By 1778, with three exceptions, all of the ships previously authorized that would be completed had not only been laid down, but had been launched. Only the ship of the line *America*, laid down in May 1777, still awaited completion. Just two other ships would be started, the frigate *Bourbon* and the sloop-of-war *Saratoga*, both laid down in 1779. Of these, *Bourbon* would languish unfinished on the stocks until after the war's end.

The Continental Navy did not go away: it evaporated. Existing ships were captured or sunk by the Royal Navy. Commodore Whipple's squadron, consisting of *Providence*, *Boston*, *Queen of France*, and *Ranger*, was sent to Charleston in December, 1779. All four, along with many privateers and ships of the South Carolina Navy, were lost when the British took Charleston that spring. In 1781, *Trumbull*, *Confederacy*, and *Saratoga* were lost.

The gun deck of the USS Warren, one of the new Continental frigates launched in 1776. The ship was armed with 12-pdr and 18-pdr guns. (Tony Bryan © Osprey Publishing)

IN CONGRESS.

The DELEGATES *of the* UNITED COLONIES *of* New-Hampshire, Massachusetts Bay, Rhode-Island, Connecticut, New-York, New-Jersey, Pennsylvania, *the Counties of* New-Castle, Kent, *and* Suffex *on* Delaware, Maryland, Virginia, North-Carolina, South-Carolina, *and* Georgia, *to,*

Abraham Whipple Esquire

WE reposing especial Trust and Confidence in your Patriotism, Valour, Conduct and Fidelity, DO by these Presents, constitute and appoint you to be *Captain* of the Armed *Ship* called the *Columbus* in the service of the Thirteen United Colonies of North-America, fitted out for the defence of American Liberty, and for repelling every hostile Invasion thereof. You are therefore carefully and diligently to discharge the Duty of *Captain* by doing and performing all Manner of Things thereto belonging. And we do strictly charge and require all Officers, Marines and Seamen under your Command, to be obedient to your Orders as *Captain* And you are to observe and follow such Orders and Directions from Time to Time, as you shall receive from this or a future Congress of the United Colonies, or Committee of Congress, for that Purpose appointed, or Commander in Chief for the Time being of the Navy of the United Colonies, or any other your superior Officer, according to the Rules and Discipline of War, the Usage of the Sea, and the Instructions herewith given you, in Pursuance of the Trust reposed in you. This Commission to continue in Force untill revoked by this or a future Congress. *Philadelphia December &c.*

By Order of the Congress

John Hancock PRESIDANT.

Attest. *Cha Thomson secy*

Abraham Whipple's Continental Navy commission. Whipple rose to the rank of commodore in the Continental Navy, and was the last captain of the frigate Providence. (Naval History & Heritage Command)

The frigates were captured while cruising, and *Saratoga* sank in a storm. Ironically, Trumbull was captured by HMS *Isis* and HMS *General Monk*, both former American warships that had themselves been previously captured. By the end of 1781 the Continental Navy consisted of only two frigates.

Yet American victory was gained by seapower French seapower. In 1781, a French fleet sent to North America succeeded in blockading a British army trapped in Yorktown. On September 5, 1781, a great battle was fought off the mouth of the Chesapeake. It ended indecisively but allowed the French to continue their blockade of Yorktown; the British in Yorktown, the last field force available to Britain, surrendered, effectively ending the land phase of the American War of Independence.

Peace negotiations dragged on for two more years, however, and the naval war continued until peace was signed in 1783. The Continental Navy gained two sloops-of-war via purchase in 1782: *General Washington* (formerly *General Monk*), and *Duc du Lauzan*. While these saw some action, they were obtained primarily to give the Continental Navy a means of transporting negotiators to and from Europe.

AFTERMATH

The war's end removed any immediate need for a United States Navy—not that there was much of the Continental Navy left by that point. Only the frigates *Alliance* and *Deane* and sloops-of-war *General Washington* and *Duc du Lauzan*

Royal Navy attempts to relieve Conwallis's force at Yorktown were checked by the French Navy in a battle off the Virginia Capes, on September 5, 1788. (Granger, NYC/Topfoto.co.uk)

were still in commission. A frigate, *Bourbon*, and the ship of the line *America* were awaiting completion. The United States had gained its independence but was deeply in debt. Keeping warships in commission was expensive, but the new nation could not even afford the lesser expense of maintaining the hulls in reserve.

Consequently, the remaining ships were disposed of. *America* was given to the French, *Bourbon* was launched in 1783 to clear the building ways and immediately sold, and *Deane*, *General Washington*, and *Duc du Lauzan* were sold soon after. Finally, in 1785 *Alliance* was sold and the navy dissolved. The officers, too, scattered. Some returned home. Most returned to prewar careers in the merchant service. A few, having acquired a taste for naval rather than mercantile service, became mercenaries. Joshua Barney, bored with peace, provided his services to Revolutionary France, at one point commanding a ship of the line before returning to the United States when that nation reconstituted its navy. John Paul Jones served briefly as an admiral in the Imperial Russian Navy, then went to France. He, too, sought a position as an officer in the navy of Revolutionary France but died before serving. Britain likewise disposed of all the prizes it had taken from the Continental Navy by 1783, following a peace settlement with its European foes. Only *Hancock*, renamed *Iris*, remained as part of the French Navy. By the time the French Revolution initiated a new round of naval conflict only three ships of the Continental Navy were still afloat—*Delaware* and *Alliance* in merchant service, and *Iris* as a powder hulk in the French Mediterranean naval base of Toulon.

In 1793 *Iris* had a last brush with history. *Toulon* had been taken by Royalist forces, then occupied by the British and Spanish. However, a Republican artillery officer, one Napoleon Bonaparte, forced these intruders out of the port. Set afire during the evacuation of Toulon, *Iris* exploded, defeating British efforts to scuttle the French Mediterranean fleet. The following year, *Delaware*, fitted out as a privateer by the French, sank in a storm. *Alliance* foundered in 1800.

Despite all this, the Continental Navy's contribution was not purely ephemeral. The format of 38 guns with main battery of 18lb long guns became the standard for frigates for the rest of the Age of Fighting Sail a change prompted by Continental

Of all of the ships of the Continental Navy, few had as much impact as USS Hancock. *It was never a lucky ship, having the distinction of being the only ship built for the Continental Navy that served in three navies (Continental, British, and French), with its transfer each time attendant on defeat in battle. (Tony Bryan © Osprey Publishing)*

frigates such as *Warren* and *Alliance*. Many Continental Navy officers, including John Barry, Joshua Barney, Stephen Decatur Senior, and Edward Preble became officers in the new United States Navy when it was reconstituted in 1798.

BRITAIN AND FRANCE

For the Royal Navy, then the world's greatest and most venerable navy, the onset of the War of Independence initially placed only a limited draw on its resources. Some Royal Navy assets were required to protect communications and move supplies, but again, ships large enough to stand in the line of battle were not required. Indeed, the two-decker was an ideal ship for the navy's responsibilities between 1775 and 1778, leading to a revival of that class by the Royal Navy.

Everything changed following Saratoga. Britain had decisively defeated France in the Seven Years' War of 1756 to 1763 following a set of brilliant naval victories and amphibious landings. France wanted to avenge this humiliating defeat. France saw British preoccupation in North America as an opportunity to regain some of the earlier losses, especially when Saratoga showed that the rebelling colonials had staying power. France signed a treaty of alliance with the United States in February 1778; the rebellion in North America was now a major war that would be fought globally.

Having European involvement changed the naval war. European allies provided the United States with a base close to their enemy's home. Continental warships and privateers could openly operate out of France. It also brought them a source of supply for both their armies and their naval forces, albeit a generally parsimonious source. For Britain, the situation became dire.

From March 1778 onward Britain was fighting for its own survival as much as it was fighting to retain its rebelling North American colonies. France had a formidable navy. It had spent much of the 1760s and early 1770s building up its navy, reforming naval administration, and replacing the ships lost during the Seven Years' War. When France mobilized its fleet, Britain did likewise, and focused its attention on the French threat across the narrow Channel. Soon both nations

"Great" or "long" gun. After this weapon was discharged, it recoiled inboard, with ropes restraining the ordnance to prevent it from moving out of control. (Science & Society Picture Library/Getty Images)

The Battle of the Kegs', 6 January 1778 Kegs filled with gunpowder float down the Delaware River near Philadelphia in an attempt to explode British ships. (Granger, NYC/Topfoto.co.uk)

had large fleets of ships of the line facing each other. Initially each navy had a fleet only in the Channel, but both nations dispatched fleets to the Caribbean, the Mediterranean, and eventually the East Indies, either to gain an advantage in those theaters or in response to the other nation's threat. Britain was also faced with the task of expanding, outfitting, and supplying its fleet. The need for expansion would become more critical in April 1779, when Spain also declared war on Britain.

The frigate action between the French Belle Poule *and British* Arethusa *in July 1778 marked the opening of active hostilities between Great Britain and France. (Mark Lardas)*

In the 1770s and 1780s Britain was largely self-sufficient. It had one of the world's largest iron industries, allowing the British to manufacture the artillery and iron fittings required for their navy. They still possessed sufficient oak to build warships. Local sources of pine were nearing exhaustion, however. Pine provided masts used for propulsion, as well as turpentine and pitch, used to waterproof wooden ships. Furthermore, the Royal Navy's need for new masts was exacerbated because the supply of masts had been allowed to dwindle following the Seven Years' War as an economy measure.

Prior to the American Revolution, the Royal Navy's major sources of pine lay in Britain's North American colonies, particularly those in New England, the heart of the rebellion. Their Canadian colonies, gained during the Seven Years' War, provided an alternative source of these naval stores, but at the time of the American Revolution these had not been developed. With France allied against Britain, the remaining sources of masts, pitch, turpentine, and other naval stores lay in the Baltic states: Sweden, Denmark, and Russia.

To assure delivery of these critical strategic materials, British merchantmen sailing to and from the Baltic sailed in convoy. Royal Navy warships escorted these convoys to protect them from enemy warships and privateers. As Britain could not afford to weaken its line of battle in the face of the French naval threat and needed its frigates for fleet scouting, these convoys were usually escorted by two-deckers and sloops-of-war.

In France, when Choiseul took the naval portfolio in 1761, there was hardly a navy left. The stores were empty, there was no money, the few ships of the line existing were abandoned in ports, sailors were scarce, officers were dispirited,

A naval engagement, 1779, showing the close promixity of the ships when at fighting distance. (Granger Historical Picture Archive/Alamy Stock Photo)

NAVAL CLOSE-QUARTERS WEAPONS

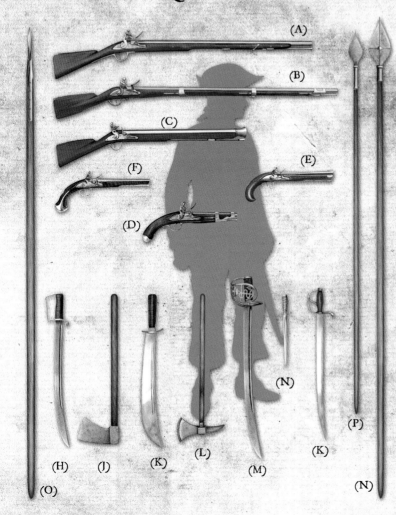

Because naval artillery of the sailing era rarely sank ships, most battles were ultimately decided by hand-to-hand combat, with the crew of one ship boarding a second in an attempt to take possession of it. Additionally, the range at which the artillery duel was conducted was often within range of the smoothbore muskets of the era. To supplement the efforts of the great guns ships would place musket-armed marksmen in the fighting tops and on the upper works. These men focused their fire on officers and gun crews, to reduce the fighting efficiency of their opponents. The weapons used by the crews included: long arms used by marksmen—(a) British Sea Service Brown Bess musket, (b) French Sea Service Charleville musket, (c) French blunderbuss; pistols issued to boarders and officers— (d) French pistol, (e) Dutch pistol, (f) British pistol; and a wide assortment of edged weapons— (g) French naval cutlass, (h) British naval cutlass, (i) French boarding axe, (j) British boarding axe, (k) French naval sword, (l) British naval sword, (m) British naval dirk, (n) French boarding pike, (o) British boarding pike, (p) French half-pike. Commissioned officers were armed with swords and pistols, midshipmen substituting a dirk for the sword, while sailors would either carry a pike or a pistol with a cutlass or boarding axe, depending upon the individual sailor's preference. Marines fought with muskets with fixed bayonets. As the pistols and muskets of the era were single-shot weapon that took time to reload, boarders carrying firearms also needed an edged weapon. (Giuseppe Rava © Osprey Publishing)

The Royal Dockyard at Deptford at the start of the American Revolution. Extensive shore facilities enabled the Royal Navy to keep its large fleet at sea. (Library of Congress)

and remnants of marines and colonial troops repatriated from fallen colonies hovered about the seaports. The duke incorporated the sea-soldiers into the line infantry at the end of 1761; then went to work on a naval program assisted by Admiral Truguet which called for a fleet of 80 ships of the line and 47 frigates. Choiseul appealed to the public for money to help. The response from the humiliated nation, which sensed the importance of naval power, was enthusiastic. The province of Languedoc contributed first in 1762 to build an 80-gun ship, an example followed by Brittany, Burgundy, Artois, Flanders; by cities such as Bordeaux, Paris, Marseilles; and by groups of financiers and individual subscriptions sponsoring mostly 74-gun ships.

While construction was under way, the first great naval regulation since 1689 was signed on March 25, 1765. Incapable officers were retired, training became a high priority, and naval artillery was improved. The navy became an independent ministry again in 1766. As in the army, the successors of Choiseul followed his lead, the most talented and energetic being Gabriel de Sartines, minister from 1774, and Marsja de Castries from 1780. As noted, by 1778 some 52 ships of the line were afloat, and this grew to 73 by 1782.

From late 1762 the duties of sea-soldiers were assigned to army regiments with debatable success; in 1769 some marine "brigades" were raised, which became regiments in 1772, but the regimental organization did not work too well. On December 26, 1774, de Sartines reorganized the whole force into 100 companies of a *Corps royal d'infanterie de la Marine*, and the elite artillerymen into three companies of *Bombardiers de la Marine*. It had an establishment of 12,248 officers and men.

These troops provided excellent services during the war; but there was a considerable shortage of marines which could only be compensated by using thousands of army soldiers—mostly volunteers—as marine detachments. There was a reorganization with an increased establishment in 1782, but this does not seem to have been carried into effect before the end of hostilities. The navy also had a coast guard militia, which was reorganized on December 13, 1778, as independent companies of coast guard artillery, which were partly activated during the war.

The reverses suffered by Great Britain during the American War of Independence were directly related to the fact that the French navy managed to keep the Royal Navy at bay. The lines of communication with America and Asia were kept open and the British put on the defensive. In this the French were helped by the Spanish from 1779, and the Dutch to a lesser extent from 1780. But without the French navy the chances of success against the world's most powerful fleet were unthinkable.

The Netherlands had one of the four top-tier navies in the 1770s and 1780s. Dutch ships, including this frigate (c.1781), tended to have shallower drafts than ships of the other major European Continental navies. (USNA)

The French Navy off Newport, Rhode Island, in 1778.
The entry of France as an American ally transformed the Revolution into a global war, which reduced the need for a Continental Navy. The French fleet provided the seapower badly needed by the United States. (Library of Congress)

Flogging. Discipline aboard ship was harsh, with sometimes dozens of lashes with a cat-o'-nine-tails administered for drunkenness, sleeping on duty, brawling, and other infractions. (Universal History Archive / Getty Images)

French admirals did fairly well on the whole: Admiral de Grasse's victory at Chesapeake Bay sealed the fate of the British army trapped in Yorktown in 1781. De Grasse lost the Battle of the Saints and was captured by Admiral Rodney in April 1782, an event that prevented a Franco-Spanish assault on Jamaica and not much else. The British press of the time (and historians since) made much of this battle; but while it did check the French, it certainly did not vanquish them, or their Spanish allies. And in the Indian Ocean, Admiral Suffren, a brilliant naval tactician, kept the Royal Navy on the defensive.

THE MEN

In the 18th century, a full-rigged warship—whether a ship of the line, a two-decker, or a frigate—was one of the world's most complicated machines. Nothing else had as many interconnected, moving parts, all of which had to be used properly, with a complex set of actions. (In the analysis below, we will focus mainly on exploring the lives and skills of British and American naval personnel, which shared a high degree of commonality.)

There was a role for the unskilled on a warship. Perhaps half of the activities on a ship could be done by them—hauling the lines to run guns in and out, pushing on capstan bars to raise anchor, or heaving on rigging lines while on deck. All of these tasks required supervision, from someone in the know: an experienced sailor. Although everything was operated by muscle power, brute strength alone was insufficient.

An experienced sailor "knew the ropes" (understood the ship's rigging) and could set, furl, and shorten a ship's sails, and operate the ship's rudder—whether using a tiller, or, as on a two-decker, a ship's wheel. Men who could do that were said to be able to handle, reef, and steer. They were prized by a ship's captain, regardless of nationality or whether the captain commanded a warship or a merchant vessel.

The most skilled seamen were the topmen, those who worked aloft in the rigging. They did some of the most necessary and dangerous work on a sailing ship, manipulating the sails, spars, and upper masts, while anywhere from 50ft (15m) to several hundred feet above the deck. It was a young man's game. Topmen were often in their teens, and light, small men were preferred. Each mast's activities would be directed by the "captain of the top," an enlisted sailor, typically in his twenties. Older sailors usually worked on the deck, doing skilled work or supervising the unskilled.

While the life of a sailor of that time is considered hard today, it was not hard by the standards of the 18th-century working man. The work was physically demanding, but sailors, unlike laborers, were aided by machinery. The pay was generally better than a man could get ashore, and a sailor had a place to sleep and regular meals. Despite the wretched reputation of seagoing rations, sailors generally ate better than laborers or farmhands of the era, getting meat regularly, as well as a generous quantity of other food. It might be monotonous, but sailors rarely starved.

It was extremely dangerous. The hazards of the sea offered the greatest peril to a sailor, greater even than combat. Storms and shipwreck destroyed more ships and killed more men than combat, even during major wars. Disease took an even greater toll. While scurvy had finally been conquered in the decades prior to the American Revolution, epidemic diseases had not. Typhus, yellow fever, and other tropical diseases killed more sailors than combat or the hazards of the sea combined. However, in the second half of the 18th century, the life of a naval sailor was easier than that of a merchant sailor. Warships had large crews, allowing work to be distributed among more men. Navy discipline was less harsh than it would become during the Napoleonic era. Navies, including the Royal Navy, granted sailors shore leave, sometimes for extended periods.

Heaving the line, one of the innumerable tasks performed by sailors in the operation of a ship. (© Look and Learn/ Valerie Jackson Harris Collection/Bridgeman Images)

A sailor from the American colonies. While native-born Americans were always the largest fraction of the crew of Continental warships, sailors born in Britain and Ireland also formed large parts of Continental warship crews. (Mark Lardas)

While the Royal Navy sometimes used impressment a form of seagoing conscription most manpower needs were satisfied by volunteers except during major wars, when the navy expanded to the largest size possible. Even in the opening stages of the American Revolutionary War, most Royal Navy sailors were volunteers. It was only after French entry into the war that impressed sailors began to outnumber volunteers. In the revolutionary Continental Navy crews were all-volunteer, primarily because the Continental Navy had no means of enforcing conscription. During this period, men technically did not join the navy. Sailors joined ships. A sailor signed on to a ship's company for the length of a cruise. If the ship was a warship whether of the Continental or the Royal Navy the sailor was in the navy, but his enlistment lasted only as long as a ship was in commission. When the ship paid off at the end of the cruise—or the moment a ship was wrecked or captured in combat—that sailor became a free agent, outside the navy.

All navies tended to draw sailors from the same pool of mariners, regardless of nationality, especially since a sailor's allegiance then tended to lie with his ship rather than the nation of his birth. This was especially true of the Royal Navy and Continental Navy, which shared a common language, and for whom national allegiance tended to be due more to personal choice than to birth. Many born in Britain preferred to think of themselves as American, while many in the rebelling colonies chose fidelity to the Crown.

Sailors who showed aptitude in a required skill—carpentry, sail-making, navigation, or gunnery—could advance into the ranks of petty officers as a mate. A sailor who was skilled in shipboard carpentry could become a carpenter's mate, one with ability in shiphandling and navigation a master's mate, and those skilled in making and maintaining barrels could become cooper's mates. (The latter was a critical skill on a ship where food and water was stored in barrels.) Petty officers were appointed by a ship's commissioned officers.

The next step for an enlisted sailor was to become a warrant officer, who was in charge of some specialist aspect of the ship's operation. These included the ship's carpenter, cooper, and armorer, and the boatswain, in charge of the ship's rigging. The most senior warrant officer was the master, who was in charge of a ship's navigation and treated with the dignity accorded a commissioned officer. Other warrant ranks included the surgeon, purser (responsible for a ship's finances), and chaplain. These

244   IMPROBABLE VICTORY

warrants, along with the master, dined with the officers. The term "warrant rank" came from the warrants issued by the naval board to those holding these positions. In the Royal Navy, the senior warrants remained with a ship to look after it even when it was laid up out of commission.

THE OFFICERS

The ships of both the Continental and Royal navies were led by commissioned officers. These officers were responsible for directing a ship's operation and leading it in battle. These men held office through a commission issued to them by the government. In the Royal Navy, the commission was issued by the Board of the Admiralty, the governmental department that ran the Royal Navy. In the Continental Navy, it was issued by the Continental Congress. Both navies used a similar structure for their officer corps and drew their officers from similar strata of society. At least in part, this was due to the Continental Congress drawing on the Royal Navy as an example when it created its navy.

The lowest-ranking officers aboard a warship, the midshipmen, were officer trainees. Both navies wanted capable officers and created a flexible path to the quarterdeck. Royal Navy officers began as volunteers, typically at ages as young as 12 or 13. These boys were carried on the books as captain's servants but spent their time learning the basics of seamanship, navigation, and leadership. Most of these candidates gained their appointments through influence: they or their parents knew someone commanding a king's ship, who gave them the position.

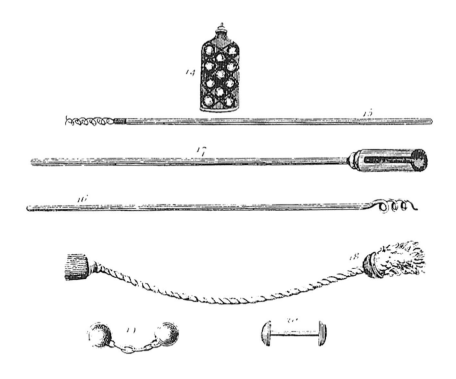

Gun tools and ammunition, showing, from top to bottom: case shot, a scouring worm, a ladle, a worm, a flexible rammer and sponge, chain shot, and bar shot. (Angus Konstam)

Midshipmen during this period were also drawn from promising members of a ship's crew as well as the gentry more usually associated with the Royal Navy officer corps. Competence was more valued than birth, as capable watch officers were critical to a ship's safety. A captain could sleep better with low-born but competent men running the watch, rather than incompetent relatives. In short, survival trumped nepotism, and as a result, the Royal Navy offered British society a degree of social mobility.

In the Continental Navy, midshipmen were appointed by Congress, although captains could fill vacancies. A midshipman who demonstrated competence could ascend the next step in the ladder of command—the rank of lieutenant, the lowest commissioned rank. In the Royal Navy, a midshipman could not be commissioned until he had accumulated six years' service and had passed an examination before a board of captains. The Continental Navy lacked both requirements, with Congress issuing commissions based on personal recommendations from those believed knowledgeable: a process that occasionally misfired.

A two-decker had between three and five lieutenants. These men were responsible for running the ship. Lieutenants had to understand all aspects of a ship's operations—sail handling, seamanship, gunnery, and navigation—to do their job effectively. Good lieutenants could do these tasks as well as the seamen that normally did them. An incompetent or lazy lieutenant could endanger a ship's safety, often by failing to recognize hazards or by ordering an improper action. This placed a premium on experience, and a ship's lieutenants were ranked by seniority, from the most senior (the first lieutenant) to the most junior (fourth or fifth lieutenant), based on the date of their commission.

One lieutenant, the watch officer, took charge of running the ship, acting for the ship's captain. In combat, the first lieutenant filled this role, but otherwise the junior lieutenants rotated as watch officer, taking the deck for four- or two-hour shifts. Crews were divided into two or three watches, which were further subdivided into divisions; each junior lieutenant was responsible for one of these divisions, in charge of welfare and training for the men of his division. In addition, the first lieutenant was in charge of ship's discipline and supervised the more junior lieutenants. In combat, the junior lieutenants commanded the guns, generally with one on each gun deck, while the first lieutenant acted as the captain's deputy. The most junior lieutenant was generally given responsibility for seeing that signals were sent properly, although if a ship

THE MARINES

Naval combat of the era was fought at close quarters. As a result warships carried marines to assist. They were stationed in a ship's fighting tops, the platforms where the top of the lower mast met the bottom of the topmast, or along a ship's bulwarks, particularly along the quarterdeck.

In close combat, marines fought hand-to-hand, either to defend their ship, or take the enemy's. Marines formed the core of the boarding parties, and any landing parties, if a ship's crew were committed to an action on land. They handled lines on the deck, and worked the great guns, but were not used aloft to handle the sails. Marines also provided shipboard security, and were used to maintain shipboard discipline. Marine sentries guarded the magazines, arms, and spirit room. Marines were posted at hatches during battle to prevent sailors from seeking refuge in the hold.

Marines were drawn from a different pool of men than sailors, and enlisted in a unit rather than on a ship. Some rivalry between marines and sailors was fostered by ships' officers, as one function of the marines was to put down mutiny, and it was feared that if the two groups became too friendly, they might be unwilling to do so. Marines messed and slept between the officers (who lived aft) and the sailors (who were berthed forward) to provide distance between officers and the crew. The marines, as soldiers, wore uniforms, while sailors of the era did not.

Admirals and captains regarded gunnery more as an art than a science, and hence paid little attention to the study of ballistics. What mattered to them, as well as to warrant officer gunners, was that a gun crew could perform their drill as quickly and as efficiently as possible. (Philip Haythornthwaite)

were short of lieutenants, this task would be assigned to a senior midshipman. A lieutenant could also command a small warship, those mounting 22 or fewer guns. In that role, the lieutenant served as captain, and was called "captain" or "commander" (from lieutenant-commanding) while in this role. The modern ranks of commander and lieutenant-commander did not then exist, and these were courtesy titles.

Any ship larger than 24 guns was commanded by the next rank up the chain of command, that of full captain. To reach that rank, an officer had to distinguish himself in some way that marked him as superior to the other lieutenants. Distinguishing oneself in combat or an emergency was one way to do this. The first lieutenant of a warship winning a notable battle was often promoted to captain. Being the most competent lieutenant available when a vacancy for a captain existed was another way of achieving promotion to captain. Given the death rate in naval service, this offered frequent opportunities for promotion, although it required the favor of the admiral commanding the station.

Captains were in charge of all aspects of a ship and were responsible for everything that happened on or to his command. If a ship ran aground due to an incompetent watch officer or sleeping lookout, it was the captain's fault, even if the captain had been asleep in his cabin and delegated responsibility. The captain should have picked better men. As a result captains had extraordinary powers. They could order a man flogged or give the entire ship's crew leave. Most importantly, they commanded the ship in combat.

To be a successful officer required a man to be brave, intelligent, and physically capable. Navigation, one of the primary responsibilities of an officer, required the ability to master spherical trigonometry. The role also required physical bravery. In a boarding action, naval officers were expected to lead their men. While every promotion took an army officer further from danger, each promotion put an officer closer to danger. The junior lieutenants commanded the gun decks, sheltered by the bulwarks. The captain's and first lieutenant's station in combat was the most exposed and visible on the entire ship: on the quarterdeck, by the helm. Throw in the hazards posed by seagoing life—disease and shipwreck—and a naval officer of the 1700s had a 50 percent chance of dying violently during his service in the navy. Competence improved the chances, but luck helped.

Sailors floating on debris. Contrary to popular belief, ships rarely sank in battle; storms and shoals were the principal culprits. (Philip Haythornthwaite)

CONCLUSION

$\mathcal{T}$HE AMERICAN REVOLUTION AROSE OUT OF a dispute that began with Great Britain's change in policy towards her colonies. The trend towards a cohesive worldwide British empire, commercially and strategically powerful, was not checked by the outcome of the war. Rather, it meant that Britain shifted her focus from the Thirteen Colonies as the centerpiece of this empire, and began to concentrate on the potential of India instead. The drive for empire, would shape the fate of Britain, and of most of the world, throughout the 19th century and beyond. In the wake of defeat in North America, Britain was also forced to assess once again the strengths and weaknesses of her army and navy. This evaluation led to reforms, which prepared the British Army and Royal Navy for further conflict with France, Britain's traditional enemy, during the French Revolution and the reign of Napoleon.

As described above, France suffered economically from her participation in the war, even though she fought on the winning side. The debts incurred in supporting the Americans with money and arms contributed to the steadily worsening economic situation at home and are frequently cited as one of the root causes of the revolution that inflamed France only a few years later. There is a popular belief that the French Revolution was motivated by events in

OPPOSITE

The battle of Blackstock's Farm, November 20, 1780. (Steve Noon © Osprey Publishing)

America, and it is ironic that this may be true, although not necessarily for the reasons commonly cited. After the Treaty of Paris, the newborn United States of America was left independent and possessed of the rights for which she had fought to trade freely, impose her own taxes, and determine her own military requirements. Possessed of a flourishing economy and boundless national resources, her opportunities appeared limitless. Indeed, the United States would succeed, with the help of liberal trade policies and the recruitment of successive waves of enthusiastic immigrants, in transforming itself into the most powerful English-speaking country on Earth in less than two centuries.

The infant nation was also left in 1783 with the delicate problem of bringing together 13 distinct entities with diverse and sometimes contradictory needs and views into a cohesive unit, and of reconciling the power of the local assemblies with the creation of an effective national representative government. The issue of where states' rights ended and federal power began was the greatest consideration in structuring this new political entity. The decisions made concerning states' rights, particularly with regard to the legality of slavery, were to have ramifications that would dominate the first hundred years of United States history. They culminated in a conflict that brought the young country to the brink of destruction: the War Between the States (the American Civil War) in the mid-19th century.

FURTHER READING

PRIMARY SOURCES

Military Guide for Young Officers containing a System of the Art of War, London, 1776.

Regulations for the Order and Discipline of the Troops of the United States, Philadelphia, PA, 1779.

Allaire, A., *Diary of Anthony Allaire*, New York, 1968.

Anburey, T., *With Burgoyne from Québec: An Account of the Life at Québec and of the Famous Battle at Saratoga*, Toronto, 1963.

Andre, J., *Major Andre's Journal: Operations of the British Army under Lieut. Generals Sir William Howe and Sir Henry Clinton*, Tarrytown, NY, 1930.

Balch, Thomas, ed., *The Journal of Claude Blanchard*, trans. William Duance, Arno Press, New York, 1969

Balderston, M., and D., Syrett, *The Lost War: Letters from British Officers during the American Revolution*, New York, 1975.

Barker, J., *The British in Boston: Being a Diary of Lt John Barker*, Cambridge, MS, 1924.

Barrett, A., *The Concord Fight: An Account*, Boston, MS, 1901.

Byers, William V., ed., *B and M. Gratz: Merchants in Philadelphia, 1754-1798*, 1916

The British Library, *Journal of Lt. William Digby*, Add. Mss. 32413

Clinton, H., *The American Rebellion: Sir Henry Clinton's Narrative of his Campaigns, 1775–1782*, New Haven, CT, 1954.

Closen, L., *The Revolutionary Journal of Baron Ludwig von Closen*, Chapel Hill, NC, 1958.

Collins, V., (ed.), *A Brief Narrative of the Ravages of the British and Hessians at Princeton in 1775–1776*, Princeton, NJ, 1906.

Dearborn, H., *Revolutionary War Journals of Henry Dearborn*, New York, 1969.

Deux-Ponts, C., *My Campaign in America: Journal Kept by Count William de Deux-Ponts*, Boston, MA, 1868.

Duncan, Louis C., *Medical Men in the American Revolution, 1775-1783*, Carlisle, PA, Medical Field Service School, 1931

Evelyn, W., *Memoir and Letters of Captain W. Glanville Evelyn of the 4th Regiment*, Oxford, 1879.

Ewald, J., *Diary of the American War: A Hessian Journal*, New Haven, CT, 1979.

Fletcher, E., *The Narrative of Ebenezer Fletcher*, New York, 1970.

Gibbs, Robert, *Documentary History of the American Revolution*, vol. 2, New York

Greenman, J., *Diary of a Common Soldier in the American Revolution, 1775–1783*, DeKalb, IL, 1978.

Hadden, J., *Hadden's Journal and Orderly Books: A Journal kept in Canada and upon Burgoyne's March*, Albany, New York, 1884.

Haskell, C., *Diary of Caleb Haskell*, Newburyport, MA, 1881.

The Historical Magazine and Notes and Queries Concerning the Antiquities, History and Biography of America, vol. III, 2nd ser., p. 202

Hulton, A., *Letters of a Loyalist Lady*, Cambridge, MA, 1927.

Huntington, Ebenezer, *Letters Written by Ebenezer Huntington During the American Revolution*, New York, 1914

Irving, Washington, *Life of Washington*, 1876 Jones, C., (ed.), *Siege of Savannah by Count D'Estaing*, New York, 1968.

Journal of Alescambe Chesney, Add. Mss. 32627, British Library

Journal of the Siege of Charleston, G. 380. 20, Boston Public Library, Manuscript Division

Kapp, Frederic, *The Life of F. W. von Steuben... with an introduction by G. Bancroft*, 2nd ed., 1859

Kemble, S., *Journals of Lieutenant-Colonel Stephen Kemble and British Army Orders 1775–1778*, Boston, MA, 1972.

de Lafayette, Marquis, Gibert Du Mortier, *Correspondence and Manuscripts of General Lafayette*, vol. 1, 1837

Lee, Henry and Robert E. Lee, *The Revolutionary War Memoir of General Henry Lee*, 1812

Letter to Gov. Thomas Johnson of Maryland about Militia Rules, 1779, Ch. F. 7. 78, Manuscript Division, Boston Public Library

Lister, J., *The Concord Fight: Narrative of Ensign Jeremy Lister*, Cambridge, MA, 1931.

Mackenzie, F., *Diary of Frederick Mackenzie: Being a Daily Narrative of his Military Service*, 2 vols, Cambridge, MA, 1930.

Major General Lincoln Papers, G. 380. 38. 207b, Boston Public Library, Manuscript Division

Martin, J., *Private Yankee Doodle Dandee: Being a Narrative of Some of the Adventures, Dangers, and Sufferings, of a Revolutionary Soldier*, Boston, MA, 1962.

Moré, Charles-Albert, *The Chevalier de Pontgibaud: a French volunteer of the War of Independence*, 1898 Moultrie, W., *Memoirs of the American Revolution so far as it related to the States of North and South Carolina and Georgia*, 2 vols, New York, 1802.

Munro, I., *Narrative of the Military Operations on the Coromandel Coast Against the Combined Forces of the French, Dutch, and Hyder Ally*, London, 1789.

Munro, I., *The Munro Letters*, Liverpool, 1988.

National Army Museum, *Letters of Lord Howe, General Burgoyne and Lord George Germain*.

Nelson, William, ed., *Documents Relating to the Revolutionary History of the State of New Jersey*, vol. III, Trenton, 1906

Papers of Baron Friedrich von Steuben, New York Historical Society

Peterson, Harold L., *Arms and Armour in Colonial America, 1526–1783*

Putnam, Israel, 'Letter Condemning Harsh Treatment of Loyalists', Ch. F. 7. 85, Boston Public Library

Recicourt, L., "American Revolutionary Army: A French Estimate in 1777," *Military Analysis of the American Revolutionary War*, Millwodd, New York, 1977.

Rice, H., and Brown, A.S.K., (eds), *The American Campaigns of Rochambeau's Army*, 2 vols,

Richards, Henry M. M., *The Pennsylvania-German in the Revolutionary War, 1775-1783*, vol. 17, 1908

Princeton, NJ, and Providence, RI, 1972.

Saavedra, D., *Journal of Don Francisco Saavedra de Sangronis during the Commission which he had in his Charge from 1780 until 1783*, Gainesville, FL, 1989.

Samuel Shaw papers, 1775-1887, Massachusetts Historical Society, Boston, MA.

Scheer, G., and Rankin, H., *Rebels and Redcoats*, New York, 1957.

Seymore, William, *A Journal of the Southern Expedition, 1780-1783*, Wilmington, DE, 1896

Siege of Charleston, Add. Mss. 57715, British Library

Simcoe, J., *Journal of the Operations of the Queen's Rangers, from the End of the Year 1777 to the Conclusion of the Late American War*, Exeter, 1787.

Simcow, John G., *Simcoe's Military Journal*, 1844

Smith, John, *The 1777 Continental Army Diary of Sergeant John Smith, First Rhode Island Regiment*, transcribed by Bob McDonald

Tallmadge, B., *Memoir of Colonel Benjamin Tallmadge*, New York, 1858.

Tarleton, B., *A History of the Campaigns of 1780 and 1781, in the Southern Provinces*

of North America, London, 1787.

Tennant, Lieutenant Colonel Jean Baptiste, *A project to enforce uniformity among American troops*, Ch. F. 8. 55A, Manuscript Division, Boston Public Library

Uhlendorf, B., trans., *The Siege of Charleston: Diaries and Letters of Hessian Officers*, Ann Arbor, MI, 1938.

Uhlendorf, B., trans., *Revolution in America: Confidential Letters and Journals 1776–1784 of Adjutant General Major Baurmeister of the Hessian Troops*, New Brunswick, NJ, 1957.

Wright, E., *Fire of Liberty*, New York, 1983.

SECONDARY SOURCES

Allen, R.S., *Loyal Americans: The Military Role of the Provincial Corps*, Ottawa, 1983.

Atwood, R., *The Hessians*, Cambridge, MA, 1980.

Black, J., *War for America: The Fight for Independence*, Stroud, 1991.

Bowler, R.A., *Logistics and the Failure of the British Army in America*, Princeton, NJ, 1975.

Brobrick, Benson, *Angel in the Whirlwind: The Triumph of the American Revolution*, 2011, p. 334

Caney, Donald L., *Sailing Warships of the US Navy*, US Naval Institute Press, Annapolis, MD, 2001.

Christie, I., and Labaree, B., *Empire or Independence*, Oxford, 1976.

Conway, S., *The War of American Independence*, London, 1995.

Curtis, E., *The Organization of the British Army in the American Revolution*, New Haven, CT, 1926.

Duffy, C., *The Military Experience in the Age of Reason*, New York, 1988.

Dull, J., *The French Navy and American Independence: A Study of Arms and Diplomacy, 1775–1787*, Princeton, NJ, 1975.

Dull, J., *A Diplomatic History of the American Revolution*, New Haven, CT, 1985.

Gardiner, Robert, *The Heavy Frigate: Eighteen-Pounder Frigates, 1778–1800*, London, 1995.

Higginbotham, D., *The War of American Independence: Military Attitudes, Policies, and Practices 1763–1789*, New York, 1971.

Higginbotham, D., *War and Society in Revolutionary America*, Columbia, SC, 1988.

Houlding, J. A., *Fit for Service: Training of the British Army*, Oxford, 1981.

Kalyvas, Stathis N., *The Logic of Violence in Civil War*, Cambridge, UK, 2006.

Kennett, L., *French Forces in America*, Westport, CT, 1977.

Lynch, J., *Bourbon Spain 1700–1808*, Oxford, UK, 1989.

Mackesy, P., *War for America*, 2nd edition, London, 1993.

Marston, J.G., *King and Congress: The Transfer of Political Legitimacy, 1774–1776*, Princeton, NJ, 1987.

Millar, John F., *American Ships of the Colonial and Revolutionary Periods*, New York, 1978.

Nordholt, J.W.S., *The Dutch Republic and American Independence*, Chapel Hill, NC, 1982.

Peckham, Howard, *The War for Independence: A Military History*, Chicago, 1958

Royster, C., *A Revolutionary People at War: The Continental Army and American Character*, Chapel Hill, NC, 1979.

Shy, J., *A People Numerous and Armed: Reflections on the Military Struggle for American Independence*, Oxford, 1976.

Smith, P.H., *Loyalists and Redcoats: A Study in British Revolutionary Policy*, Chapel Hill, NC, 1964.

Syrett, D., *The Royal Navy in American Waters*, Aldershot, 1989.

Weigley, R., *Towards an American Army*, New York, 1962.

Wright, R.K., *The Continental Army*, Washington, DC, 1983.

RELATED OSPREY PUBLICATIONS

This volume has been compiled from a number of previously published Osprey publications. The key book used was Essential Histories 45 *The American Revolution* by Daniel Marston as well as Campaign 192 *New York 1776* by David Smith, Warrior 42 *Redcoat Officer* by Stuart Reid and Warrior 176 *Patriot Militiaman* by Ed and Catherine Gilbert. A full list of all the Osprey publication used in this compilation is provided at the start of the book.

INDEX